Ada: Managing the Transition

Proceedings of the Ada-Europe International Conference
Edinburgh 6-8 May 1986

Edited by

PETER J.L. WALLIS

School of Mathematics,
University of Bath.

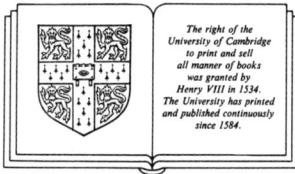

The right of the
University of Cambridge
to print and sell
all manner of books
was granted by
Henry VIII in 1534.
The University has printed
and published continuously
since 1584.

CAMBRIDGE UNIVERSITY PRESS

Cambridge

London New York New Rochelle

Melbourne Sydney

Published by the Press Syndicate of the University of Cambridge
The Pitt Building, Trumpington Street, Cambridge CB2 1RP
32 East 57th Street, New York, NY 10022, USA
10 Stamford Road, Oakleigh, Melbourne 3166, Australia

First published 1986

Printed in Great Britain at the University Press, Cambridge

Library of Congress cataloguing data available

British Library cataloguing in publication data:

Ada-Europe International Conference
   (1986 : Edinburgh)
   Ada : Managing the Transition : Proceedings
   of the Ada-Europe International Conference,
   Edinburgh, 6-8 May 1986.   (Ada companion
   series)
   1. Ada (Computer program language)
   I. Title   II. Wallis, P.J.L.   III. Series
   005.13'3   QA76.73.A15

   ISBN 0 521 33091 2

Contents

Contents

Foreword

This was the 5th conference in which Ada-Europe has played a major
role with support from the Commission of the European Communities
Information Technology and Telecommunications Task Force and with the
colllaboration of SIGAda, the relevant ACM Special Interest Group. Apart
from the 3 days devoted to the conference, many Ada-Europe Working
Group meetings and a meeting of the International Standards
Organisation Working Group ISO/TC97/SC22WG9-Ada took place in
Edinburgh during the week of the conference.

The 1986 conference theme "Ada - Managing the Transition" aims to
identify the problems which organisations may encounter when they
decide to change to Ada, and hopefully to identify some solutions to
these problems. These proceedings, therefore, provide invaluable
advice to the managers and technicians involved in the Management of
the Transition.

In selecting the technical presentations that are given in this volume,
papers were sought which would illuminate current or anticipated
problems with the transition to Ada and ways of dealing with them.
However, contributions were solicited from any relevant subject area
within this general brief, and it will be seen from these Proceedings that
a wide range of different issues were addressed. The design,
implementation and introduction of Ada has been remarkable for the way
it has stimulated both technical and managerial developments in every
branch of software engineering, and it is pleasing to see this work now
bearing fruit in the consideration of the concrete practical problems of
the transition to Ada.

Over 50 abstracts were received, and selection was made difficult by the
high quality of many of them.   Each contribution was refereed by up to
three members of an international panel of referees, and the final
program, which included the 26 technical papers, was drafted in the
light of the referees reports by a program committee consisting of:

> G Glynn
> M Boasson
> J-P Rosen
> P Kruchten
> P Wallis
> I Richmond
> K Lester
> J Nissen
> K Ripken.

We are most grateful to the Program Committee, to the referees and to
the sponsoring organisations.   Special mention should be made of the
local arrangements for the conference organised by Iain Richmond, and
of all those who have provided secretarial and organisational support for
us. Finally, our thanks to Cambridge University Press for their
co-operation in arranging the publication of these proceedings in their
thriving Ada Companion Series.

The 1987 Ada-Europe Conference will be in Sweden in May and (for the
first time) will be in collaboration with Ada in Sweden, when the theme
will reflect a maturing use of the language.

> Garth Glynn
> Ada-Europe Chairman
>
> Peter Wallis
> Programme Chairman

Part I Management Issues

ADA EVALUATION AND TRANSITION STUDIES

Peter J. Robinson
European Space Agency (ESTEC)
Postbus 299
2200 AG Noordwijk ZH
The Netherlands (01719-83813)

1. INTRODUCTION

As part of its Technical Research Programme, in preparation for using Ada, the European Space Agency has just completed a study to evaluate the use of Ada in a typical space-oriented software project, with particular emphasis on the impacts on METHODOLOGY and the prospects for PORTABILITY, REUSABILITY and development at multiple sites. The study was based on rewriting in Ada the Attitude and Orbit Control Software and the simulation of the satellite dynamics and operators environment of a recent satellite, which were previously implemented in Assembler and Fortran.

As a result of this study, we now have a set of Ada packages which has been used to evaluate many of the existing Ada compilers and Ada supporting toolsets. This proved to be a valuable way of identifying some of the key aspects for providing portable software, and for identifying strong and weak features of existing and potential APSEs.

It is planned that Ada will be used extensively in the European Space Station (Columbus), both onboard and on the ground. A Software Management Plan has been developed to define the activities needed to manage this large project, including the transition to Ada. In addition, ESA has started several projects to apply Ada in the relevant application areas for this and future programmes.

This paper reports on the study, the Ada compiler and toolset evaluation, and the planning for the Columbus project.

(Ada is a registered trademark of the U.S. Government)

2. ADA EVALUATION STUDY PROJECT

The study project was performed by Informatique Internationale (France) and CESELSA (Spain) under the direction of ESA Technology Centre (ESTEC). The Main activity was to rewrite in Ada (a) the Attitude and Orbit Control Equipment (AOCE) software of a recent satellite, from the existing design written in Caine, Farber Gordon PDL and the listings of the RCA1802 Assembler programs, and (b) the simulation of the satellite dynamics and operators environment which were previously implemented in Fortran. this was a well-defined project, which had already been completed in a different environment, typical of the work of our Simulation Section at ESTEC.

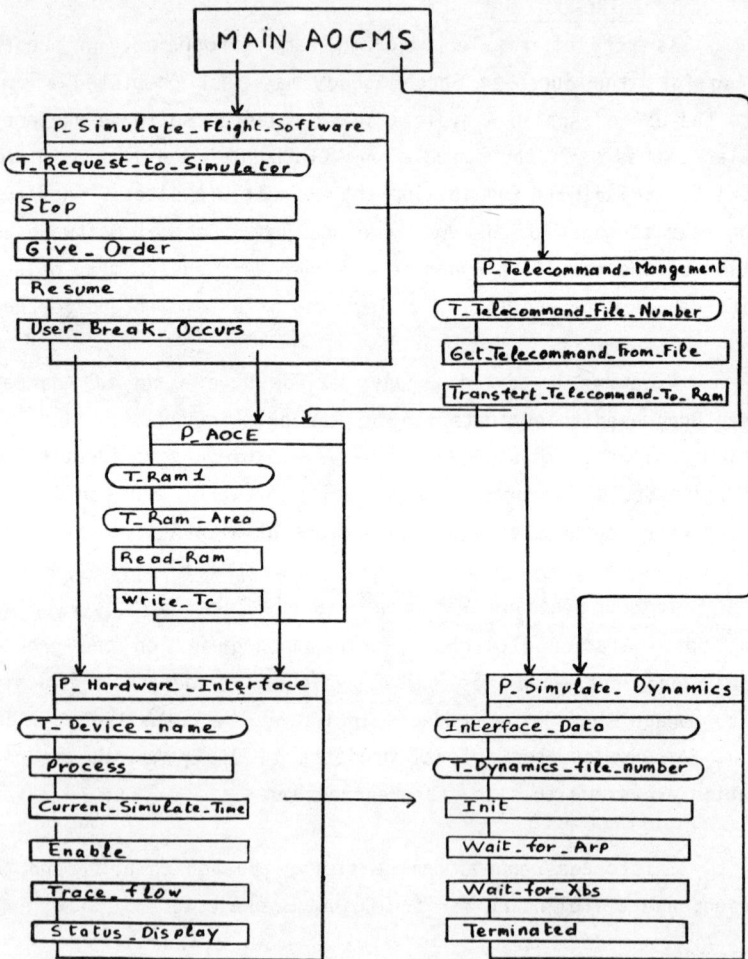

```
                    ┌─────────────────────┐
                    │    MAIN AOCMS       │
                    └─────────────────────┘
```

MAIN AOCMS

P_Simulate_Flight.Software
- T_Request-to-Simulator
- Stop
- Give_Order
- Resume
- User_Break_Occurs

P_Telecommand_Mangement
- T_Telecommand_File_Number
- Get_Telecommand_from_File
- Transfert_Telecommand_To_Ram

P_AOCE
- T_Ram 1
- T_Ram_Area
- Read_Ram
- Write_Tc

P_Hardware_Interface
- T_Device_name
- Process
- Current_Simulate_Time
- Enable
- Trace_flow
- Status_Display

P_Simulate_Dynamics
- Interface_Data
- T_Dynamics_file_number
- Init
- Wait.for_Arp
- Wait.for_Xbs
- Terminated

Figure   1: Aocms Architectural Design

The Ada program consists of 6 components (see Fig. 1). The core of the program is the package P_AOCE containing the satellite software. The RAM is visible to provide access to data for operator display, and part of the RAM (T_RAM1) is available to write telecommands. This package is embedded in a simulation of the real world environment, consisting of telecommand management, hardware interface, dynamics simulation and operator command/display interface. The satellite configuration definition and controlling telecommand streams are defined in disk files, so that several simulations can easily be run.

ESA standards for the software life-cycle [1] were followed to assess their suitability for Ada. These consist of phases for software requirements, architectural design, detailed design and implementation, each phase terminating in a formal review. Full documentation was produced.

The Software Requirements Document was written by II to pull the requirements together and as a familiarisation task to provide a clear definition of the work to be done.

As an experiment, 2 Architectural Designs were produced, at both II and CESELSA. Each consisted of narrative, design diagrams and Ada Specification parts. In addition, the major task structure was prototyped using TEXT_IO to provide a listing of the flow of control, thus demonstrating that the overall architecture is correct, and that the Specification parts were consistent and compilable. After the review, the ADD which was based on Object Oriented Design was selected since this provided the more coherent and complete view of the design. It was decided to use OOD on the detailed design of the dynamics part in the next phase to gain more experience of this technique.

The Detailed Design was also repeated by the two contractors, using the same architecture as a baseline for each. The main difference was that II decided to use SEPARATE compilation extensively in the design of the larger packages. This has the benefit of reducing the time for recompilation due to changes in only one procedure during module testing. It results in more source files and a slightly more complex library structure, with therefore more need for Ada Program Library tools to manage the re-compilation and configuration management activities.

To try out the multi-site aspects of the project with a set of independently coded packages, the satellite software was programmed in ESA and the simulation parts were programmed at a contractor in Spain (CESELSA). These were then integrated at a third site in France (Informatique Internationale), with the help of all parties. The effort at CESELSA was larger than expected due to inexperience in this application and in Ada, and the lack of proper definition of the purpose of each module (the main source of functional requirements was the equivalent Fortran source from the previous implementation). Each module was tested individually. As compensation, there was a low effort required in the integration phase for the simulation packages. The only problem was due to a requirement misunderstanding caused by misreading a badly photocopied sheet in the definition of the algorithms.

On the other hand, the Ada packages coded by ESA were not module tested for two reasons (a) since there was insufficient manpower available, and (b) that as the code came from verified PDL and Assembler, there would be less need. In any case, one purpose of the simulation is to test the AOCE code. The AOCE packages were compiled and executed end-to-end with stubs for the interfaces. Consequently more effort was needed to integrate these packages into the simulator. Errors were found due to misplaced END IF statements (these compiled correctly but produced wrong logic flows), and incorrect boolean logic interpreted from the PDL design - these should have been detected by module tests.

Acceptance was based on 10 test cases from the ESTEC Assembler/Fortran implementation, which produced identical plots in 9 cases and a better result at the 5th significant digit in the 10th case. Differences between computers were therefore insignificant.

The main part of the study produced working software, and the software development lifecycle worked satisfactorily. Module testing at package level lead to easy integration, with good support from the symbolic debugger. There is a clear conclusion that it pays to do module testing, and that the resulting integration effort with Ada is relatively low in that case. OOD was found to provide a natural method of producing a clear picture of the design, which leads easily into Ada definition, implementation and integration.

[A "module" in Ada is defined as package, for which each visible part (data, procedure, functions) is tested.]

A summary of the statistics of the project is shown below.

Item	Fortran	Ada
Simulator lines	4800	4174
P_AOCE lines	--	2738 = 6912
Lines of test code	--	886 = 7798
Comment lines	1600	3677 = 11475
Compile time	5 min	113 min
Execution time	80 sec.	350 sec.

Phases	Man days	
Requirements	40	
Architectural design	77	
Detailed design	101	
Code, test & integration	152	
TOTAL	370	= 31 lines/day

3.   EVALUATION OF ADA COMPILERS AND TOOLSETS

3.1 Compilers

The software was developed on the Telesoft compiler Release 1.3 at ESA on VAX/Unix 4.1bsd and on the Data General (Rolm) ADE Rev. 2.20 on MV10000 at II and CESELSA. Integration took place on the DG machines, which worked well but were slow due to multiple users operating over Transpac in France. The symbolic debugger was used from Holland over DN-1 and Transpac packet switched network.

The completed programs were then transferred to the ESA VAX. By this time (August 1985), Telesoft compiler 2.1 was delivered after validation, but it would not run on Unix 4.1, so the VAX/VMS version was installed for the porting test. This was a complete failure due to three major problems:

a) This compiler version did not support subprogram as formal parameters of generic units.
b) This compiler version could not generate code for an instantiation of a generic package whose body contains a task declaration.
c) Mathematical functions SIN, COS, SQRT and ARC_TAN and the pragma INTERFACE were not provided. These functions have since been written, but in view of the previous problems, there was no point in continuing the effort at that stage. The study ended at this point.

A series of trials were then performed on the following compilers (mostly on VAX/VMS), with the overall result that only the DEC compiler proved capable of compiling and executing the delivered code, with minor modifications for the implementation dependent aspects of the Ada compilers:

- DEC V1.0-7 compiler worked well, with only a problem with the attribute COUNT of task entries, which did not increment.
- Softech Ada Language System V1.34 (ALS) was so slow that trials were restricted; in addition, the use of generic instantiations lead to stack overflow.
- Dansk Datamatik Centrum Rel 2.2 (DDC) worked well at the module level, but again too many generic instantiations caused stack overflow in one package.
- Karlsruhe/Systeam V1.3 had many size restrictions that caused compiler errors.
- Alsys/Apollo (ready for validation at the date of test) compiler failed.
- Gould/SEL Irvine compiler (not validated) showed the ease with which the pragma INTERFACE to the C library could be used.

These results demonstrate that early ACVC suites were inadequate, and that one day is not long enough to transfer a working program of 7000 lines onto an unfamiliar system.

The portability problem areas found during this exercise were minor and consisted of:

a) INTEGER was defined as 32-bit, or as 16-bit with LONG_INTEGER as 32-bit. The solution for types requiring more than 16-bits is to use LONG_INTEGER in all cases, with the extra statement for compilers that have 32-bit Integers:

subtype LONG_INTEGER is INTEGER;

b) Naming of the Maths Library functions SIN/SINE etc. is not consistent, or they are missing and pragma INTERFACE had to be used to a Fortran or C library. This can be resolved by using RENAMES.

c) Use of pragmas - certain foibles appeared such as the need for the package SYSTEM for pragma PRIORITY on Karlsruhe compiler. PRAGMA MAIN was required on Data General ADE, and ignored elsewhere.

d) Differences of source file naming defaults (extensions .text or.ada expected), command names for compiler and linker (ada, ada/mpp,...). Unix and VMS provide alias and command file facilities to simplify execution.

e) Differences in implementation of TEXT_IO procedure PUT_LINE, which in one case did not have an implicit NEW_LINE. Once these differences are found, overloading allows resolution.

f) Use of generics was the most difficult area, with failures due to generics not being fully implemented, or the heavy compilation effort of instantiation which caused stack overload on ALS and DDC compilers.

The main features of Ada that are relevant for our typical applications are:

- generics to allow transporting standard packages to hardware of different types;
- multiple packages, since all software is built by a combination of contractors in different countries;
- tasking, since much software is real-time or on-line.

3.2 Toolsets

Part of the evaluation activity was to investigate the tools provided with each compiler, with the following results:

a) The VAX/VMS editor EDT was standard, slightly enhanced by DDC, and with the option of the Language Sensitive Editor from DEC.

b) Symbolic debuggers worked well and are valuable when debugging a strange system.

c) Cross-reference generator all produced different reports.

d) Compilers produced different listing and statistics.

e) The ALS execution overhead brings into question the level at which APSE activities should be incorporated into a database.

3.3 Evaluation Methods

It is a difficult and important task to determine how to decide which compiler to buy. Support for compiler evaluation from suppliers was generally willing but weak. Possible methods that are being considered are:

- shortlist possibilities by needs (host and target);
- produce some typical Ada code;
- try them out at the distributor;
- have an open system, that can accept other compilers later as they become available, or as needs for targets change.

Buying a compiler is a critical and very costly decision, justifying considerable effort. We are fortunate in having a research budget to allow us to undertake this task, but it is clearly going to be more complex to evaluate cross-development systems.

4.   TRANSITION ACTIVITIES

4.1 Columbus Project Planning

The European Space Station project Columbus is now in its initial planning and requirement stages. Following NASA's decision to use Ada as the preferred programming language for application software connected to the Space Station Data Management System onboard, ESA has made a similar decision for Columbus, so Ada will be used extensively throughout the project, both onboard and on the ground. A Software Management Plan has been developed to define the activities needed to manage this large project, including the transition to Ada. While most of the topics relate specifically to this project as a multinational project with many software contractors, Ada is seen as helping in the following ways:

- A standard Software Development Environment needs to be defined and adopted at each software contractor. Using Ada as the main language reduces the alternatives while the development of APSEs provides the necessary environments. While absolute commonality is not essential, all software must be delivered to a central site so that commonality implications have to be met.

- Central to the maintenance requirements is Configuration Management, for which methods need to be established. The Ada package provide an obvious level for control.

- At this stage it is accepted that multi-language development is necessary (primarily Ada, with C and Assembler only if needed for performance reasons). Thus there will be a sound structure to the software system.

- Commonality of language and SDE will require extensive training for staff of all levels, which is seen as a necessary and productive investment.

- Standards need to be adopted for all activities, including new features like OOD, Ada as a PDL, prototyping, as well as quality assurance, verification and validation. Ada language features (such as exception handling, generics) will help this process.

4.2 Studies

In addition, as part of the ESA Applied Technology Programme, ESA has started several projects to apply Ada in the relevant application areas for this and future programmes. These projects will run for 1986/7, providing a base of experience for ESA, and a pool of skilled staff for the contractors. These projects cover the following areas:

- Data Management Testbed, in which all the nodes of the Columbus on-board data management network will be simulated in a hardware and software prototype, using a mixture of computers and software languages, including C and Ada.

- Crew Work Station, a simulation of the crew interface for Columbus.

- Ada Pilot project, to convert a section of a Coral 66 VAX/VMS real-time program to Ada to evaluate the potential for a mixed language system, in order to improve maintainability; for each space project, part of the system has to be tailored to the needs of the individual satellite, so the long term need is to phase out Coral.

- Onboard HOL study to investigate the implications for distributed systems, including a pilot implementation.

- In addition, 3 compilers will be used in ESA to continue to folow the progress and to have them available for new projects as soon as the compilers are fully effective.

- "Lessons on Ada" from Alsys is installed on a IBM-PC and is being used for language training. It is easy to use and more effective than just reading a manual, since it contains examples to be done. It is expected to have a useful life-time of many years and is therefore worth the investment.

Correlation of the results of these projects will result in standards and methodologies for Columbus, including techniques for problem areas like portability.

There is currently much activity in the development of cross compilers, Ada tools and target development systems, so that it will take a considerable evaluation effort to select the best available environment when program production begins in 1988/9. It is therefore planned to use the AOCE Simulation code in more environments during 1986, especially with Intel 8086 as target, to look for the best solution to our needs.

5. CONCLUSIONS

Most Ada compilers were not good enough in the autumn of 1985 for production work on space applications. There are detailed differences between compilers and supporting tools which are simple to overcome. ESA continues to investigate development methods and tools, and is starting to prepare staff and methods for the first operational projects.

Bibliography

[1] ESA Software Engineering Standards BSSC(84)1 Issue 1.

GLOBAL ISSUES IN REUSE FROM A REAL PROJECT

T. D. Arkwright
Lockheed Missiles & Space Company, Inc.
Sunnyvale, CA

ABSTRACT
Recent experience at Lockheed suggests that management receptiveness to Ada is commensurate to engineers' ability to speak to the classical management concerns: cost, schedule, quality, control. This case study, one of fifty-five, shows how Lockheed addressed a single issue—relative maintenance costs, thus developing the foundation for the first major contractor/customer acceptance of Ada.

1.0 OVERVIEW

The emerging Ada technology has surfaced first in Sunnyvale, California, at Lockheed Missiles & Space Company, Inc. (LMSC), where Ada has been in use on a multibillion dollar project since September of 1984. [Ada is a registered trademark of the U.S. Government (AJPO)]

A businesslike and intellectually honest flavor characterized the voluntary Ada acceptance process at LMSC. However, we believe that the acceptance of Ada hinged on the underlying structure of our acceptance procedures, which followed two concurrent tracks, the global and the local.

When we speak of global issues we reference themes that affect the bottom line. Global issues agitate or comfort decisionmakers. When we speak of local issues, we reference those themes that affect the implementation. Local issues motivate the technical judgements of the implementors.

Chart 1 enumerates some selected global issues in reuse. The purpose of this paper is to report that, in our experiences, the ability to project for decisionmakers the expected benefits of our maintenance cost reduction program was perhaps the biggest factor in the acceptance of Ada for one major project (MILSTAR). In our experience, LMSC and military decisionmakers have had strong concern for reuse's impact on maintenance costs, to the point that LMSC's maintenance cost reduction program is now perceived as the most influential global issue in reuse. Accordingly, we have selected that topic as the basis for illustrating this article.

A shared feature of the issues in Chart 1 is that they are intelligible to the class of higher decisionmaker that no one would expect to discuss the details of Ada and software engineering. For example, a software engineer should be able to assert whether or not the preparation of implementors is being accomplished. A second shared property of each global issue is the availability of an observable impact that a decisionmaker may attempt to control.

Chart 1. Selected Global Issues In Reuse
Achieving Universal Buy-In on Ada Software Reuse
Publishing a Schedule of Benefits
Implementing a Development Cost Reduction Program
Implementing a Maintenance Cost Reduction Program
Preparing the Implementors

2.0 DYNAMICS OF GLOBAL ISSUES

Global issues are important because a successful review of these features is a precondition for the managers who occupy the most responsible positions to give their approval to implement the local issues. In general, a decisionmaker will not fund a technically elegant new solution if an adequate old solution is less costly. On the other hand, a businessman is virtually compelled to follow a cheaper elegant solution if the global and local issues appear manageable.

We shall see in this paper that reuse appears to be of immense importance on the global level because of its effects on cost; whatever the individual decisionmaker's personal opinion, if all other global and local issues are equal, cost will generally carry the day.

3.0 CASE STUDY OVERVIEW: QUANTIFYING THE IMPACT OF REUSE ON MAINTENANCE COST REDUCTION

As noted above, the MILSTAR project at LMSC recently decided to use Ada instead of its original baseline, JOVIAL, to implement its software. In retrospect, after all the other issues feeding the decision had been addressed, we were able to reach a decision only after quantifying the maintenance phase costs with a projection. Building on LMSC's earlier work in reuse we built a model which reflects our perception of the role of reuse on the project. By our calculation, *the largest contributor to maintenance phase savings would be software reuse*.

Our case study projected the maintenance cost of coding in JOVIAL and that of coding in Ada. The projections were performed using two sets of assumptions which we call the *nominal* case and the *worst-for-Ada* case. The actual projected values conform in the aggregate to generally accepted notions of the cost of maintenance (see section 6.1, Calibration). Some values are not based on the literature; for example, the software reuse experience lies largely in the future rather than in the past. However, our assumptions are clearly laid out in section 3, and alternative values can be readily submitted to the model, on demand, in order to assess the sensitivity or impact of alternate values for selected parameters. To reduce the need for multiple alternative analyses, we have worked through a second set of assumptions significantly less optimistic for Ada.

A key feature of this model is its realistic accommodation of *de facto* practice, in that error removal and *new* requirements are likely to continue to be somewhat difficult to distinguish in the maintenance timeframe of the project being discussed. This feature reflects the fact that while maintenance budgets are programmed in advance of need, the maintenance effort has two legitimate components from the budget officer's point of view: the uncontrollable component associated with errors, and the controllable component which responds to requirements.

We have formulated a uniform model suitable for projecting maintenance costs of various languages. We have included terms in the model which take into account special features of Ada such as the ability to accommodate a significant amount of software reuse. An instance of this model is given for JOVIAL in Table 1, and an instance for Ada is given in Table 2.

The possibility of extracting a delta is based on the idea of applying the rules of the model to a *baseline* set of data (JOVIAL) and to a *treatment* set of data (Ada). In reality, every output of the model is a virtual delta. For example, the total lines of JOVIAL code on hand in 2005 A.D. could be compared with the total lines of Ada code on hand in that year. This richness facilitates the review of assumptions, and enables a fuller interpretation of the ultimate cost impact of language selection during the maintenance phase.

The data mentioned above represent the best available information. For example, the divisor (2000 lines of code) used to compute the JOVIAL unadjusted yearly maintenance manyears (see column L) is a DoD historical statistic for the average number of lines of code (LOC) maintained (serviced) per year. This agrees roughly with LMSC experience. Other data are more solid; for example, the timespan (1992 – 2010) is the current planned-for maintenance phase. Still other data fall unequivocally into the realm of assumptions. For example, the staff attrition curves for each language are presented as inversely proportional. This and all other assumptions are equitable and logically defensible, but clearly are not subject to strict empirical confirmations: the future lies ahead of us, and projections interpret the future.

3.1 Nominal Case Assumptions

The following subparagraphs describe the assumptions used in the nominal case for each language. The exposition proceeds from left to right for each term (column) of the model. For each datum subject to and/or resulting from computation, the formula for its term is shown beneath the column heading. When no formula is given, the values of the column are strictly expository, and may (see column N) enter into other formulas. Please examine Tables 1 (JOVIAL Projected Maintenance Costs: Nominal Case) and 2 (Ada Projected Maintenance Costs: Nominal Case) while reading sections 3.1.1 through 3.1.11.

3.1.1 Year (Column A). Each year is listed consecutively, starting with 1992, the start of the maintenance phase, and continuing through 2010, the last year of maintenance.

3.1.2 Total Lines Of Code (LOC) On Hand (Column B). Our working assumption is that in 1992 there will be 500,000 lines of code on hand, regardless of implementation language. Thereafter, the total LOC on hand will be the LOC on hand from the previous year (Column B) minus the LOC supplanted from the previous year (Column F) plus the new LOC actually composed from the previous year (Column K). Total LOC on hand is at the start of the year. A LOC is defined as an executable high order language (HOL) instruction, *exclusive of reusable off-the-shelf modules.* Earlier work at LMSC by our group showed that the comparability of LOC across languages can be increased by making a distinction between declarative and executable lines of code, in the sense of the RCA Price S cost estimation tool.

3.1.3 Predicted Yearly Errors (Column D). The predicted yearly errors (LOC that will have to be serviced due to errors) is defined as being two per cent or less of the total LOC on hand. The formula for determining where, in this range, the predicted yearly errors will fall is as follows: Two per cent of the total LOC is determined, and then multiplied by a factor. Those factors are listed at the bottom of Tables 1 and 2 as variable V1. They are figured as follows:

3.1.3.1 Factor For Jovial. Errors decay smoothly over a nineteen year period down to ten per cent (of two per cent).

3.1.3.2 Factor For Ada. Debugging is assumed to be less than the effort of JOVIAL due to Ada's ability to avoid global scopes, to reduce module interactions, and to deliver other benefits discussed in the literature. With Ada, errors are assumed to be removed over a four year period. Subsequently, errors level off at a nominal five per cent (of two per cent).

3.1.4 Supplanted Code Removed (Column F). For both JOVIAL and Ada, the supplanted code removed as new lines are added (we assume that errors removed is a tit for tat replacement) is assumed to be twenty-five per cent of the new LOC required. This percentage has been

Table 1. JOVIAL PROJECTED MAINTENANCE COSTS: NOMINAL CASE

A	B	D	F	H	I	K	L	N	P	Q
Year	Total Loc On Hand	Predctd. Yearly Errors	Supplntd Code Removed	New Loc Required	Reusable Loc For New Reqt	New Loc Actually Composed	Unadjstd Maint. Manyears	Project Attritn. Per Cent	Adjusted Yrly Maint. Manyears	Cumulative Adjusted Manyears
	Prev(B) − Prev(F) + Prev(K)	B*.02*V1	H*.25	(B*.1)-D	0	H-I	K/2000 + D/2000		(L*N/6) + L	Prev(Q) + P
1992	500,000	10,000	10,000	40,000	0	40,000	25	.33	26	26
1993	530,000	10,070	10,733	42,930	0	42,930	27	.33	28	54
1994	562,198	10,120	11,525	46,100	0	46,100	28	.35	30	84
1995	596,773	10,145	12,383	49,532	0	49,532	30	.37	32	116
1996	633,922	10,143	13,312	53,249	0	53,249	32	.39	34	150
1997	673,859	10,108	14,319	57,278	0	57,278	34	.41	36	186
1998	716,817	10,035	15,412	61,646	0	61,646	36	.42	38	224
1999	763,052	9,920	16,596	66,386	0	66,386	38	.44	41	265
2000	812,841	9,754	17,883	71,530	0	71,530	41	.47	44	309
2001	866,489	9,531	19,279	77,117	0	71,117	43	.49	47	356
2002	924,327	9,243	20,797	83,189	0	83,189	46	.5	50	406
2003	986,719	8,880	22,448	89,791	0	89,791	49	.52	54	459
2004	1,054,062	8,432	24,243	96,974	0	96,974	53	.54	57	517
2005	1,126,793	7,888	26,198	104,792	0	104,792	56	.57	62	578
2006	1,205,387	7,232	28,327	113,306	0	113,306	60	.59	66	645
2007	1,290,366	6,452	30,646	122,585	0	122,585	65	.6	71	715
2008	1,382,305	5,529	33,175	132,701	0	132,701	69	.62	76	792
2009	1,481,831	4,445	35,934	143,738	0	143,738	74	.65	82	874
2010	1,589,634	3,179	38,946	155,784	0	155,784	79	.67	88	962
Sums:		161,108	402,157	1,608,630	0	1,608,630	885		962	

V1 Takes On The Following Values: 1, .95, .9, .85, .8, .75, .7, .65, .6, .55, .5, .45, .4, .35, .3, .25, .2, .15, .1

Total Lines Of Code On Hand In 1992 Is 500,000

Table 2. ADA PROJECTED MAINTENANCE COSTS: NOMINAL CASE

A	B	D	F	H	I	K	L	N	P	Q
Year	Total Loc On Hand	Predctd. Yearly Errors	Supplntd Code Removed	New Loc Required	Reusable Loc For New Reqt	New Loc Actually Composed	Unadjstd Maint. Manyears	Project Attritn. Per Cent	Adjusted Yrly Maint. Manyears	Cumulative Adjusted Manyears
	Prev(B) − Prev(F) + Prev(K)	B*.02*V1	H*.25	(B*.1)-D	H*V2	H-I	(K/3000) + (D/3000) + (I*.5/3000)		(L*N/6) + L	PREV(Q) + P
1992	500,000	10,000	10,000	40,000	0	40,000	17	.67	19	19
1993	530,000	4,240	12,190	48,760	19,504	29,256	14	.67	16	35
1994	547,066	875	13,458	53,831	22,071	31,760	15	.65	16	51
1995	565,369	565	13,993	55,971	23,508	32,463	15	.62	16	67
1996	583,839	584	14,450	57,800	24,854	32,946	15	.6	17	84
1997	602,335	602	14,908	59,631	26,238	33,393	16	.59	17	101
1998	620,821	621	15,365	61,461	27,658	33,804	16	.57	18	119
1999	639,259	639	15,822	63,287	29,112	34,175	16	.54	18	137
2000	657,612	658	16,276	65,104	30,599	34,505	17	.52	18	155
2001	675,841	676	16,727	66,908	32,785	34,123	17	.5	18	174
2002	693,238	693	17,158	68,631	35,002	33,629	17	.49	19	192
2003	709,709	710	17,565	70,261	37,238	33,023	17	.47	19	211
2004	725,166	725	17,948	71,791	38,767	33,024	18	.44	19	230
2005	740,243	740	18,321	73,284	40,306	32,978	18	.42	19	249
2006	754,899	755	18,684	74,735	41,852	32,883	18	.41	19	269
2007	769,099	769	19,035	76,141	43,400	32,741	18	.39	20	288
2008	782,804	783	19,374	77,498	44,949	32,549	19	.37	20	308
2009	795,979	796	19,700	78,802	46,493	32,309	19	.35	20	328
2010	808,587	809	20,013	80,050	48,030	32,020	19	.33	20	348
Sums:		26,240	310,987	1,243,947	612,365	631,582	231		348	

V1 Takes On The Following Values: 1, .4, .08, .05, And Remains Constant At .05., .45, .4,
V2 Takes On The Following Values: 0, .4, .41, .42, .43, .44, .45, .46, .47, .49, .51, .53, .54, .55, .56, .57, .58, .59, .6 IS 500,000

deemed *rational* by experienced hands at LMSC, but it could not be grounded in any known data. The assumption favors JOVIAL, in our opinion. JOVIAL programmers are sometimes reluctant to jettison code that just might be needed elsewhere. In Ada, this can be determined more readily. We are not convinced that all supplanted JOVIAL code will actually be removed.

3.1.5 New LOC Required (Column H). The new LOC required values for JOVIAL and Ada are assumed to be ten per cent of the total LOC on hand minus the predicted yearly errors. Thus, ten per cent of the total LOC on hand will be serviced annually. That ten per cent will be split between LOC serviced due to errors (uncontrollable maintenance) and LOC necessary due to new requirements (controllable maintenance). Note the explicit claim that the total level of effort is mostly a reflection of the budget available, rather than the number of errors or the number of new requirements in need of service.

3.1.6 Reusable LOC For New Requirements (Column I). This term quantifies the LOC not composed, due to reusable code that already exists.

3.1.6.1 For Jovial. Jovial does not constructively support reusability, so this entry is zero.

3.1.6.2 For Ada. For Ada, the number of reusable LOC is determined as a percentage of the new LOC required. This is 40 per cent, starting in 1993, with a straight line growth curve to 60 per cent in 2010.

An earlier LMSC study gathered estimates in a survey of LMSC Ada programmers. Their consensus was that eventually the maintenance reuse factor would be eighty per cent. The sixty per cent eventual reuse factor used here is a more conservative assumption. To further reduce any potential overestimation of software reuse in Ada, we have started with a forty per cent factor in 1992, increasing in a fairly straight line through 2010, as described by the vector, V2, at the bottom of Table 2 [See also Ramachendra, P. (1984) *Software Development Evolves into Software Engineering,* Computer Design 23, 10, pp. 165-176, for a more optimistic scenario.]. The reusability level in the first year of maintenance (1992) is assumed conservatively to be zero, due to overhead costs. Such overhead may include establishing a data base for cataloging modules or establishing procedures for reuse.

3.1.7 New LOC Actually Composed (Column K). This term expresses the LOC that will actually have to be composed for each language.

3.1.7.1 Jovial. The new LOC actually composed is the new LOC required minus the LOC that are reusable. Since JOVIAL has no reusability, this figure is the new LOC required.

3.1.7.2 Ada. The new LOC actually composed is the new LOC required minus the LOC that are reusable.

3.1.8 Unadjusted Yearly Maintenance Manyears (Column L). This is the LOC for new requirements divided by the productivity rate for new development plus the predicted yearly errors divided by the productivity rate for error correction. In the case of Ada, a burden is included that amounts to half of the cost of actually compassing the code reused.

3.1.8.1 Jovial. The productivity rate for new development of JOVIAL is assumed to be 2000 lines per year per person (see 3.0). The productivity rate for JOVIAL error correction is assumed to be 2000 lines per year per person, also.

3.1.8.2 Ada. The productivity rate for new development of Ada is assumed to be 3000 lines per year per person, and that of Ada correction is assumed to be 3000 lines per person per year.

The reason for adding in the burden is that reuse is not free. We have to include the cost of locating, evaluating, purchasing, integrating, testing, and documenting the reusable code. As expressed here, the burden is almost certainly too high, but does relfect our desire to avoid any unduly liberal conclusions.

3.1.8.3 Note. The Ada/JOVIAL differentials are conservative with respect to the recent literature [e.g.,Boehm, B. and T. Standish (1983) *Software Technology in the 1990s,* IEEE Computer, 16, 11, pp. 30–37.], which uniformly suggests productivity improvements might be up to an order of magnitude greater, based on standardization, program generators and so on. These are likely to be more available to Ada. Recently, usable data have started to emerge from the aerospace firms' experience with Ada. While encouraging, the interpretation of interlanguage coding rates is beyond the scope of this paper.

3.1.9 Project Attrition Percentage (Column N). This represents the fact that people will leave the project.

3.1.9.1 Jovial. We assume that a person will stay on the project for three years at the start of maintenance, i.e., 33 per cent of the maintenance staff will turn over annually; at the other extreme, 2010, we assume that the maintainer will endure 1.5 years, i.e., a 67 per cent turnover rate. Attrition percentages are straightlined between these endpoint values during the maintenance phase.

3.1.9.2 Ada. We assume the inverse of JOVIAL, starting with a 67 per cent turnover rate in 1992 straightlined to 33 per cent in 2010. This reflects increasing availability of Ada programmers over time, and the converse for JOVIAL. It would be plausible to argue that Ada programmers will be readily available in 1992; this would be a less conservative assumption, but more favorable to Ada.

3.1.10 Adjusted Yearly Maintenance Manyears (Column P). We assume equal costs for training a new staff member for JOVIAL and Ada. Thus the adjusted yearly maintenance manyears is the unadjusted maintenance manyears plus the cost of training the new staff members. Training cost is determined by multiplying the unadjusted maintenance manyears by the project attrition percentage and dividing by six. (Training costs are assumed to be 300 hours or 1/6 manyear for classroom and on the job development.)

3.1.11 Cumulative Adjusted Manyears. This value represents the accumulating sum of individual yearly projections.

3.2 Worst-Case-For-Ada Assumptions

The following subparagraphs describe those assumptions which differ from the nominal case in that they are considerably more pessimistic for Ada than the already conservative nominal case assumptions.

We believe this set of assumptions represents the lower bound on reasonable Ada assumptions, in that stricter assumptions begin to appear improbable, and would simply represent a future failure to follow all of the Ada methodology guidance developed for our project. In that case Ada would have been applied as if it were a traditional language; this would lead toward a traditional maintenance cost profile.

3.2.1 Changes To The Ada Nominal Case. We have introduced two changes to the Ada nominal case set of assumptions to derive this still more conservative projection.

First of all, the error removal rate for Ada is assumed to be less than that of the
Ada nominal case, leveling off at .05 (of two per cent) after six years. This change would be
expressed in the vector variable, V1 (1, .7, .4, .25, .08, .06, .05).

Second, the productivity differential of Ada programmers is moved to 2500
from 3000, nearer parity with JOVIAL (2000 lines per year).

3.2.2 Changes to the Jovial Nominal Case. The single change to the set of nominal case
JOVIAL assumptions is that the yearly predicted errors will reach .1 (of two per cent) in nine
years (via intervals of .1 (of two per cent) in all nine years) rather than in nineteen years, and
stabilize at a lower .05 (of two per cent) in the tenth year.

4.0 METHOD
We made an *a priori* decision to base our findings on two deltas, the cumulative
delta of the year 2010, and the cumulative delta of the year 2001. The latter delta is of considerable interest because historically, large systems are frequently abandoned after ten years of
deployment.

On the other hand, because of the presumed higher maintainability of Ada code
we might expect that total system replacement would be forestalled, or that the step function
replacement concept could give way, because of Ada and the associated methodology, to a
continuous refresh concept which would obsolete the idea of totally replacing a system. Be that
as it may, by evaluating both the 2001 and 2010 deltas we are adopting the most conservative
possible posture, based on a plausible set of assumptions which are clearly laid out and available for alternative simulations.

5.0 RESULTS
Key findings of the model are given in Table 3, and described in sections 5.1–
5.4. Section 5.5 presents the dollar impact in present dollars. Finally, section 5.6 describes the
relative contribution to savings of software reuse, as shown in Table 4.

5.1 The Nominal Case In The Year 2010
The model predicts 962 manyears of maintenance phase effort for JOVIAL,
versus a lesser 348 manyears for Ada.

5.2 The Nominal Case In The Year 2001
The model predicts 356 cumulative manyears of effort in the maintenance phase
through 2001 for JOVIAL, versus a lesser 174 manyears for Ada.

Table 3. CUMULATIVE MAINTENANCE PHASE COSTS JOVIAL/ADA
IN 1999 AND 2008 (IN MANYEARS)

	YEAR	JOVIAL	ADA
NOMINAL CASE			
	2010	962	348
	2001	356	174
WORST-FOR-ADA-CASE			
	2010	998	416
	2001	359	208

5.3 The Worst-For-Ada Case In The Year 2010

The model predicts 998 manyears of effort for JOVIAL in the maintenance phase through 2010, versus a lesser 416 manyears for Ada.

5.4 The Worst-For-Ada Case In The Year 2001

The model favors Ada through the 2001 timeframe with 208 manyears of maintenance phase effort versus a greater 359 manyears for JOVIAL.

The reader will note that even though the rate of removal of JOVIAL errors speeds up in comparison with the JOVIAL nominal case, the manyears projected increase somewhat. The accelerated reduction in errors speeds up the servicing of new requirements, which leads to a larger JOVIAL code body after 1993 under assumptions intended to favor JOVIAL!

5.5 Dollar Impact Of Ada Versus Jovial

In the most conservative plausible scenario, (the worst-for-Ada case in 2001) a savings of over eighteen million dollars would arise from selecting Ada. In the most probable scenario (Nominal case in 2010) the dollar differential would grow to seventy-four million dollars. These dollar estimates are based on constant present manyear costs of $120,000. A $150,000 figure might have been more appropriate, but the lesser figure gives a more conservative result.

5.6 Contribution of Reuse

We can isolate the contribution of reuse to the maintenance phase savings of Ada. In the nominal case, through the year 2010, a fifty-six per cent of the savings are due to reuse. Through the year 2001, forty-three per cent of the savings are due to reuse. To develop these results we simply altered column I and column L in Table 2. The coefficients for V2 (see 3.1.6.2) were set to zero in column I; the cost of reuse (see 3.1.8 and 3.1.8.2) was removed from column L.

In the worst-for-Ada case, sixty-nine per cent of the savings is due to reuse by 2010, while sixty-two per cent is attributable to reuse through 2001. These findings are reflected in Table 4.

Table 4. CUMULATIVE MAINTENANCE PHASE COSTS, JOVIAL/ADA, WITH AND WITHOUT ADA REUSE (IN MANYEARS)

	YEAR	JOVIAL	ADA	ADA, NO REUSE	SAVINGS DUE TO REUSE
NOMINAL CASE					
	10	962	348	689	56%
	2001	356	174	253	43%
WORST-FOR-ADA CASE					
	10	998	416	817	69%
	2001	359	208	301	62%

6.0 DISCUSSION
6.1 Calibration.

A conventional rule-of-thumb is that seventy per cent of a system's cost (assume a ten year life cycle) is maintenance. If we assume 500,000 lines of JOVIAL code were produced at 2000 lines per manyear then 250 manyears would have gone into development. A total of 356 years is predicted by the model in Table 3 to be the maintenance cost. Adding the development and maintenance figures gives 606 manyears of which the maintenance portion is nearly sixty per cent. This *a posteriori* calibration suggests that the assumptions applied to the model are both realistic and conservative.

A second *a posteriori* calibration comes from a nearby firm which was able to demonstrate 40% reuse *during development*, on a 4,000 line (est.) project. The vector, V2 described in 3.1.6.2, appears to be unduly conservative in light of this experience, related to us as this paper reached its final form.

6.2 Cost Impact Of Management's Reuse Policies In the Maintenance Phase

The recent LMSC MILSTAR Ada Study expended significant effort to spell out development procedures that would promote maintainability. Discussions there in more than fifty trade studies of *safe structures*, cost impacts, reusable generics, coding techniques, maintenance, management, training and methodology were designed to communicate software development strategies that can yield highly modular code suitable for a future maintenance technique of *swapping in* reusable modules. We assume that management can control to some extent the exploitation of software reuse technology. Clearly, managers could suppress the practice entirely; presumably, they could also encourage reuse; this is what we see happening now at LMSC.

6.3 Conclusion of Case Study

Based on the assessment presented above, we conclude that the maintenance phase cost of using Ada on the project being examined here will be considerably less than the maintenance cost of using JOVIAL. We expect reuse to be the main contributor to the lesser cost.

7.0 GENERAL CONCLUSION

Our review of maintenance costs' sensitivity to reuse is telling. While our projections must be treated as highly tentative, global issues in reuse can have (and have had at LMSC) a decisive influence on the acceptance of Ada (and therefore the acceptance of reuse). We are currently developing and analyzing recent data which indicates that the reuse profile presented here may be too conservative. We shall present some of this data at the conference.

Many times we in the technical Ada community have not been meeting the needs of decisionmakers for understandable impact projections associated with global issues. As noted at the outset of Section 2.0 above, local issues can not gain funding unless the global issues have a green light from the people in the most responsible positions. We at LMSC *have* faced the global issues, and the result is that use of Ada has been funded for a major program.

EVALUATING ADA IMPLEMENTATIONS - SMOOTHING THE
TRANSITION TO ADA

R H Pierce
Software Sciences Ltd.
London & Manchester House
Park Street
Macclesfield
Cheshire, SK11 6SR

Abstract. This paper describes the recommendations of a study
carried out for the UK Ministry of Defence into the
requirements for an evaluation service for Ada
implementations. The aspects of Ada compilation systems which
are to be evaluated are described, together with the methods
to be adopted to perform such evaluations. The tools
considered are the Ada compiler, program library management
system, linker, loader and symbolic debugger. Performance,
capacity, code quality, usability and completeness of
implementation are examined.

1. INTRODUCTION

One of the prime concerns of an organisation which is thinking
of making the transition to Ada, or of a project manager who has the
job of running a project using Ada, is the availability and quality of
Ada compilation systems for the host and target computers to be used.
The possession of a validation certificate is no guarantee that a
particular compiler is usable. An assessment of the quality of the
compilation system which is not derived either from the compiler
supplier, or from hearsay, will be of great value in allowing an
objective choice to be made between competing systems, and
alternatively ensuring that a chosen system would be adequate for the
job.

Software Sciences Ltd has completed a study into the provision
of an evaluation facility for "Ada machines" under a contract from the
UK Ministry of Defence. The MOD intends to set up an evaluation
service as part of its overall quality assurance operation which will
conduct evaluations of Ada machines which are of interest to MOD
(further details on the operation of this service are given in
section 10). The goals of the study were to assess the desirable

attributes an Ada machine and to recommend the method of evaluating how well an Ada machine meets these requirements. In addition, an outline specification of the test and supporting software to be used by the evaluation service has been produced.

Sources for the study included existing MOD Coral 66 and MASCOT evaluation suites, the US E&V effort (Castor, 1984), the Ada-Europe selection guidelines (Nissen & Wichmann, 1984) and the paper by Bassman et al (1985).

2. SCOPE OF THE EVALUATION PROPOSALS

The "Ada machine" is defined as the means of creating, compiling, linking and testing Ada programs. It includes the following components

(a) Text editor

(b) Ada compiler

(c) Program library management system

(d) Linker

(e) Loader or down-line loader

(f) Symbolic debugger

(j) Target assembler or other appropriate low level language.

The evaluation facility does not attempt to prescribe how the facilities of the Ada machine are subdivided between tools, since this would be both presumptuous and unnecessary. The underlying functionality is the important thing, although the way in which the facilities are split between tools, and the degree of integration of these tools (for example in the commonality or otherwise of their human-computer interface style) may well affect the usability of the Ada machine.

While the terms of reference for the study were to address MOD´s requirements it was concluded that these do not differ in any marked respect from those of any other producer of large scale real-time software. The evaluation criteria and software identified by the study are thus of interest to users of Ada in general.

3. REQUIREMENTS FOR THE ADA MACHINE

We have identified a number of requirements which an Ada machine should satisfy if it is to be usable for a typical large real-time project. There are also a large number of implementation characteristics which must be highlighted so that project teams are not faced with unpleasant surprises when the Ada machine is used for the first time. Tasking and Ada predefined input-output are two areas, for example, where the Ada standard allows a wide latitude to the implementor. Some of the requirements set out below can obviously be relaxed for projects of a less stringent nature.

3.1 Compiler usability

To be usable for a large project, the compilation system must have a reasonable speed to avoid development delays. Even more important is capacity - the system must be able to compile large compilation units, units with large context clauses, and large language constructs such as aggregates. The Ada linkage and loading system must also be able to handle very large programs composed of tens or hundreds of units.

The compiler and other tools must be easy to use, with clear commands and parameters. Error reporting and robustness in the face of user errors must be good. The compilation system must provide a variety of information output such as object code listings, data maps, and cross-reference listings.

Documentation must be complete and easily usable.

3.2 Implementation characteristics

The general requirement is that the Ada implementation must exploit all the hardware features which have an Ada equivalent (e.g. precisions of arithmetic, both integer and floating point). Conversely, implementations should not impose restrictions or limits which are not warranted by the hardware or operating system. Where the Ada definition allows some latitude, the most useful and practical interpretation should be adopted; generally this requirement affects pragmas and representation aspects of Ada.

3.3 Object code efficiency

Clearly, most projects require good efficiency from the generated code and in some cases (such as avionics systems), only the very best will do.

3.4 Run-time systems

Storage management, tasking and exception handling must all be adequately implemented. For example, UNCHECKED_DEALLOCATION must be provided, and STORAGE_ERROR raised correctly, e.g. when a stack overflow arises on a subprogram call (the author knows of one validated implementation where neither of these requirements is currently met).

The nature of the tasking implementation is important - it should be usable and not merely minimally compliant with the language standard. For an embedded target system, the following conditions should be met.

(a) PRIORITY must be available.

(b) Where appropriate interrupt entries must be implemented.

(c) A task performing input or output must not cause suspension of the whole program.

(d) Cooperative scheduling should not be relied upon.

(e) Selective wait statements should give equitable service to each entry accepted in the wait statement.

(f) SYSTEM.TICK should not be unreasonably large; in particular, it should be not greater than 20 ms (as for DURATION 'SMALL). Delay statements should be meaningful with a duration of at least this small.

The time taken to execute an Ada rendezvous should be as small as possible (a goal of 0.5 ms is desirable).

The compilation system should either recognise, or allow the user to nominate by means of a pragma, tasks which are "monitor tasks" used purely for mutual exclusion or buffering, and implement such tasks in a specially efficient way.

4.   EVALUATION METHODS

The evaluation procedure is designed to measure the Ada machine against the requirements in as objective a manner as possible, using a questionnaire and a set of tests and benchmarks. It is also designed to reveal implementation characteristics (such as the scheduling method used for tasks) not identified by the validation suite, and possibly not documented by the supplier. Some evaluation criteria, such as documentation quality, are subjective, but guidelines for these areas are to be provided.

Since it is intended that evaluations will be conducted by the same full-time staff, the degree of subjective variability should be reduced.

The aspects of the Ada machine to be evaluated can be classified as follows:

(a) PERFORMANCE – the host resources (time, memory, I/O transfers) used by the compiler and other tools.

(b) CAPACITY – how large a compilation unit or program can be handled by the Ada machine.

(c) USABILITY – the convenience, level of facilities supplied, robustness and quality of documentation of the tools.

(d) COMPLETENESS – how many optional facilities of Ada are implemented, and how well these match the target hardware.

(e) OBJECT CODE QUALITY – the compactness and speed of the generated code. Included in this area is the numerical accuracy of the implementation.

(f) RUN-TIME SYSTEM QUALITY – the performance and behaviour of the exception handling, tasking, storage management and input-output systems.

(g) ADDITIONAL SUPPORT PACKAGES – the extent and quality of additional library packages supplied with the Ada machine.

Many of the evaluation criteria can be objectively assessed by means of tests (which elucidate the behaviour of some aspect of the Ada machine) and benchmarks (which measure performance). Other aspects such as documentation quality are only amenable to subjective assessment, but here the assessor will be guided by checklists of features to look for.

The remainder of this paper provides some more details of the proposed evaluation topics.

5. COMPILER EVALUATION

For Ada compilers, performance in terms of both CPU and elapsed time is to be measured for a variety of compilation unit sizes from the null package up to many thousands of lines of declarations and statements. The effect of the separate compilation scheme will be measured by making the same set of declarations visible directly and by means of with clauses (with and without use clauses).

The efficiency of generic instantiation will also be measured. The effect on elapsed time of running simultaneous compilations will be assessed, as will the memory used by the compiler. For capacity evaluation, we are interested in the total amount of Ada that will be accepted, and also in limits on individual constructs such as the maximum number of enumeration literals in an enumeration type, or the total number of identifiers in a compilation unit. On the whole, Ada compilers do not impose arbitrary "brick walls" due to the design of the compiler, but some limits may be imposed by target hardware. On the usability front, the error handling and recovery of the compiler will be evaluated by using standard text containing common Ada errors. An important aspect of usability is the nature and quality of compiler outputs such as source listings, object listings and cross-reference listings; the assessor will try to generate all the outputs claimed to be available and examine the results. The various compiler options will also be exercised to ensure that they work as stated. The robustness of the compiler in the face of user errors, such as supplying the name of a non-existent source file, will also be assessed.

On the important topic of reliability i.e. the absence of errors for correct input, it is recognised that this is currently a major problem with Ada compilers, but that it cannot be checked by this evaluation facility. Any errors discovered will be noted in the final evaluation report.

6. OTHER TOOLS

The evaluation of other tools follows the same headings as that of the compiler, with variations as appropriate.

6.1 Program library system

This will be assessed largely by checklist, since Ada does not stipulate the facilities to be supplied by the program library tools. Features to be looked for include support for sharing compiled units between libraries, reporting dependencies between units, automatic recompilation of obsolete units, and support for configuration management. Performance of program library tools is usually of lesser importance, but the capacity of the program library system in the sense of the number of compilation units which a library can contain will be assessed since real projects may easily generate very large program libraries.

6.2 The linking and loading system

The Ada linking and loading system will be evaluated for capacity, which means both the number of compilation units forming the program to be linked, and also the total size of the executable program. The performance of the linking system will be assessed by measuring the time to link, build and load (including down-line loading where appropriate) programs of reasonable size. The evaluation will consider the options and facilities provided to control such things as placement in memory and support for ROM/RAM working.

The information output by the linking system (such as a memory map or a note of the elaboration order chosen) will be evaluated. Finally, Ada linkers will detect a few errors such as absence of a legal elaboration order and missing or obsolete units; programs to provoke these errors will be used to assess the quality of error reporting.

6.3 Symbolic debugging

An Ada machine may not include a symbolic debug tool; in this case the evaluation will note this fact. However, sufficient Ada machines have or are planned to have a symbolic debug capability, so that it is legitimate to include it in the scope of evaluation. Standard programs will be used to allow the assessor to set breakpoints, examine variables, examine the state of tasks and so on, to enable him to check the expected facilities and form an opinion on the tool's usability.

7.   COMPLETENESS OF IMPLEMENTATION

The object of this part of the evaluation is to see how many of the implementation-defined features are implemented, to decide how sensibly their implementation matches the target hardware and to reveal implementation-dependent features. The features to be examined include the predefined numeric types, representation clauses, unchecked conversion and deallocation, machine-code inserts, pragmas and attributes.

8.   COMPILED CODE EVALUATION

The evaluation of the quality of the object code generated by the compiler is clearly important to many kinds of application. This will be assessed by three complementary methods - standard synthetic benchmarks such as the Ada version of "Whetstone" (Curnow and Wichmann, 1976) and "Dhrystone" (Weicker, 1984), benchmarks to assess the time taken to execute individual language constructs such as assignments of various types, allocators and procedure calls, and tests of the compiler's optimisation capabilities. In the latter case, examples of Ada which give the compiler the opportunity to perform standard optimisations will be compiled, and the resulting object code examined to see if the compiler has taken advantage of these opportunities.

The optimisations to be checked include the important ones of removing redundant constraint checks and loading only those subprograms from library packages which are actually used.

Tests of the numerical accuracy of the implementation, primarily for floating-point types, are proposed.

9. RUN-TIME SYSTEM EVALUATION

The size of the run-time system will be examined, and also how this varies, if at all, according to whether tasking, allocators and other language constructs which normally call the run-time system are used in the program.

9.1 Tasking

The tasking system of the Ada machine will be evaluated for performance and for implementation characteristics.   Among the performance measurements of interest include the time taken to execute a simple rendezvous, the effect of using various forms of selective wait, and the variation in tasking overheads with the number of tasks in use. The characteristics of the tasking implementation are of great importance to users, since they may affect the design of a real-time system.   The evaluation suite will try to decide whether the requirements given in section 3.4 are met.

9.2 Storage management

This is another area in which implementations have wide latitude while remaining in conformance to the Ada language standard. The time taken to execute allocators is measured by the compiled code benchmarks, but the behaviour of the storage management scheme will be tested. For example, tests will check whether STORAGE_ERROR is correctly raised when the main program or a task stack is exhausted.

The places at which heap objects are recovered (if at all) will be determined, and tests will attempt to decide whether adjacent free areas of memory are merged to form larger areas. The space overheads for heap objects will also be measured (where possible).

9.3 Input-output evaluation

This is the area of Ada where implementations are likely to differ most. The evaluation suite will determine what is implemented (i.e. what operations will raise USE_ERROR), the implementation-defined features such as the "FORM" parameter, and also the performance of input-output operations.

10. THE TESTING SYSTEM

The goal of the testing system is to make the process of conducting an evaluation as automatic as possible, since the amount of work involved is considerable and it is essential to minimise the workload on the MOD assessor and the disruption to the site at which the evaluation is conducted. The system is based on a test controller running on the host which selects and sequences the test and benchmark programs to be compiled and run. Some tests are generated automatically (e.g. certain capacity tests which require large and possibly variable amounts of Ada code). The test controller is written in Ada and must give scope for considerable manual intervention, for example to cater for the cases where it is not possible to invoke the Ada compiler from another program, or where timings must be obtained via the assessor's stopwatch.

The test and benchmark programs, which run on the target machine, store their results in a database on the host using standard support packages. This database is also used by the test controller to store host-based measurements and results, and to store the answers to the vendor's and assessor's questionnaires. The database is used by the test controller to choose alternative paths e.g. if a test reveals that a particular feature of Ada is not implemented, further tests of this feature can be skipped. The test results database is also used by the report generator program, which takes a standard evaluation report template and inserts values from the database to produce the evaluation report for the Ada machine being assessed. The assessor will then edit this report to incorporate his own observations and qualifications, and will add a "management summary" which will provide an abstract of the main body of the report and conclusions on the suitability of the Ada machine for MOD use.

11. RELEVANCE OF THE EVALUATION SERVICE

While the MOD evaluation service is intended to assess the quality of Ada machines and to approve them for use in MOD projects, the test suite will be published to enable other users to perform assessments for themselves. The objective parts of evaluation reports prepared by MOD should be generally available, although the management summary dealing with the overall assessment of quality and approval or otherwise for MOD use will be confidential. It must be borne in mind that an evaluation is of a particular version of an Ada machine and that improvements may be made with time.

It may also be the case that having a full-time evaluation service in operation may stimulate Ada suppliers into achieving higher standards than would otherwise be the case.

12. ACKNOWLEDGEMENTS

The author would like to thank: K. Phillips, K. Hayter and P Taylor of MoD(PE) for their contributions to the study, Dr B A Wichmann of NPL for valuable discussions, and his colleagues I. Marshall and S. Bluck for their sterling efforts.

REFERENCES

Bassman M.J., Fisher G.A. and Gargaro A. (1985).
An approach for evaluating the performance efficiency of Ada compilers. In Ada in use, ed. J.G.P Barnes & G.A. Fisher, pp 151-63. Cambridge: Cambridge University Press.

Castor V.L. (1984). Evaluation and validation (E&V) team public report, volume 1.
Washington DC: Ada Joint Program Office.

Nissen J.C.D. & Wichmann B.A. (1984). Ada-Europe guidelines for Ada compiler specification and selection. In Ada: language, compilers and bibliography, ed.
M.W. Rogers. Cambridge: Cambridge University Press.

Curnow H.J., Wichmann B.A. (1976). A synthetic benchmark. Computer J., 19, no 1, pp 43-49.

Weicker, R.P. (1984). Dhrystone: a synthetic systems programming benchmark. CACM, 27, No. 10, pp 1013-30.

ADA COMPILER PERFORMANCE BENCHMARK

Gregory. A. Riccardi
Department of Computer Science, The Florida State University
Tallahassee, Florida USA

Audrey A. Hook
Computer and Software Engineering Division, Institute for Defense
Analysis, Alexandria, Virginia USA

Michael J. Vilot
General Systems Group, 51 Main Street, Salem,
New Hampshire USA

Abstract. This paper is a report on a study of Ada compiler
performance benchmarking which was done at the request of the Ada
Joint Program Office. Included is a discussion of the preliminary
design of an Ada Compiler Evaluation Capability (ACEC) which
integrates benchmark tests and support software. The strategy
adopted is to measure the cost of individual language features and to
use these figures to determine which compilers may be suitable for
particular applications. A prototype ACEC was implemented with
support software written in Ada. The prototype tests were compiled
from existing Ada benchmark tests; these tests were modified to fit
the testing strategy.

1 Introduction

Before there were any validated Ada Compilers, much of the Ada community viewed validation as the mark of a good compiler. That is, if a compiler
had been validated, then it would be useful for applications programming. Those
programmers and program managers who had experience with validation efforts for
other languages, such as Jovial, knew better. Validation simply means that a compiler can successfully process a collection of test programs. This is not a measure of
the quality of the generated code nor of the ease of use of the compiler.

What then is a program manager to do? In order to commit to a major
development in Ada, one must have some confidence that the product to be developed
will meet the system requirements. These requirements include the speed and space
of the compiled system as well as the amount of computer resources which will be
needed to implement it. There must be a way to evaluate compilers with respect to

compilation and execution resources required for the intended application.

In June, 1983, the Ada Joint Program Office established an Evaluation and Validation (E & V) task to provide the ability to evaluate the utility of the Ada language and Ada programming systems for a specific class of applications. The E & V team developed a set of criteria for evaluation of the usability of various components of an Ada Programming Support Environment (APSE). One of the most critical components is the compiler. To date, various attempts have been made to "measure" Ada compilers. None have established definitive characterizations of Ada language performance.

This paper is a report on the development of a strategy for evaluating Ada compilers and of a Prototype Ada Compiler Evaluation Capability (ACEC). The purpose of this project was to analyze Ada compiler performance benchmarking in the context of the larger E & V effort, to conduct a preliminary design of the ACEC, and to provide a prototype compiler benchmark test suite. The following sections cover the scope of the effort, the background of previous work on the topic, the approach taken, the suggested ACEC architecture, and conclusions we have drawn from the experience of building the Prototype ACEC.

2 Scope

The primary goal of this project was to investigate methods of evaluating Ada compilers and to recommend a specific method to be used for the ACEC. As part of this investigation, we were asked to collect and analyze existing Ada performance tests available in the public domain and to put these tests together in a Prototype ACEC. A key result was to be a catalogue of the tests with respect to the E & V criteria list.

The other main goal of the project was to test the feasibility of the performance benchmark suite concept. The result was to develop an initial prototype of the benchmark software in Ada, to discover any difficulties with developing such a system.

The development of the Prototype ACEC proceeded in several phases. The first phase was to collect the available tests, eliminating duplicates. Next, develop a classification scheme for the performance tests. Then design and implement a prototype benchmark system. This involved the selection and modification of tests from the available ones. Finally, use the prototype to collect statistics on available Ada compilers.

3 Background

There were two key areas of activity which were relevant to the early phases of this project: E & V criteria definition, and previous Ada benchmark efforts.

3.1 E & V Effort

The charter for the E & V group proposes an ambitious plan for a comprehensive strategy for evaluation and validation of APSEs. Among their objectives is to provide a complete catalog of available Ada environments and their components. See [EV84].

The components would all be *validated* for conformance to the standard for that component, if one exists, and *evaluated* for function and performance. The intended audience of this catalog are those applications developers considering the use of Ada. The purpose is to provide them with readily available information that will aid their selection of suitable APSE tools. This framework must be flexible enough to provide significant results across a wide range of Ada environments. The characterizations must be sufficiently precise to allow an objective basis for comparison and selection.

A decision was made to develop an ACEC to be used to evaluate Ada compilers. Before the AJPO could contract for the development of the ACEC, some preliminary work was needed. The Institute for Defense Analysis was asked to develop a prototype ACEC and to write a report outlining the requirements for the full ACEC. We were asked to collect the existing Ada benchmarking programs from a variety of sources and to put them together into a benchmarking test suite.

3.2 Previous Work

One thing that is apparent in all of the existing benchmark test suites is their orientation to the various applications under development at the time. There is no unifying concept standardizing the tests or their results. Tests developed for one application are difficult to apply in another context. Features that are crucial in one system may be irrelevant to another.

The most prevalent notion of "synthetic" benchmarks assumes a "typical" language feature distribution to represent a class of applications. Even if the subjectivity can be removed from this formulation, another problem remains: some specific applications are likely to be atypical. A performance benchmark suite should allow these application developers a reliable measure of the costs and benefits of their use of Ada.

Such tests can be useful for ranking alternative solutions. Their value is limited to providing only a gross comparison between systems (e.g., how "fast" is Ada vs. Fortran at solving the Whetstone problem [Ha84]. However, general measures of program running time are not enough to answer the important questions about compiler performance [Mo82].

This has some important implications for any proposed performance benchmark prototype. The users of the performance tests will be constructing profiles of their applications, and using the results of performance tests to predict performance. The purpose of a performance benchmark is to come up with a set of objective, quantifiable attributes that can be used to evaluate the *usefulness* of a particular Ada compiler and runtime environment.

For characterizing a compiler, the key "stress loads" are the most frequently used language constructs. A difficulty with synthetic benchmarks is that their choice of language profile may not be relevant to any particular embedded application [We84].

The combinatorial complexity of trying to measure each language feature with each data type and parameter mode is clearly unmanageable. The solution is to offer consistent measures of the *overhead* of any particular Ada language feature. The key to establishing a reliable measure of this overhead is the use of *differential* statistics [Ba85].

There are several attributes that can be measured with this approach. Chief among these is the *elapsed* time for a measurement, since this is what the users of the compiler have to deal with.

4 Approach

We begin discussing our approach to evaluating Ada compilers by describing the Prototype ACEC. Our strategy for the full ACEC follows. This section of the report reviews the results of each of the phases of the project: Analysis, Architecture, Design and Implementation, and Data Collection.

The first phase of the project analyzed Ada compiler performance benchmarking, as part of a larger APSE evaluation capability. It examined the requirements for performance evaluation, and the approaches taken to date towards measuring Ada compiler performance. Analysis of existing tests revealed the need to carefully define performance measures, considering the relevance of these measures to an applications developer.

A test architecture was developed to be used for the ACEC. A preliminary version was implemented for the Prototype ACEC. Section 5 gives the details of this test architecture, which includes a collection of support software as well as performance test programs.

The Design and Implementation phase produced Ada code to implement an initial benchmarking support system. The key requirement for this software was portability to a number of available Ada compilers. The Prototype ACEC was tested on three different Ada compilers for two different computers.

5 Suggested ACEC Architecture

The ACEC should be a self-contained compiler benchmarking system. Support software must be provided to collect compilation and execution statistics, and to provide access to this information in report form. This section outlines the strategy which we suggest for the ACEC, and which is used in the Prototype ACEC.

5.1 Performance Tests

The ACEC will have a large collection of preformance test programs. We have used two types of tests: the *normative* tests, which measure specific language features, and the *optional* tests, which measure combinations of language features. Traditional synthetic benchmark programs are in the optional class.

We have adopted a method of measuring the cost of individual language

```
with INSTRUMENT;              with INSTRUMENT;
use INSTRUMENT;               use INSTRUMENT;
procedure test_add is         procedure control_add is
x,y : integer := 5;           x,y : integer := 5;
begin                         begin
START("test_add");            START("control_add");
for i in 1 .. N loop          for i in 1 .. N loop
   LET(x,y);                     LET(x,y);
   x := x + y;                   -- x := x + y;
   -- x := y;                    x := y;
end loop;                     end loop;
STOP;                         STOP;
end test_add;                 end control_add;
```

Figure 1: Programs to Calculate the Cost of Integer Addition.

features using differential statistics. Bassman, Fisher and Gargaro give a detailed description of this method in [Ba85]. Each preformance test has a test and a control version. The only difference between these versions is the presence of code to use the language feature in the test version and its absence in the control version. An example program is given in Figure 1. The package INSTRUMENT contains the support software which records execution statistics. Procedures START and STOP use the system clock to record the elapsed time of the for loop. The call to procedure LET, which is also part of package INSTRUMENT, is included to avoid the loop optimization and to keep the value of x from overflowing. The programs are parameterized by the number of iterations (N). This allows the tests to be tailored to specific compilation systems. The difference in the execution times recorded by procedures START and STOP of the test version and the control version is the cost of (N iterations of) the language feature.

5.2 Support Software

The support software provides a mechanism for compiling and executing the preformance tests, and for collecting and reporting the associated costs. Parts of the support software are system dependent, and must be modified (or completely rewritten) for each new compilation system. The calculation of time and memory requirements for compilation and execution are necessarily system specific, as are the operating system commands required to compile and execute Ada programs.

Whenever possible, the support software should be written in Ada. For the Prototype ACEC, we implemented a data base package for test information – including test descriptions and other attributes as well as the compilation and execution statistics. The data base files are all text files and are processed using text_io. We also implemented an instrumentation package which is used by the preformance tests to collect and report execution statistics, and a report writer which provides access to the test information.

The Prototype ACEC was tested on three different compilation systems. This allowed us to develop support software which would execute correctly on any Ada system and to analyze the effort required to install the ACEC on new systems.

The support software includes an instrumentation package which is used by the test programs to report their execution characteristics, a database program for maintaining information about the tests, and a report writer which produces reports about the test programs and their compilation and execution.

6 Conclusions

Complete dependence on the traditional synthetic benchmarking approach is not adequate for the type of analyses of compiler preformance envisioned for the ACEC. The results of such tests cannot yield precise answers to the questions posed by system developers concerned with choosing a compiler or implementation strategies. The issues involved are a complex interaction of factors, and demand detailed results.

To gain the insight needed, applications developers must have the ability to construct their own language profiles. With this capability, they must also have reliable measures of performance which are consistent across a number of Ada compilation environments. Only when these two conditions are met will system developers have a sound basis for comparison.

The strategy which we recommend for the ACEC, that of developing tests of individual language features, provides the applications developers with tools to predict the costs of Ada implementation without having to design, implement and debug new synthetic benchmarks. The development and testing of the ACEC on multiple compilation environments will provide reliable and consistent statistics about any Ada system.

The Prototype ACEC is a good first step towards evaluating Ada compilers. However, there were significant implementation restrictions which had adverse affects on its usefulness. We were tasked to collect and analyze existing benchmarking tests for Ada, and there were insufficient time and funds available to develop new tests. Most of the existing tests were examples of synthetic benchmarks, with very few which could fit into our normative class of language feature tests. Hence, the Prototype ACEC has only limited coverage of language features.

The software and tests developed for the Prototype were run on the three available Ada environments. The data collected was analyzed for consistency and accuracy. This effort yielded the most insight concerning an eventual performance benchmarking suite. The major conclusions from this analysis are:

- It is possible to collect the costs of specific language features using differential statistics.

- A great deal of care must be used to keep compiler optimizations from distorting execution times.

- A careful analysis of system clocks and calendar.clock is required to allow interpretation of statistics.

- Our suggestions do not include a reasonable method to evaluate compile time costs. Such a method is an important facet of the ACEC.

- The ACEC will be a very large collection of test programs in order to adequately cover language features and synthetic benchmarks.

- The ACEC must be tested on a variety of compilation systems in order to expose inconsistencies in tests and support software.

The full report on the performance benchmarking study [Ho85] will be distributed by the AJPO. This document contains a detailed view of the test architecture, a catalog of the performance tests, specification of the support software, and detailed analysis of the approach we have taken and of the Prototype ACEC.

References

[Ba85] Bassman, M., G. Fisher and A. Gargaro, "An approach for Evaluating the Performance Efficiency of Ada," *Proceedings of the Ada International Conference*, Cambridge University Press, 1985.

[DoD80] *Requirements for the Programming Environment for the Common High Order Language, STONEMAN*, AJPO, 1984.

[EV84] "Requirements for evaluation and validation of Ada programming support environments," AJPO, 1984.

[Ha84] Harbaugh, S. and J. Forakis, "Timing studies using a synthetic Whetstone benchmark," *Ada Letters*, IV 2, 1984.

[Ho85] Hook, A., G. Riccardi, and M. Vilot, "Rationale for the Prototype Ada Compiler Evaluation Capability (ACEC) Version 1 and Recommendations for Research and Development of Successive Versions", IDA Memorandum Report M-139, December, 1985.

[Ke84] Kean, E., "Evaluation criteria for Ada compilers," Rome Air Development Center, 1984.

[Mo82] Morris, M. and P. Roth, *Computer Performance Evaluateion: Tools and Techniques for Effective*, Van Nostrand Reinhart, 1982.

[We84] Weiker, R., "Dhrystone: a synthetic systems programming benchmark," *CACM, 27* 10, 1984.

THE MAGNAVOX TRANSITION TO ADA

D. J. Gaumer, Senior Staff Engineer
Magnavox Electronic Systems Company
1313 Production Road
Fort Wayne IN 46808 USA

ABSTRACT. The transition to the effective use of the Ada
computer programming language in a medium-sized U.S. firm is
compared to other major technology transitions. The transition to Ada appears to be different in that it supports a
transition rather than being one in its own right, and its
importance and magnitude are not so clearly evident. The
actual Ada transition steps are then reviewed, ending with
the lessons learned.

1 *PREVIOUS TECHNOLOGY TRANSITIONS*

Significant aspects of both technology and technology-
related business transitions are described here in sequence although
many of these transitions overlap one another in time. Some of these
transitions are related to the current Ada transition.

1.1 *Transistors Vs Vacuum Tubes*

This rapid change began in the late 1950s, with half of the
industry small signal circuits transistorized by about 1959 (Packard
1973). It required different design and development skills. Instead of
designing circuits as voltage amplifiers, designers now had to base
designs on electric current amplification. The user saw immediate
differences in size, weight, and power. This transition had to be made
rapidly for a company to remain competitive. The same may be true of
the Ada transition.

1.2 *Digital Vs Analog Circuitry*

This more gradual transition (continuing today) began in the
1950s, with the introduction of digital circuitry and the evolution of
sequential logic into systems that previously had used only analog circuitry. This occurred in different applications at different times,
depending on how successfully and economically digital techniques could
be realized for a particular application. The developers of these
systems also had to learn new design and development skills.

Over the years, more digital circuitry has been integrated into a single semiconductor chip, with half of the industry products built with integrated circuits by about 1973 (Packard 1973). With small scale integration, logic designers used pretty much the same techniques that were used before integrated circuits; i.e., very detailed minimization of individual logic functions. With large scale integration, the design process changed. The designers attempted to make the most of functions on available chips, whether or not much of the capability of a particular chip might go unused. Their high-level design concepts were thus implemented more directly and in less time.

This is analogous to the possibilities with the reuse of Ada software. Currently, almost all of a system must be designed in detail while reusing only some low-level components. As greater selection becomes available in reusable components, the nature of the design process will change. A vast number of available components may require that automated aids be used to put a system together.

1.3 *Software Vs Hardware*

Starting in the 1960s, the use of software in early embedded systems was limited to relatively small programs. It was customary for the hardware developers to also produce the software on the same project. Most of the developers were electrical engineers with no formal software training. Company-sponsored training was limited to classes in assembly language, with selected individuals being sent to outside classes and seminars.

1.4 *Embedded Computers Vs Hard-wired Logic*

Advantages of embedded computers over hard-wired logic circuitry included, among many other things, the ability to more easily change the system functions. This greatly shortened the time to evaluate and modify system concepts. Unfortunately, much industry software had the inadequacies - low quality, skant documentation, etc. - that may be expected from a rapid prototype, although it was considered to be of final production quality.

There was abuse of this advantage of software. If it is easy to change, then it is easy to fix. And if it easy to fix, then a careful design is not important since all the problems can be fixed during debug. Small software systems could emerge with some measure of success under such a philosophy. The larger ones needed today cannot.

1.5 *Microprocessors Vs Other Embedded Processors*

Microprocessors became the dominant embedded processors as
they became more capable and better adapted to the field environment.

1.6 *Software Engineering*

Initial software engineering education was provided by
outside seminars. Later, education experts were brought in. The
initial courses were by Yourdon Inc. in 1979 through 1982. Ada
education has been taught more recently, and is described below.

1.7 *The First Project With Preliminary Ada*

Starting in 1981, Phase 1 of the Enhanced Modular Signal
Processor (EMSP) used preliminary Ada (1980 version) with the Intel 432
processor. The application did real-time signal processing with 15
processors, and had interfaces to two array processors and a large
Magnavox signal processing and display system.

1.8 *Projects Using Standard Ada*

Projects using standard Ada were initiated in rapid suc-
cession. These included the Advanced Field Artillery Tactical Data
System (AFATDS) awarded by the U.S. Army in 1984, Regency Net awarded by
the the U.S. Army in 1985, and Satellite Communication Ground Terminal
(SCOTT) awarded by the U.S. Army at the end of 1985.

2 *DEFINING THE ADA TRANSITION*

The transition to Ada is perhaps different from previous
ones in that the magnitude of the needed transition is much less
apparent. Previously, it was more clear that a transition must result
in a specific outcome if a company were to enjoy continued profit-
ability, and that significant resources would have to be expended to
continue as an effective contender. The main questions were how rapidly
to achieve the transition and how to apply it to one's own business.

In the transition to the Ada language, actions may range
widely depending on how the transition is perceived. The minimal
extreme is to simply acquire a suitable compiler, language reference
manuals, and text books, but otherwise develop software systems as
before. This simple substitution of one language for another appears to
be too minor to even qualify as a technology transition.

The opposite extreme is to attempt whatever change is needed
in order to permit Ada to make its maximum contribution, while bringing
all connected activities to the same level of sophistication. Such
activities include requirements analysis, software engineering,
automatic document generation, computer-aided test, and any other
aspects of producing a software system. The overall goal of effective
use of Ada is not just a switch to a new language, but to use that language to more cheaply produce reliable systems, even though such systems
perform functions that are ever more complex and more critical.

From this we may conclude that introduction of Ada does not
alone constitute a transition. In fact, it was not intended for that to
be the case. The purpose of Ada was to facilitate a broader software
transition. If this is not sufficiently understood, a company may
completely fail to make a significant transition, but think that it has.
No one would have tried to plug transistors into vacuum tube sockets.

As with previous transitions, changes in the technology of
electronic systems can result in developing systems by different
methods. Such transitions may thus be thought of as not just the
emergence of a major technical mechanism, but as a major change in the
nature of human activities.

Another difference with the Ada transition is that new
aspects may be added without replacing old ones. Even though much has
been written and spoken about software engineering and software development methods, it appears that software engineering has been little
understood by system developers, and that software development methods
have been poorly applied even when they were supposedly well established
in a particular company. One reason for this might be that the established development methods only poorly served the needs of the developers. For an effective Ada transition, we must finally do well some of
those things that in the past we only thought we were doing well, if
indeed they were being done at all.

3 ADA TRANSITION PLANS IN DETAIL

Our early approach was to follow closely the development of
the new language, starting with the initial DoD activities that
identified the need for a single high-order language in the 1970s
(Gaumer 1985). Over the years, we were largely in agreement with the

rationale, motivation, and standardization. As a result, Magnavox is
now a strong supporter for the incorporation of this language into our
DoD systems. For further early Ada involvement, see the section on Ada
Education below.

Understanding Ada developments was done by participation in
the Special Interest Group on Ada (SIGAda, then called AdaTEC);
attendance at a class on Ada in 1980; use of the SofTech Ada-to-Pascal
translator; early Ada education as described below; field testing the
Intel 432 Ada compiler in 1981; selection of an Ada text book in 1983;
acquisition of the TeleSoft-Ada compiler in 1983; and development of an
Ada Language Test Bed in 1984, which was used to gain experience with
some of the types of software that go into Magnavox systems.

When it became certain that Ada was going to have a major
influence on our products, it was decided to maximize this transition.
Intensive education in Ada and in modern software engineering was
started early in 1984. In addition, a new software development method,
Object Oriented Design (OOD), was introduced into the Company. OOD was
chosen because among those methods available at the time which were
adapted to Ada, it had experienced education available.

A recent turning point for the Company was that of becoming
a prime contractor for a number of larger electronic systems. This made
even more important an effective Ada transition because the larger
systems are also more complex and more critical than many earlier
systems. It was felt that drastic measures would be required to ensure
success, and that much attention should be given to software since it
has assumed a dominant role in many such systems.

In preparation of an Ada project larger than EMSP, Magnavox
trained key developers in Ada software engineering; started development
of a Data Base Management System (DBMS) in Ada since it would be needed
on the project; extensively rewrote the Software Standards and
Procedures Manual (SSPM); adapted the Intermetrics Byron (trademark of
Intermetrics, Inc.) Program Development Language (PDL); contracted for a
new OOD handbook (EVB 1985); wrote an OOD development manual; and wrote
standards for developing portable and reliable Ada code. These tasks
required and received a strong management commitment.

The standards and procedures were revised to apply Ada to
the best advantage. In the process, there came to light serious
conflicts with the U.S. DoD software development and documentation
standards, not just with respect to Ada but mostly relating to modern
software engineering. It was decided to take the difficult path of
applying Ada and software engineering as best we could, document the
development in the most direct and useful way, and fulfill the intent of
the DoD documentation requirements. This required an adventuresome
spirit on the part of management, dedication on the part of the methodology developers, and cooperation from the customer. To alleviate
future requirements mismatches, Magnavox is taking an active part in
helping modernize the DoD software requirements through the Software
Development Standards and Ada Working Group (SDSAWG) of SIGAda.

4   ADA EDUCATION

Ada education is one of the most significant factors in
making the transition to effective use of Ada. Outside education
specialists were secured by the two initial projects, AFATDS and Regency
Net. Different training courses were used because AFATDS is to
implement Ada fully, while Regency Net uses it only as a PDL.

A study of the university courses chosen by individuals
under the Company's education subsidy showed that almost all individuals
were taking courses most relevant to established technology, generally
building on previous education. Therefore, specific training selected
by the company is seen as essential for a new technology transition.

5   LESSONS LEARNED

5.1   Establish The Magnitude Of Your Transition

The transition to effective use of Ada is a major one, but
is not exceptional in its impact on a "high-tech" company compared to
other technology transitions that have occurred over the past few
decades. As with any other major technology transition, the Ada transition must be anticipated early enough to allow for careful planning and
to ensure that enough information is available to those who will make
the controlling decisions about the transition. As discussed in section
2 above, the magnitude of the transition is largely established by
deliberate decision rather than by definite external forces.

5.2 *Establish Goals*

Well in advance of the first large Ada project, understand
the purposes of Ada and the benefits it is intended to provide so that
you may define goals to be attained as the transition is accomplished.
Establish what needs to be changed to realize the full potential of Ada.
It may be that a company has been well served by software development
standards, procedures, policies, and facilities which are not adequate
for Ada. We have benefited from a continuous involvement in a wider
community outside the Company, principally through SIGAda conferences.
If you don't start work before management asks for answers, it is
already too late to learn enough about this complex field to provide
sound advice if answers are needed quickly.

5.3 *Don't Over-Sell*

Realistically identify startup costs and inefficiencies due
to the immature state of compilers and other tools. Realize that you
may not have available a high quality, tested, and complete run-time
environment for embedded computers. Note that a wide selection of
reusable components is only gradually going to come about. Emphasize
that portability is not automatic with Ada but can only be achieved with
careful design and implementation. Expect that the first time anything
new is tried, enough mistakes will be made that some early attempts will
have to be discarded and started again.

5.4 *Go Beyond The Language*

Ada embodies some software engineering aspects that probably
cannot be realized fully with established Company practices. Do portability guidelines need to be rewritten for this language which is
designed to enhance portability? Is software reusability sufficiently
encouraged for this language that is intended to foster a new industry
in reusable software? Do the software modularity requirements give
developers freedom to exploit the package facilities of Ada? Does the
software development method foster use of all features of the language
as appropriate to the application, especially packages, generics and
tasking? Do the documentation requirements need to be updated, even if
it requires convincing a customer to allow adaptation of existing
standards? After answering these questions, be aggressive in revising
company software standards, procedures, and policies.

5.5 *Initial Management Commitment*

If the above items have been done well, present to higher
management the facts which support the need to commit people and
resources to planning and implementing the transition, as detailed in
some of the following items. Do this well before hard decisions have to
be made so that they can assimilate the information more gradually and
so that you will have time to answer any questions that arise.

5.6 *Don't Skimp On Education*

Use Ada education not just in how to use the language but as
a way to upgrade the entire software development staff in software engineering principles and Ada testing, especially since Ada provides a
more natural way to implement a design which was done using good software engineering.

5.7 *Devote Sufficient Resources To The Transition*

Provide the staff to rewrite software development standards,
procedures, and policy; to organize and fill a library of reusable software; to study the embedded software limitations which are due to the
relatively immature state of compilers and run-time systems; to
institute or adapt software project data collection; to develop quality
and complexity measures, tools, and analysis procedures; to adapt test
support to Ada, especially since test and debug tools may be limited or
immature; to study the improvements that may be needed in the host
computer environments, tools, and throughput. The impact on development
system resources should be expected to come well in advance of actual
project use of Ada because of employee education and early installation
and development of tools. Whatever host computer system resources are
expected for a project, double them if Ada is to be used, at least with
the present maturity of Ada support tools and environments.

5.8 *Choose Innovative Managers*

For the early projects, choose managers who are not afraid
of innovation. A manager who avoids innovation cannot contribute to a
technology transition. The purposes will be thwarted. The enforcement
will be lacking. Developers will be encouraged to ignore or circumvent
the new practices. The tools and facilities, such as for reusability or
metrics, will not be applied well, if at all. Those developers who
could contribute the most will be frustrated and discouraged. Those
developers who don't easily take to new ideas will not be pulled along.

When difficulty is experienced with the new aspects, the developers will not be encouraged and supported to try again and perhaps create improvements to the requirements placed on them. In short, with non-innovative management, the transition just won't happen.

5.9 Expect Managers To Be Technically Involved

Choose managers who can relate well to the technical aspects of the new standards, procedures, and methods. Only then can they have the resolve to insist on the new methods even when some of the developers resist. Only then can they recognize when the new methods need improvement or do not apply to a particular situation. Only then will they advance the transition beyond the early plans and goals, both during the first project and into later ones.

5.10 Methods

Ada should be introduced only with a compatible software development method. An attempt to adapt most existing methods will result in Ada being poorly applied, perhaps with great detriment to any large job. Ensure that the documentation follows directly from the design process without being contorted to fit obsolete requirements.

5.11 Foster Professionalism

Most software developers will perform professionally in a professional climate. They must be given adequate and proper education. They must be supplied with tools to enhance their productivity and creativity. They must have standards, procedures, and policies which help them work in an orderly fashion and which require documentation that clearly has value to the developers, testers, managers, maintainers and to the customer. They must know that the goal of their organization is to produce a quality product which satisfies the customer's need. They must be rewarded for quality, thoroughness, correctness, and meaningful documentation and not just for hastily producing the minimum program code to satisfy the mere letter of the requirements. When they are having difficulties or can improve something, they must be heard. In short, it is the joint responsibility of the management and the managed to create an environment in which people can have the satis-faction of creating cost-effective and quality products instead of just earning wages as "code crafters".

5.12 *Customer Requirements And Documents*

Be prepared to cooperate with customers in adapting the requirements on software development methods and documentation related to Ada and to software engineering in general. The older U.S. Department of Defense software development methods state good intentions in terms of assembly language and FORTRAN programs common in the 1960s. It is possible to fulfill those good intentions by adapting the development and documentation requirements. Although Ada is widely considered to be the reason for these changes, the real reason is often because of software engineering issues which have gained prominence along with Ada.

Don't assume that the structure of the software can be made to match the structure of requirements documents. Requirements are structured, section and subsection, in terms of functional decomposition, which is counter to the object-oriented nature of Ada.

5.13 *Management Consistency*

Having carefully laid the groundwork for a project caught in a technology transition, software managers must consistently enforce the policies and methods that were established. Otherwise, those policies and methods mean nothing, the transition goals will not be attained, and the end product will likely be late, more costly, and of lower quality. Of course, sufficient flexibility must be exercised so that improvement is made when needed.

6 *REFERENCES*

Booch, G. (1985) - not yet published. Software Components with Ada.
          Fort Collins CO 80526 USA: Benjamin/Cummings Publishing Co.
EVB Software Engineering (1985). An Object-Oriented Design Handbook for
          Ada. Fredrick MD: EVB Software Engineering Inc., 5303
          Spectrum Drive, Fredrick MD 21701 USA
Gaumer, D.J. (1985). Case Study of a Military Ada Project: AFATDS. In
          proceedings of: Using Ada - Getting Results, pp.90-117.
          U.S. Professional Development Institute, 1620 Elton Road,
          Silver Spring MD 20903 USA.
Packard, K.S. (1973). Impact of an Emerging Technology on Company
          Operations. In A Practical Guide to Technological
          Forecasting, ed. Bright and Schoeman, pp. 55-68. Englewood
          Cliffs NJ USA: Prentice-Hall.

THE ECONOMICS OF ADA

Keith Southwell

Logica International Ltd, London W1A 4SE, England

1. INTRODUCTION

This paper describes an approach to evaluating the likely costs and benefits of introducing Ada, both in the short term and in a 'stable-state' long term. It draws heavily on Barry Boehm's 'Software Engineering Economics' (Boehm 1981) to look at the impact which Ada is likely to have on software cost drivers. However, it also looks at other costs and benefits arising during the development process, at the effect Ada is likely to have on the predictability of the software development process, and at costs and benefits over the remainder of the life-cycle.

Many of the actual costs and benefits are inevitably unknown at this stage. Some are very dependent on the individual case (eg on the effectiveness of a given compiler); for others more general research is needed. However, the approach described provides a framework into which data can be inserted as it becomes known. An example of its use is provided by inserting estimated parameters. Software estimating is inevitably at best an inexact science. Many of the effects descussed in this paper can be no better than guesses. However, the fact that we find a shortage of hard quantitative evidence for some parameters should not blind us to their existence. Magnusson (1986) and Orme (1986) provide useful data.

2. THE COCOMO MODEL

'Software Engineering Economics' identifies a range of factors which affect the cost of software projects. Fifteen of these factors, covering product, computer, personnel, and project attributes are incorporated into the Cocomo model, allowing their effect on the cost of a given project to be estimated.

Readers unfamiliar with the model should read Boehm (1981). In summary, the model relates the effort required to product software to the quantity of 'Delivered Source Instructions' (DSI). For embedded systems, the formula is:

$$MM \text{ (Man-months)} = 2.8 \text{ (KDSI)}^{1.20}$$

The resulting effort estimate is then modified by the cost drivers. For example, depending on the use of software tools, the estimate will be multiplied by a factor ranging from 0.83 to 1.24. Each cost driver is clearly and objectively defined, and the model was calibrated on 63 projects, covering a wide range of applications and sizes.

3. SOFTWARE COST DRIVERS

We must be careful to consider what we are comparing Ada with, and for what type of system. It is proposed that a wide range of systems will in future by developed using Ada; at present they are based on an equally wide range of languages, such as Assembler, Pascal, CORAL 66, and COBOL. The appropriateness for the job in hand varies, and this should affect our view, both of cost-driver values and of the amount of code generated.

In many cases, the Cocomo cost drivers are likely to be significantly affected by a transition to Ada. The 'Programming Language Experience' driver is likely to be low (= high cost) initially, for example, as new projects start with largely inexperienced staff. As time progresses, however, the effect is likely to move in the opposite direction, as the benefits of a single standard language take effect. Similarly, the whole Ada initiative will both facilitiate and stimulate developments in tools and methods, thereby affecting those cost drivers. However the short-term effects may once again be adverse.

The main cost drivers potentially affected are:

TIME (Execution time constraint)
STOR (Main storage constraint)
VIRT (Virtual machine volatility)
TURN (Computer turnaround time)
PCAP (Programmer capability)
VEXP (Virtual machine experience)
LEXP (Programming language experience)
MODP (Use of modern programming practices)
TOOL (Use of software tools)
SCED (Required development schedule - this interacts with the effort
       estimate and there may therefore be a feedback effect).

The other cost drivers, which are unlikely to be affected, are RELY (Required software reliability, although of course Ada could assist in achieving this), DATA (Database size), CPLX (Product complexity), ACAP (Analyst capability), and AEXP (Analyst experience). The relationship between all of the costs considered is shown in figure 1.

3.1 Hardware Constraints

These correspond to the cost drivers TIME (Execution Time Constraint) and STOR (Main Storage Constraint). Both cost drivers are potentially affected by the compilers and run-time libraries being used. The actual effect will depend on how severe a constraint, if any, there is in the first place. Often there will be no effect at all.

Some compilers now available appear to produce object code which executes as efficiently as that produced by good compilers for other high level languages. This is likely to be increasingly the case, so that the tendency will be for Ada to have no effect on the TIME cost driver. In the short term, some compilers can be expected to produce inferior code. In an extreme case, this could for example increase the execution time constraint from a starting point of 'very high' (x1.30) to 'extra high' (x1.65).

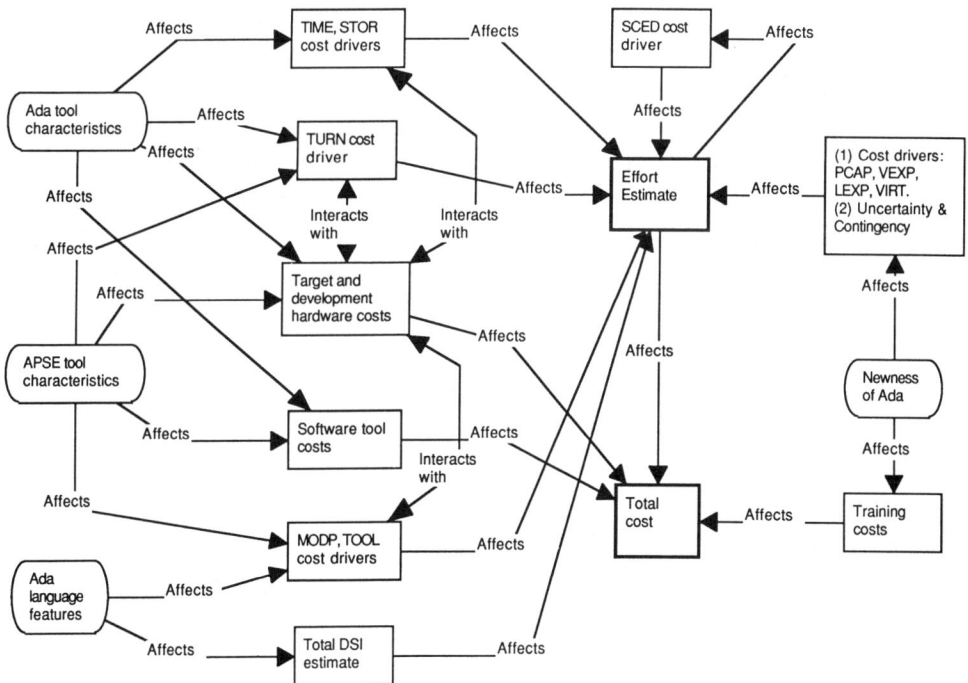

Figure 1: Relationship between factors affecting total project cost

Turning now to STOR, there is no reason why code generated by Ada should be any less compact than that produced by, say, a good CORAL compiler. Ada is likely always to need a larger run-time library than simpler languages, but the impact of this would normally only be noticeable in small systems. Memory availability is increasing rapidly; the tendency will therefore be for Ada to have no effect on this cost driver. Magnusson (1986) provides some interesting comparisons between Fortran and Ada in this area.

3.2 Development Systems

This corresponds to the cost drivers VIRT (Virtual Machine volatility) and TURN (Computer Turnaround Time).

VIRT is a measure of the (lack of) stability of the combined development and target environments. Clearly the long-term effects will be neutral, and possibly even positive. In the short-term, the cost driver will depend very much on the system being used. In some cases, one could probably already use a cost driver of low (0.87), whereas other environments are likely to range from low to very high (1.30).

TURN measures the effect on productivity of the turnaround time available for development work. In the Cocomo model as currently published, all interactive facilities are rated in the same way (= low). However, work in IBM by Lambert (1984) has shown that response time in interactive facilities has a significant effect on productivity. Reducing the response time from 2.2 secs to 0.8 secs was found to increase productivity across a large part of the project (start of detailed design through to end of integration) by 58%. If Ada development tools were to require more development system power, therefore, this could either increase development system costs or decrease productivity.

The evidence is that the best Ada compilers now available compare well with those for other high-level languages in this respect. This is not true of all compilers, however. In some cases they can easily be 10 times slower than the best. Over the next few years, it is quite likely that the biggest impact of Ada on this driver will be in the use of early APSEs. These will themselves bring benefits (see 3.4), but we have observed a tendency for existing PSEs to be heavy users of development system power (see also Orme 1986). If one believes the IBM numbers, it would therefore be easy to achieve a 40% reduction in productivity across the whole project as a result of inefficient compilers and PSE. In practice, a rational project manager would reduce the total cost to the project by buying more hardware (see 5.1).

3.3 Team Experience and Ability

The cost drivers potentially affected are PCAP (Programmer Capability), VEXP (Virtual Machine Experience), and LEXP (Programming Language Experience).

In the long term, it seems unlikely that PCAP will be affected. In the short term, however, it is quite possible that Ada projects will attract and retain a higher-than-average calibre of staff. This is a matter on which individual organisations would need to take a view. If that effect is considered to be likely, then the PCAP cost driver might, for example, go from nominal (1.00) to high (0.86). This subject is discussed further in Orme (1986).

Lack of experience of Ada and APSEs will clearly in the short term lead to low values of VEXP and LEXP. In the long term, standardisation on one language can be expected to produce a larger pool of experienced programmers than that which exists for any embedded-system high-level language today. However, even in the short term, there is a large stock of Pascal programmers, who will take to Ada more quickly than, say Coral or Assembler programmers. (See Judge 1985).

At present one might expect, for Coral, an average LEXP of nominal (1.00) and, for Ada (making some allowance for Pascal experience) an average LEXP of low (1.07). In the future one might expect LEXP to be high for Ada (0.95). Similar figures can be expected for VEXP.

3.4 Tools and Methods

This covers the cost drivers MODP (Modern Programming Practices) and TOOL (Use of Software Tools).

Boehm defines modern practices in terms of what are, by now, not very revolutionary procedures, such as Top-down Analysis and Design, Structured Design Notation, and so on. He adds that, more than with most other factors, it is difficult to distinguish these gains from those due to other factors, and that (slightly paraphrased): "Software development systems are evolving towards a coalescence of interactive access, use of extensive software tools, and support of modern programming practices. This will make it more difficult in the future to separate the effects of the Cocomo TURN, MODP, and TOOL factors, but easier to achieve enhanced software productivity".

We can distinguish three separate effects. First, Ada itself can be seen as a tool in that, for example, interfaces can be checked at an early stage, and integration problems thereby decrease (Magnusson 1986, Orme 1986). Secondly, the whole Ada movement is stimulating the development of PSEs and tools. Thirdly however, in the short term, Ada is often less well served with tools than existing languages. Although one could take the view that programming practices are independent of the language, most experience seems to contraadict this, particularly in the case of Ada. Furthermore, the adoption of good practice is likely to be stimulated by availability of tools in each of the three cases described above.

Most CORAL projects probably have a TOOL value of 'nominal' (1.00) at present. In the short term, Ada projects will probably be somewhere between 'nominal' and 'high' (0.91), rising in due course to 'very high' (0.83). A similar effect can be expected on the MODP cost driver. It is worth noting that, as one would hope, both of these cost drivers have their greatest effect on the integration and test phase. (Boehm 1981).

To offset these gains, it is to be expected that these tools will not be cheap, either in terms of the purchase price or their use of development hardware. This is discussed further in sections 5.1 and 5.2.

3.5 Project Timescale

If the amount of development effort required for a project is modified by any of the above factors, then this will affect the relationship between the schedule and the effort, which is another Cocomo cost driver (eg a project with a tight timescale costs more). Alternatively, the project schedule itself could be modified.

4. DELIVERED SOURCE INSTRUCTIONS

Most of the projects used to calibrate Cocomo used earlier high-level languages, such as Fortran and Cobol. In extrapolating to Ada, we need to reconsider both what constitutes a source instruction and how the quantity of source instructions will change.

The original definition of DSI relies heavily on the assumption that one DSI = one line of code. Block-structured languages such as Ada allow considerable freedom of layout, however. We have therefore defined a Format-Independent DSI in terms of semi-colons, logical expressions, and begin/end pairs.

Views conflict on the quantity of source instructions needed for a given problem in Ada, compared with other languages. Orme (1986) considered Ada to be 25% more verbose than 'other languages' because of data declarations. Magnusson (1986) found that 'systems in Ada require significantly fewer statements than in Fortran'. This is an area which requires considerably more work, to establish not only how many DSI are required in each language but also whether we can still assume that "effort per source statement is highly independent of language level" (Boehm 1981). There are two main issues:

- How to treat data declarations; Boehm himself introduces an arbitrary correction for COBOL to correct for "large numbers of often redundant non-executable statements".

- Whether effort per DSI increases when the full power of Ada is used to produce the "incredibly dense" code observed by Magnusson (1986).

In the presence of such confusing evidence, I have assumed in my example that the net effect of Ada is neutral in this respect.

5. OTHER SOFTWARE DEVELOPMENT COSTS

There are other costs associated with software development, such as the cost of the development system and the cost of the software tools to run on it. If one looks at the total system being developed, the hardware for the target system needs also to be considered. This could and often should also be influenced by the choice of programming language, although frequently the reverse is true.

In the short term, development systems are likely to be expensive - the tools will be expensive and probably inefficient in their use of hardware. In the longer term, hardware costs are still coming down; software tools should do the same as the size of the market for them increases. Furthermore, Ada may use the target system less efficiently than some earlier languages.

5.1 Hardware Costs

The issues involved here are discussed in 3.1 and 3.2 above. Instead of modifying our productivity estimates, it may be possible to modify the hardware which we buy, both for the development system and the target system. For development systems, this will nowadays normally be the more cost-effective solution. There can also be second-order effects: if other benefits lead to a smaller team size, then less hardware will be needed to support their activities. For target systems there is a wide range of possible situations from:

- Simple one-off systems, were buying more hardware is cost-effective, to
- Heavily-embedded systems built in large quantities, where it may be impossible without massive changes elsewhere.

5.2 Software Tool Costs

At present, a VAX Ada compiler costs £20,000, whereas a Pascal compiler costs £6,000 and a Coral 66 compiler costs £8,000. On a large embedded system, this may not be a major factor in itself, and in the UK the MoD have made some compilers freely available to organisations using them on MoD contracts.

The early APSE systems are likely to be very expensive however. Figures in excess of £100,000 for software alone have been quoted, and bearing in mind their development costs, one can understand why. They are also likely to be heavy users of development hardware (see 3.2 and 3.4).

5.3 Training Costs

Ada is new, and is a more complex language than most of those currently used for real-time systems. The training costs will therefore be higher, to be offset in due course by the benefits discussed elsewhere in this paper. Training typically has two components:

- A formal training course, followed by
- A period of on-the-job familiarisation during which productivity will be lower than usual.

The second of these is covered by the LEXP cost driver (see 3.3). Many commercial language courses last for 5 days, and cost around £600 per person, independent of the language taught. To learn Ada properly, however, one typically needs two such courses. To this must be added the value of the time spent on the course, typically £100/day for an inexperienced programmer. Initially all programmers will need training in Ada, compared with, say, 25 - 50% in the more commonly-used existing languages.

5.4 Uncertainty and Contingency

One view of the software process depicted in 'Software Engineering Economics' is that of an activity during which one is gradually gaining more information about the system one is developing. For example, when one has a 'good' specification, one clearly has more information about the system then beforehand; similarly when the system has been fully tested. At each stage, there are unknown factors, which must be eliminated by the expenditure of money and/or effort. There can therefore be a trade-off between carrying out a project cheaply and carrying it out predictably.

Ada will change this trade-off. On the one hand, its greater power should permit inconsistencies to be detected at earlier stages, as should the tools which will emerge from APSE-like activities. On the other hand, in the short term, the project management uncertainties will clearly increase owing to unfamiliarity. It turns out that both of these effects are covered by existing Cocomo cost drivers;

- The ability of Ada and APSEs to detect errors at an early stage is covered by MODP and TOOL (see 3.4)
- The contingency which one would wish to build into cover Ada's newness should be covered by LEXP and VEXP.

6. LONGER-TERM EFFECTS

Much of the published justification for Ada rests on hoped-for savings on a wider scale than those provide within individual development projects. The two main categories are reduced maintenance costs and savings owing to re-use of software.

6.1 Maintenance Costs

Many existing defence systems are highly unstructured, and written in programming languages which are little-known and badly-supported. This leads to high maintenance costs, at least in those cases where maintenance is still possible.

Defining software maintenance is difficult enough, and estimating maintenance costs is an even blacker art than estimating development costs. In particular much of the work frequently referred to as maintenance within the context of major defence systems actually consists of major extensions to the capability of the system.

The Cocomo model for estimating maintenance effort is similar to that for estimating development effort, with a number of minor modifications. In particular:

- The total maintenance effort incorporates an 'Annual Change Traffic' (ACT) factor
- The effect of the MODP cost driver is increased, particularly for large projects.

There is not space here to work through all of the implications of this, but as a basic indication, one would expect Ada projects to show up even better here than in the development phase, for two reasons:

- Most projects will not reach the maintenance phase until Ada has matured; many of the short term effects will therefore not apply.
- MODP is one of the factors particularly affected by Ada and APSE's (see 3.4).

The strategic benefits arising from an improved responsiveness in modifying defence systems must also of course be taken into account.

6.2 Software Re-use

A further objective of Ada is an increase in portability and in our ability to re-use software. Ada in itself is not sufficient to achieve this, but it does help to remove some of the barriers. In Cocomo terms, this appears as a reduced number of source instructions required for new systems and, for modified code, as the adaptation adjustment factor (AAF).

It is difficult at this stage to forecast quantitatively the extent to which Ada will bring about an increase in software re-use. One can however make the following observations:

- Where true re-usability can be achieved (ie without any modification), the percentage benefits are better than the percentage reduction in code, since productivity increases with decreasing DSI; there are also secondary effects such as a relaxation of pressure on the SCED cost driver.
- Where true re-usability is not achieved, the hoped-for benefits can disappear rapidly. To quote Boehm (1981), "be very conservative".

Design for reuse and portability also has a cost (see Orme 1986).

7. EXAMPLE

The following example is based on one in which the decision on using Ada had to be made. The project is to produce an embedded system, of 60000 DSI (assumed constant - see section 4), on a reasonably mature host and target (eg VAX/VMS).Three cases are presented; CORAL 66, Ada now, and Ada a few years hence.

The total nominal effort, taking into account those cost drivers not covered below, was estimated at 381 Man-months, with an ideal schedule of 17 months, and a maximum team size of 31. The effects of the various languages are summarised in Table 1. Note that this is purely an example, and may be competely unrepresentative of many particular cases.

8. CONCLUSIONS

- In any individual case, the economics of Ada will depend on a number of factors specific to that system.

- It is fairly clear that in the long term, based on an unscientific extrapolation from Cocomo, Ada can be expected to have a beneficial effect not only on life-cycle but also on development cost.

- In the short term, viewed solely from the piont of view of development costs on one project, the position is likely to be less clear-cut.

Table 1 - Example Calculation, using estimated values.

Cost Drivers:	CORAL 66	Ada Now	Ada Future	Notes
TIME	1.00	1.00	1.00	
STOR	1.00	1.00	1.00	(1)
VIRT	0.87	0.87	0.87	
TURN	0.87	0.87	0.87	(2)
PCAP	1.00	0.86	1.00	See 3.3
VEXP	1.00	1.07	0.95	See 3.3
LEXP	1.00	1.07	0.95	See 3.3
MODP	1.00	0.91	0.82	See 3.4
TOOL	1.00	0.91	0.83	See 3.4
Development Hardware Costs	£100,000	£150,000	£150,000	(3)

Target hardware: not allowed to change

	CORAL 66	Ada Now	Ada Future	Notes
Software tool costs:	£10,000	£20,000	£50,000	(4)
Training Costs	£10,000	£40,000	-	(5)

	CORAL 66	Ada Now	Ada Future	
Total effort estimate (MM)	295	235	177	
Labour costs (@ £2500/MM)	737,500	587,500	442,500	
Total Costs (£)	857,000	797,500	642,500	

Notes on Table 1

(1) Assuming store is not critical enough for extra Ada overhead to cause a problem.
(2) Assuming extra hardware has been bought for Ada systems - some extra allowance might be made for good response time, but I am assuming this is uniform across all languages.
(3) Notional 18 months rent = 50% capital cost (including maintenance etc). For Ada in the future it is assumed that hardware requirements will increase (for APSEs) but that the cost of that hardware will decrease in real terms.
(4) These are also entered at 50% of cost, assuming write-off over two projects.
(5) Assume 1/3 of team need 1 week CORAL training; 2/3 need 2 weeks Ada training.

REFERENCES

Basili, V.R., Katz, E.E., Panlilio-Yap, N.M., Ramsey, C.L., & Chang, S. (1985)
    Characterisation of an Ada Software development. In Computer,
    18, No 9.

Boehm, B.W. (1981). Software Engineering Economics. Englewood Cliffs, NJ.:
    Prentice-Hall.

Fox, J.M. (1978). Benefit Model for High Order Language. Mclean, VA.:
    Decisions and Designs Inc.

Judge, J.F. (1985). Ada Progress Satisfies DoD. In Defense Electronics, 17, No 6.

Klein, D. (1985). A Buyer's Guide to Ada Procurement. In Defense Electronics,
    17, No 1.

Lambert, G.N. (1984). A comparative study of system response time on program developer
    productivity, In IBM Systems Journal, 23, No 1.

Magnusson, J.D. (1986). A real-time Ada Experience. In Ada User, 7, No 1.

Orme, Tony (1986). Project Management Experience of Ada. In Proceedings of Ada UK
    Conference 1986.

Whinery, D.G. & Barber G.H. (1985). Analytical Approach to Software
    Reusability. In Proceedings of Annual National Conference on Ada
    Technology 1985.

Part II   Technical Issues in
          the Transition

TWO YEARS OF ADA EXPERIMENTS : LESSONS AND RESULTS

Michel PAPAIX
CENTRE NATIONAL D'ETUDES SPATIALES, Toulouse, France
Maurice HEITZ, Bertrand LABREUILLE
INFORMATIQUE INTERNATIONALE, Toulouse, France

Abstract. We describe an Ada experiment conducted by INFORMATIQUE INTERNATIONALE for the French national space agency (CNES) in Toulouse, France. The main objectives of the experiment were to provide information on the suitability and use of the Ada language, and on the problems to be expected when introducing Ada into an industrial environment. Results and lessons learnt can contribute to a better understanding and management of an Ada technology transfer. Special care is given to education and development methods. Experimental data given have been extracted from a development effort of six people over two years with a total production of 30 000 Ada source lines.

1. EXPERIMENTATION OVERVIEW

1.1. Objectives

The experiment had to cover two main areas :
- introduction of the language (i.e. how it is used and learnt in practice by personnel with different technical backgrounds)
- suitability of the language for applications specific to the aerospace industry, particularly real-time applications.

These topics were further refined, analyzed and balanced against technical ADA constraints (mainly lack of information and training on Ada software engineering) and three evaluation areas were defined :
- learning and use of the Ada language
- development of Ada software products
- assessment of a validated Ada environment.

1.2. Experimentation tasks summary

To reach these goals within budgetary constraints, we decided to redesign and redevelop existing Fortran applications, meanwhile monitoring related activities. These applications corresponding to small-scaled projects were preferred to a single large real-time project, due to the high risks implied by such a choice, at the time the project started. A previous paper (Labreuille 84) gives an in-depth discussion of the project's tasks and the resources involved. Since a detailed presentation of the project's tasks would require far more space than permitted in this paper, we won't present them here.

2. ASSESSMENT OF THE ADA PRODUCTS DEVELOPED

2.1. Effort and Resources involved

One must emphasize the fact that the significance of the data given hereafter is highly context dependent. The development team was small, motivated, enthusiastic and experiencing the learning process of using Ada and the tools of the programming environment. Moreover the development life-cycle of our mini-projects are not similar :

- for the Automatic Effort Measurement Package (AEMP), the requirements have been defined in informal french, and refined at design phase
- for the Real-time monitor, requirements have been synthesized from the existing product documentation and the implementation restricted to the feasibility demonstration.

These data should therefore be interpreted with care and balanced against a real industrial context.

2.1.1. Productivity. A rather high productivity ratio around 1400 ASL/ m*m (Ada Source Line per man*month, comments not included) has been experienced for small developments (1 or 2 people less than 1000 ASL). On the other hand, a smaller one (< 1000 ASL/m*m) has been measured for larger projects (3 to 5 people, more than 7000 ASL). This shows that as soon as project size increases, using Ada itself is not sufficient and one must rely on good methods, allowing full use of Ada features for parallel development, as well as good use and support of the environment tools. Besides, the productivity ratio in Ada must be redefined to include reuse of existing software components as these will be more and more available.

2.1.2. Life-cycle effort. Here again, the numbers we have measured must be taken with care, since there is no uniformity on the products developed. We give only general trends :

- Compared with classical projects data, there is a significant increase in the design phase effort (up to 50 %) balanced by an associated reduced integration phase effort (up to five times).
- Some coding may already appear in the design phase due to early validation of design and interfaces through prototyping. Prototyping is easily performed by implementing step-wise the BODY parts associated to previously checked and compiled SPECIFICATION parts.

For the monitoring of machine activities, the AEMP tool was developed, and used for each mini-project. To give a more precise view, we have extracted some data from the AEMP database that was daily updated by automatic analysis of project history files. Using the AEMP tool, the data was extracted and processed in order to produce various statistics on duration and frequency of tools activation. The monitored activities (Editing, Pretty-printing, Compiling, Linking, Executing (with or without debugger) and Formatting) cover a mini life-cycle at the module level. To comply with the standard product life-cycle, our tool was able to group the low level module activities into the following phases :

. PRODUCTION   - Editing up to the first pretty printing
. STATIC VALIDATION   - Editing and pretty printing up to the first
                          compilation without errors
. FUNCTIONAL VALIDATION - Operations from the first compilation
                          without errors.
. DOCUMENTATION   - Editing & formatting of documentation files

The results upon the development of the AEMP tool itself (3 people, 7000 ASL, 7 m*m) are given hereafter and show that machine activity was 58 % of the total time spent on the project. The larger part of the STATIC VALIDATION phase is directly related to the many iterations at detailed design phase (step-wise prototyping was used). For the FUNCTIONAL VALIDATION, the relative effort spent is rather low.

- PRODUCTION ....   57.2 hours .... 23 %
- STATIC VALIDATION......   292.9 hours .... 42 %
- FUNCTIONAL VALIDATION..   193.6 hours .... 28 %
- DOCUMENTATION.........   48.4 hours .... 7 %
- TOTAL MACHINE ELAPSED TIME ..   692 hours
- TOTAL PROJECT HOURS .... 1176 hours (7 m*m)
- PRODUCT SIZE................ 7000 ASL + 1000 comments

2.2. Product evolution assessment

To assess Ada product evolutions and changes, we focused primarily our interest on compilation errors. We distinguish Evolution during development, and Evolution through use of products.

2.2.1. Evolution during development. With the AEMP tool one can also obtain statistics on compilation errors from history files analysis. Statistics on about 3000 errors (syntactic errors excluded) were gathered :

- TYPE errors.... 30 % (misuse of objects with respect to their types)
- CONTEXT errors.. 24 % (compilation of body parts, references to non
                        existing or obsolete units)
- CALL errors.... 23 % (Interfaces inconsistencies)
- Other errors.... 23 % (Specific Ada semantic errors)

Major implications are the following :
- robustness of Ada programs may be high through strong type checking
  and entry/subprogram calls checking
- a library manager should be very efficient and easy-to-use in order
  to reduce the context errors (e.g. WITH clauses)
- no significant difficulties in the use of Ada features (only 23 %
  for specific Ada semantic errors)

Another result is that more than 50 % of compilation errors take place
in the "static validation" phase.

2.2.2. **Evolution through use of products.** This issue has not been deeply
investigated, since only basic packages have been used and reused in our
projects. However, changes brought to these products required only little
effort. Indeed the need of a good configuration tool was highlighted for
the management of several versions of package bodies associated to a
same specification part.

2.3. Quality Assessments

Faced with lack of recognized software metrics specific to
Ada, simple hand-made analysis of both textual and structural aspects of
Ada programs was undertaken. It adressed statistics about declarative
and instruction parts as well as measures of structural complexity such
as number of visible definitions per unit, depth of dependency trees,
number of units per dependency level...

2.3.1. **Ada programs statistics.** Through pretty-printer automatic analysis
of the declarative and instruction parts of Ada compilation units, the
following trend has been highlighted :

```
. DECLARATIVE PARTS  : - 60 to 80 % variables
                       - 10 to 20 % types
                       -  5 to 10 % instantiations
. INSTRUCTION PARTS  : - 30 to 50 % subprogram calls
                       - 20 to 30 % assignements
                       - 10 %         IF statements
                       -  5 to 20 % loop statements
```

These results show homogeneous usage of the Ada features, with extensive
use of typing and high modularity (subprogram calls).

2.3.2. **Ada software structure.** The AEMP data show that package structuring
has a great influence on the overall structure of large Ada programs (more
than 7000 ASL), with very few nested levels, balanced however by a high
density of inter-module relationships.

Moreover, the structure of a software is different if the module decomposition is done on a package basis, or "à la Pascal" with heavy use of the "SEPARATE" feature :

- using "SEPARATE" DECOMPOSITION : up to 4 nested levels of subprograms are used with the following partition : 20 % at level 1, 20 % at level 2, 52 % at level 3 and 7 % at level 4.
- using "PACKAGES" DECOMPOSITION : up to 3 nested levels of subprograms are used with more than 70 % at level 1.

One can see here that proper use of Ada, with systematic abstraction oriented structuring, leads to a grouping of most functionalities at level 1. This software structure limiting side and propagations effects due to changes, could have a benefic impact on the maintenance effort.

3.   ASSESSMENT OF ADA TRAINING AND USE

The project team was rather balanced (Fortran/Pascal experience, seniors/juniors) and not especially predisposed towards the language, although its members had been sensitized to the problems of software engineering. The team training consisted of a formal three-day seminar, followed by a one internal week training on the ADE and completed by personal efforts, using whatever text books available (Barnes 84, Booch 84, Gehani 83, Haberman 83) in addition to the Ada Language Reference Manual (ALRM). The approach chosen to start was rather successful and was to develop simple, demonstrative packages.

3.1. Learning the language

The main concepts and features are quickly understood and assimilated, while the quality of the Ada compiler appears to be very important : a compiler must be a validated one and should not introduce any ambiguity between the language and its implementation (e.g. for features described in Appendix F of ALRM). Some problems arose in the application of detailed restrictions with some sour points such as private generic parameters, use of derived types, task termination, I/O facilities for composed types. Finally, an average training and learning period for an operational programmer could be set up to a full month, but with efficient support. Special training is however required to reach a level of expertise in particular areas (e.g. generics, tasking, I/O).

3.2. Using the language

A few features such as derived types and renaming were little or never used. One can wonder whether it is due to bad assimilation or to too simple applications which did not need any use of the full power of Ada. Difficulties appeared for using Ada according to the good software engineering principles. Almost the whole team had no proper view of how to apply correctly in practice such concepts as abstraction, information hiding, reusability,.. Sometimes, the propensity to "program first" was stronger than thinking over and discuss, but it is true that nobody was mature enough to be considered as an expert. As a result, a number of tricks in the heavy use of Ada have been discovered, such as solving inter-units visibility problems and use of private types. Moreover, Ada was found to have such richness for some solutions that formal or informal "expertise" would be of great help on any industrial Ada project, even if the team is already well trained. Finally a last word on a crucial Ada issue : tasking. Tasking concepts were found easy to grasp and to use (termination excepted).   Nevertheless, two problems arose with heavy use of tasks, related to expression of tasking semantics and performances.

Expression of tasking semantics : Putting some informal comments together with task entries specifications was found to be poor and other solutions such as graphical representation as suggested in (Buhr 84) or prototyping were investigated. The latter was successfully used and is now recommended in our development methodology.

Tasking performances : Our experimentation on the real-time scheduler for telemetry processing demonstrated clearly the full power of Ada according to system extensibility and flexibility. However, real-time system designers and programmers considered it with high skepticism with respect to possible performances increase (the current implementation overhead costs of Ada synchronisation against traditional implementation is about 1 to 10). Awaiting efficient run-time implementations for our machines, we suggest therefore to minimize the use of tasks at design and, if time constraints are too high, to use the "mixed development approach" (see below).

4.   METHODOLOGY OUTLINES

Our experiment not only highlighted the importance of using Ada in design, with a real need of methods aiming at making this usage more efficient, but also has had considerable impact on classical development methods, especially through Ada prototyping features. Possibilities and limitations of Ada in specifications have already been widely discussed in numerous papers such as in (Goldsack 85). We give only the main advantages that were actually experienced by our team, namely :

a) Ada has proven to be suitable as a long range development tool over the life-cycle. This result is mainly due to the expressive power of Ada formalism and its use from design to integration.

b) Ada allows explicit description of modularity and supports it both logically and physically :
   - logical modularity allowing powerful structuring of programs into high level abstract entities
   - physical modularity allowing parallel and formalized stepwise refinement development.

As such a typical development scheme of an Ada application is :

1° **Logical partitioning** : specification parts of packages are defined. Thus defined interfaces and unit relationships can then be validated either by compilation and/or by partial prototyping of the associated bodies. The problem here, "Design for Ada", still not satisfactory solved, is how to find out the "best" suitable packages.

2° **Physical implementation** : once the specification parts are approved and/or validated, implementation can be given to a development team. Ada is first used as PDL for detailed design of bodies and final code is derived by step-wise refinements.

4.1. Design for Ada

The so-called "object-oriented-design" (OOD) was chosen as a basis and has proved fundamental to highlight the "good" abstractions of an application. The following limitations have been discovered, and must be cited :

- Expression of control flow is not explicit and care must be taken so that its description in textual or graphical form will be produced by the designer.
- The method makes the expression of a designer's solution easier, but has no formal basis and as such does not help for identification and verification of a "good" solution.
- OOD must be practiced by reasonably well trained designers for good results since Quality Assurance rules for reviewing outputs have not been yet established and/or validated.
- Finally difficulties remain for expressing and understanding of tasking behaviour, leading to prototyping as the only mean of validation.

We are further working on improving existing OOD guidelines focussing on the upper life-cycle phases in order to achieve greater formalization.

4.2. Design and implementation with Ada

The correct compilation of Ada specification parts does not prove that the design is correct ; only syntactic consistency and unit relationships are validated. However, it is possible with very little effort, to code stub-bodies with minimal statements (needed for instance to print strings showing the control flow). If inter-task communication is involved, this approach may validate the synchronisation scheme. This technique has been successfully used giving real confidence for detailed design and implementation, and saving a lot of time at integration.
Although prototyping, before detailed design, seems to be right, it might not be applicable to all kind of problems with respect to context and size constraints. Accordingly an Ada software development methodology should be tailored to fit with previous existing ones (Rajlic 85).

5.   ENVIRONMENT ASSESSMENT

5.1. Ada compiler quality

It is worth recalling that official AJPO validation suites are still not concerned with implementation aspects such as pragmas, low-level features, optimizations, tasking implementations. There is presently far more maturity in compilers than in 1983 and it is easy now to get data and detailed description of compiler features according to the guidelines formulated in (Nissen, 84). However as more and more validated compilers are put on the market, it appears that implementation choices let free by the standard, such as pragmas, predefined environment,... become of primary importance for compiler evaluation. Availability of pragmas INLINE or SUPPRESS may be essential for developing embedded systems, while such could be the case for pragma INTERFACE (to Fortran) for numerical applications. Although compilers must respect the Ada standard, they must also have characteristics aimed at user specific needs. As such, a number of Ada specific benchmarks have been developed, testing both speed of compilation and execution performances. Synthetizing the results gives a compilation speed ranging from 100 to 400 ASL/min-cpu and a rendez-vous synchronization cost of two millisecond for our AOS-VS/ADA MV10000 system.

5.2. MAPSE Tools

Apart from the validated compiler, the following tools were found the most valuable :

. PRETTY-PRINTER : used to produce standardized code layouts and to check Ada syntax (reducing compilation costs)

. LIBRARY-MANAGER : a key tool in a MAPSE, the Ada library management is a key area for improving programmer's productivity, especially in the context of multi-programmer team. As such, indication of recompilations induced by a change, and possibly automatic triggering of recompilations, was badly missing in our environment.

. DEBUGGER : specifically tailored to Ada, this powerful tool substantially increases productivity and reliability (e.g. allows to locate exactly which instruction triggered an exception even when tasking is involved).

On the other hand, the lack of Ada oriented maintenance tools was also felt, especially to track and to master evolutions of packages and what is still more important, the induced evolutions. Although there were tools available like SCCS and MAKE from the UNIX system, they did not take into account the specific Ada relationships. Finally, the use of a number of powerful tools was found to be of significant help, but it took time and efforts to learn how to use them effectively.

6. GUIDELINES FOR THE TRANSITION TO ADA

With respect to the experience gained by our organization we give the recommendations currently assessed by CNES.

6.1. Setting up a suitable infrastructure

The goal is to provide to an organization, human and technical means for efficient use of Ada. Among these, training is the most critical for adoption by future users. This setting up should therefore address :

- **The human means** by analysing specific training needs according to the software engineering background of the personnel in order to define a training plan. This plan must be as openminded as possible for internal and outside acquisition of the state of the art.
- **The technical means** by assessment (with respect to organization's needs) of potential use and suitability of Ada, as well as the Environment tools available "off the shelf" or to be tailored to organization's needs, (such as specific code generators, run-times...) and finally by assessment of specific reusable component library development.

- **The management means by** :
  - . Analysis of impacts on development methodology and quality assurance
  - . Analysis of impacts on project management and organization

6.2. Progressive adoption of Ada

Once an infrastructure is reliably in place and gives daily demonstration of Ada uses, it can contribute to step by step dissemination of this technology as new projects start. Three approaches can be chosen :

- **crossed** : Ada is used for design, but since efficient implementations are still missing, coding is done in a different language.
- **mixed** : Ada is used for design, but only partially for implementation. The pragma INTERFACE must be available in the environment. This approach must be taken each time one wants to reuse existing libraries written in Fortran or Pascal, as well as when performance constraints are critical (e.g. a real-time loop is coded in assembler to fit in timing constraints, while deferred data processing is written in Ada)
- **Full Ada** : Ada for design and implementation. This approach will be chosen when mature programming environments, experienced people and/or training supports will be available and operational.

The crossed approach has already been successfully experienced with several small to medium sized projects. Although Ada features (tasking excepted) are only used in design phase the resulting products are of significantly higher quality (than those obtained previously) and integration and testing time is reduced by half. The mixed approach seems very promising too, especially since it allows the use of Ada at design phase with suitable Ada decomposition, and progressive use of Ada implementation with possible backing if performance constraints are too high.

7.   CONCLUSIONS

With respect to the initial objectives, we draw the following conclusions which we separate into trends (to be confirmed or not) and certainties.

a) **Trends**

High productivity ratios have been measured (up to 1400 ASL/m*m) but in our particular context. More than this absolute value, the knowledge of improving productivity factors is of highest interest and we point out :
- Early validation through use of Ada at design phase
- Automatic recompilation features supported by a good control configuration system
- Reuse of existing software components.

The structural decomposition of large Ada programs has few levels of depth of nesting and is rather "horizontal". This software structure should be of significant interest for maintenance cost reduction.

b) Certainties

Training

Our experimentation has proven that acceptable level of proficiency in Ada could be gained reasonably well (less than a month). Ada, as a programming language is not more difficult to learn than any other language, but making full use of its underlying software engineering principles requires some more efforts. Due to Ada richness, special training is required for "good use" of advanced features, as well as to avoid use of "well known" subset.

Environment

The availability of a number of tools is of great help, but one should not forget that learning how to use them effectively is almost as important as the language, and takes time and effort as well. Evidence was given that an Ada compiler must be a validated one, but the other tools must be of quality as well and should allow development and support for large Ada programs (more than 10 000 ASL).

Development methodology

Use of Ada impacts heavily on traditional methods through :
- Early and continuous use from the design phase
- Early validation of design through prototyping
- step-wise PDL refinement
- Design effort which is increased by up to 50 % while integration is reduced up to 5 times.
- Effective parallel development

8.   ACKNOWLEDGEMENTS

This work has been done in the context of a contract with CNES (Centre National d'Etudes Spatiales) and we are grateful to the following people who gave us their constructive contribution and the permission to publish the results :
Mr. P. Ricard
Division Génie Informatique/CNES/Toulouse, France

9. REFERENCES

[Barnes 84]   J.G.P. Barnes : "Programming in Ada", 2nd edition, International Computer Science Series, 1984

[Basili 85]   V. Basili, E. Katz : "Characterization of an Ada Software Development", IEEE computer, september 1985

[Booch 83]   G. Booch :"Software Engineering with Ada" The Benjamin/Cumming Pusblishing Company, 1983

[Buhr 84]   R.J.A. Buhr : "System Design with Ada", Prentice Hall, 1984

[Eliott 84]   Eliott : "APSE Tools - Rolm Experience", ADA-EUROPE, Adatec 1984, Brussels Conference, 1984

[Gehani 83]   N. Gehani : "Ada - An advanced Introduction"; Prentice-Hall, 1983

[Goldsack 84]   Goldsack : "Ada For Specifications : Possibilites and Limitations", ADA - Companion series, Cambridge University Press, 1984

[Habermann 83]   A.N. Habermann : "Ada for Experienced Programmers"

[Labreuille 84]   B. Labreuille, M. Heitz : "The Introduction of Ada in French Aerosopace Industry", ADA-EUROPE, Adatec 1984, Brussels Conference

[Nissen 84]   Nissen, Wallis : "Portability and Style Guide in Ada", ADA - Companion series, Cambridge University Press, 1984

[Rajlic 85]   V. Rajlic : "Paradigms for Design and Implementation in Ada", Communications of the ACM, July 1985

[Stoneman 80]   U.S. Departement of Defense : "Requirements for Ada Programming Support Environments", 1980

TRANSITION TO ADA FOR SUPER COMPUTERS

Gerd VÖLKSEN
Philipps-University, Marburg/Lahn, Germany

Peter WEHRUM
Siemens AG, Corporate Research and Technology, Munich,
Germany

Abstract. The issue to be discussed in this paper is how to use Ada
on modern hardware that performs high speed computation by
means of pipelining, vector processing and other mechanisms of
parallelism. There are a few alternatives of which the one that
provides hardware connection by machine code insertions or
pragma INTERFACE is - if not the best choice - the solution most
easily realized. Though Ada data type concepts cannot be fully
exploited, operator definitions, overloading of operators and infix
notation can be employed by the user.

BACKGROUND AND MOTIVATION

There is already modern hardware available which enables high
speed computation to be performed by means of pipelining, vector processing
or other mechanisms of parallelism such as those provided by multiprocessors
and multiple instruction stream - multiple data stream (MIMD) architectures.
These technologies speed up program execution at the lower level of the
computer hierarchy just as ultra large scale integration (ULSI) does with respect
to chip evolution. On the other hand, high level, i.e. algorithmic, optimization
of program execution - as carried out by compilers (or application
programmers) - has not yet been entirely successful and will not be in the
future. The new hardware aims at improvements in execution speed by factors
and even by orders of magnitude whereas the high level optimization
mentioned above attains improvements typically in the range of a few per cent
up to, say, fifty per cent (cf. Kowalik 1984). Programming language designers
and compiler constructors will have to take this into consideration.

The issue to be discussed in the present paper is how to use Ada on
vector processor systems such as the Cray 2, Cyber 205, NEC SX 2, Fujitsu VP 200/
Siemens 7.800-VP 200. More precisely, this paper investigates how, in principle,
the vector processing facilities of the hardware can be exploited by using Ada;
in a second step, prototypes of reusable software components covering the
field of basic vector operations are developed. The target machine we have
especially in mind is the VP 200, which represents a kind of single instruction

Figure 1. VP 200 hardware architecture

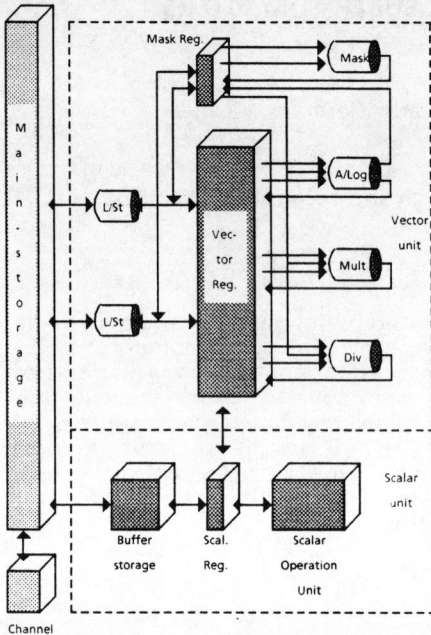

stream - multiple data stream (SIMD) architecture that employs pipelined arithmetic units to process vector data (see figure 1). The fast computation of vector data is supported by six pipelines. Up to five pipelines are able to work in parallel; these are the load/store pipelines, the mask pipeline and two of the others. Up to eight vector registers can be accessed at the same time; the scalar unit and the vector unit are able to work in parallel, too. Through these mechanisms the VP 200 executes up to 500 MFLOPS (Fujitsu 1984, Siemens 1985). The examples below refer to this machine.

To take advantage of the concurrency provided by multiprocessors it is natural to try to employ Ada tasks, cf. Hibbart et al. 1981 and Schonberg & Schonberg 1985. However, it is clear right from the beginning that Ada tasks are hardly any help to exploit vector operations when used on vector (mono-) processors.

Most of the common programming languages, except for example APL, provide a scalar structure. This means data structures for vectors are available but there are no predefined functions or operators to work with them. Programming languages dealing with vector arithmetic such as VectorC (Li & Schwetman 1985), PASCALV (Ehlich 1984) and MATRIX PASCAL (Bohlender et al. 1982) are non standard extensions of common scalar programming languages.

Which predefined "vector operations" does Ada provide? There are only a few such as relational operators, membership tests, conjunction, inclusive and exclusive disjunction of arrays of boolean components, catenation, slicing, indexing, conversions and assignment (Reference Manual of the Ada Programming Language (RM) 1983). Consider an example:

```
type VECTOR is array (INTEGER range <>) of SCALAR;
            -- Let SCALAR be a floating point type.
V1, V2: VECTOR (1..1000); ...
V1 := (1.0,1.0,others => 0.0)   -- Aggregates
V2 := V1;                       -- Array-Assignment
V1 (1..8):= V2 (3..6) & V1 (3..6);
                          -- Slicing, catenation
if V1 /= V2 then ... end if;-- Relational operators
V1 (5) := 2.0 * V2 (7);    -- Indexing
```

By means of indexing, statements as the last one above are allowed but, for instance, vector products, inner products and scalar products are not predefined in Ada. Statements like

```
V1 (1..4)  := 2.0 * V2 (3..6);
V1         := 2.0 * V2;
```
require an explicit definition of "*" according to:

```
function "*" (S: SCALAR;V: VECTOR) return VECTOR;
[pragma INLINE ("*");]
```

To express the semantics of the operator "*" by high level Ada constructs, one has to "scalarize", i.e. the vector operation must be implemented by scalar Ada code, using loops and scalar expressions. What can be done in parallel is transformed into a sequence of steps to be carried out one after the other; the vector character of "*" is lost:

```
function "*" (S:SCALAR;V:VECTOR) return VECTOR is
   RESULT: VECTOR (V'RANGE);
begin
   for INDEX in V'RANGE loop
      RESULT (INDEX) := S * V (INDEX);
   end loop;
   return RESULT;
end "*";
```

On conventional hardware the function body will be executed as required by the source code and, therefore, the runtime will be proportional to the index range. Modern vector processing hardware is able to execute the function body by invoking essentially one single instruction with a strongly reduced runtime for all index values out of a certain range (<1024 for the VP 200) according to the following piece of VP200 assembler code:

```
L      8,RANGE     Load vector length
VLVL   8           Load vector length register
LD     8,SCALAR    Load scalar factor
VLD    0,V2,0      Load source vector
VMSD   32,8,0,0    Compute scalar product
VSTD   32,V1,0     Store target vector
```

SOLUTIONS

The question is how to translate Ada code into vector machine code. Basically, one may conceive of two different solutions (ignoring a third possibility, viz the idea of realizing "language extensions" which could be introduced through implementation defined pragmas).

- Firstly, developing an Ada "vector compiler" which generates powerful vector machine code by using vectorizing algorithms (i. e. optimizing sequence source code).

- Secondly, implementing a package including basic vector arithmetic by utilizing the high level interface for the specification part and machine code insertions or pragma INTERFACE for the bodies.

Let us discuss briefly the strong and weak points of either alternative.

First alternative: vectorizing compiler

+ Better portability because there is no implementation dependent package; everything is programmed in high level (scalar) Ada.

+ Optimized execution time by pipelining because there are less procedure calls than in the second alternative (assuming no use of inline expansion).

- Compiler generated code may be of a lower quality than handwritten code.

- Since Ada compilers are hard to build, Ada vector compilers will be even harder to construct. Sophisticated vectorizing optimization techniques must be applied to recognize vector structures in pieces of scalar code (cf. Lamport 1974).

- Basic algorithms first designed in vector form by the programmer must be scalarized and implemented in (scalar) Ada code, thus enabling the compiler to vectorize it again, i.e. to restore an equivalent of the original vector operation.

Second alternative: implementation of (the bodies of) basic vector operators by machine code insertions

+ A vector package guarantees optimal hardware use.

+ It may easily be implemented as concepts like packages, separation of specifications from implementations, representation clauses and machine code insertions already exist.

± For Ada programs containing vector arithmetic written without use of such a package there is no speed-up in an Ada environment offering a vector package. (This problem can be solved by a decompiling preprocessor that is able to transform loops working on arrays into equivalent vector procedures

offered by the package. On the other hand there may be only a few Ada
software products containing vector arithmetic today.)

-   There is the possibility of pipelining efficiency loss caused by several vector
procedure calls in a sequence interrupted by other statements.

Balancing the two possibilities, the second one is - if not the better
choice - the solution easiest to realize. Furthermore, all Ada compilers which are
being developed or are available now seem to have scalar machines as their
targets. The problem of pipelining efficiency loss mentioned in the last
paragraph may be weakened by a hierarchical construction of the package.

Here we follow the second approach, which relies on the
subsequent language features: overloading of operators - Ada provides the
appropriate infix notation -, separation of specifications from implementations,
predefined and implementation-defined attributes and some low level features
such as machine code insertions and pragmas (INLINE, INTERFACE, and
implementation defined) and representation clauses.

MACHINE CODE INSERTIONS

The library package MACHINE_CODE is a prerequisite for using
machine code insertions. In general an implementation need not supply such a
package. But here, of course, we rely on its existence and its suitability for
vector processing. Among other things, this package will contain information
about vector registers, operation codes, instruction formats, the pipeline
identification, and procedures each of which can execute a machine instruction
of a specific format:

```
package MACHINE_CODE is
-- Declarations of general registers, the maximum
-- displacement, the displacement range, and
-- other hardware specific entities.
type VREGISTER is range 0..255;
-- Vector/mask registers
type VR_OPCODE is   (..,VLVL,..,VMSD,..);
for  VR_OPCODE use  (..,16#FFE90#,..,16#FR9C#,..);
-- Declaration and representation of VR-opcodes
    ...
type VX_OPCODE is   (..,VSTD,..,VLD,..);
for  VX_OPCODE use  (..,16#FF2#,..,16#FFA#,..);
-- Declaration and representation of VX-opcodes
   type ID_TYPE is   (' ','A','B');
   for  ID_TYPE use  (0,1,2);
   -- Declaration and representation
   -- of pipeline identification
```

```
type VX_FORMAT (CODE : VX_OPCODE) is
  record                        -- Declaration of
    VREG1      : VREGISTER;     -- the VX-format
    DISP       : DISP_RANGE;
    X_REG      : REGISTER;
    BASE_REG   : REGISTER;
    case CODE is
      when VIL|VILD|VILE|VIST|VISTD|VISTE
              => VREG2 : VREGISTER;
      when others
              => REG2  : REGISTER;
          ID       : ID_TYPE;
    end case;
  end record;
  for VX_FORMAT use            -- Representation
    record at mod 2;           -- of the VX-format
    CODE       at 0 range 0..11;
    ID         at 1 range 4..7;
    VREG1      at 2 range 4..11;
    DISP       at 4 range 4..15;
    X_REG      at 3 range 4..7;
    BASE_REG   at 4 range 0..3;
    VREG2      at 1 range 4..11;
    REG2       at 2 range 0..3;
  end record;

  procedure EXEC_VX_OP
  (C:VX_OPCODE;I:ID_TYPE;VR1:VREGISTER;
   D:DISP_RANGE;X,B,R2:REGISTER;VR2:VREGISTER);
          -- Procedure that executes one machine
          -- instruction of the VX-format.
     pragma INLINE(EXEC_VX_OP);
  -- Declarations and representations
  -- of the VR-format
  -- and scalar instruction opcodes and formats
end MACHINE_CODE;
```

The VX-instruction must be specified by means of a variant record which discriminates direct from indirect load and store instructions. This is caused by the fact that indirect load and store operations need a vector register specified by 8 bits to describe the variable distance instead of a 4 bit general register specification to describe the constant distance and a 4 bit pipeline specification needed by direct load and store instructions. The complete specification of all VR-instructions by the record VR_FORMAT necessitates eleven variants.

```
package body MACHINE_CODE is
    ...
    procedure EXEC_VX_OP
    (C:VX_OPCODE;I:ID_TYPE;VR1:VREGISTER;
     D:DISP_RANGE;X,B,R2:REGISTER;VR2:VREGISTER) is
```

```
begin
   VX_FORMAT'( CODE      => C,
               ID        => I,
               VREG1     => VR1,
               DISP      => D,
               X_REG     => X,
               BASE_REG  => B,
               REG2      => R2,
               VREG2     => VR2 );
   end EXEC_VX_OP;                 ...
end MACHINE_CODE;
```

Specifying vector operations by operator definitions guarantees use of infix notation and legibility. In this case the subprogram body may be implemented by a sequence of procedure calls of the kind EXEC__xx__OP, each of which invokes a scalar or a vector machine instruction. Using this method there might be a large runtime overhead caused by saving and restoring registers each time a machine code procedure is called. (This overhead should be removed by a corresponding implementation defined pragma if this is not done implicitly upon inline expansion.)

```
with MACHINE_CODE; use MACHINE_CODE; ...
function "*" (S:SCALAR;V:VECTOR) return VECTOR is
   RESULT : VECTOR (V'RANGE);
   LENGTH : INTEGER := V'LENGTH;
begin
   -- Instructions to carry out serialization
   EXEC_RX_OP(L,8,LENGTH'DISP,
                     LENGTH'X_REG,LENGTH'BASE_REG);
   EXEC_VR_OP(VLVL, 0, 8, 0, 0);
   EXEC_RX_OP(LD,8,S'DISP,S'X_REG,S'BASE_REG);
   EXEC_VX_OP(VLD,A,0,V'DISP,V'X_REG,V'BASE_REG,0);
   EXEC_VR_OP(VMSD, 32, 8, 0, 0);
   EXEC_VX_OP(VSTD,B,32,RESULT'DISP,
                     RESULT'X_REG,RESULT'BASE_REG,0);
   -- Instructions to carry out serialization
   return RESULT;
end "*";
```

Suppose there is no possibility of suppressing register saving; then, in attempting to reduce the overhead involved, vector operations may be specified directly by machine code procedures whose code statements make use of the procedure parameters as shown below. The drawback of this solution is that the infix notation cannot be applied any longer, and that length parameters must be passed explicitly.

```
with MACHINE_CODE;use MACHINE_CODE; ...
procedure SCALMULT (RESULT:out VECTOR;
     S:in SCALAR;V:in VECTOR;LENGTH:in INTEGER);
   pragma INLINE (SCALMULT);
```

```
procedure SCALMULT (RESULT:out VECTOR;
  S:in SCALAR;V:in VECTOR;LENGTH:in INTEGER) is
begin
  --Instructions to carry out serialization
  RX_FORMAT'( CODE => L, ...);
  VR_FORMAT'( CODE => VLVL, ...);
  RX_FORMAT'( CODE => LD, ...);
  VX_FORMAT'( CODE => VLD, ...);
  VR_FORMAT'( CODE => VMSD, ...);
  VX_FORMAT'( CODE => VSTD, ...);
  --Instructions to carry out serialization
end SCALMULT;
```

Obviously, by using infix notation, the first case allows a more natural presentation of vector operations than the second one, on the other hand the differences in runtime should be investigated.

```
V1 := 2.0 * V2;
SCALMULT(V1,2.0,V2,V2'LENGTH);
```

A third alternative will be the possibility of infix notation and a runtime better than in the first case (if there is no suppression of register saving). This is achieved by a hierarchical structure using operator definitions at the upper and procedures containing code statements at the lower level:

```
function "*" (S: SCALAR;V: VECTOR) return VECTOR
is
  RESULT : VECTOR (V'RANGE);
begin
  SCALMULT (RESULT, S, V, V'LENGTH);
  return RESULT;
end "*";
```

Because of the better readability, operator definitions will be used in the following section in order to specify a simple vector processing package.

SPECIFICATION OF VECTOR MODULES

In this section a package specifying vector arithmetic is introduced. It will contain definitions of basic vector operations such as negation, vector addition, vector substraction, scalar multiplication and inner product. This package is not a fully-fledged version; it is meant for demonstration purposes and kept short to save space. For a more comprehensive vector package see, e.g., the work of Klatte et al. (1985). The vector package defined below is non-generic. The predefined type FLOAT serves as the vector component type. Assuming that FLOAT is mapped onto the 64 bit floating point hardware type, which delivers the most precise arithmetic possible (if vector instructions are

involved), most of the numerical analyst's requirements will be met: user
defined floating point types will be mapped onto FLOAT anyway (or onto types
of *less* accuracy).

```
package VECTOR_ARITHMETIC is
    subtype COMPONENT is FLOAT;
    type VECTOR is array
            (INTEGER range <>) of COMPONENT;
    function "-" (X:VECTOR) return VECTOR;
    function "+" (X,Y:VECTOR) return VECTOR;
    function "-" (X,Y:VECTOR) return VECTOR;
    function "*" (S:COMPONENT;X:VECTOR)
                                return VECTOR;
    function "*" (X,Y:VECTOR) return COMPONENT;
end VECTOR_ARITHMETIC;
```

Certainly, this package might be extended by other vector
operations. For example: compute the total of vector components, determine
the values and indices of the minimum and maximum vector components,
perform component shift. One disadvantage of the Ada language definition is
the lack of combinations of characters allowed to be used in operator
definitions as for example "<-" and "->" to name shift operations.

The function bodies to be defined in the package body can be
implemented as described in the previous section. The package body represents
the hardware connection between high level vector operations and vector
machine instructions.

The use of the vector package is demonstrated by the following
piece of code:

```
with VECTOR_ARITHMETIC; use VECTOR_ARITHMETIC; ...
procedure VECTOR_USE ( ... ) is
    subtype SMALL_VECTOR is VECTOR (1 .. 1000);
    V1, V2 : SMALL_VECTOR;
    S      : COMPONENT; ...
begin  ...
    V1 := 2.0 * V1 + V2;
    S  := 2.0 * V1 * V2;   ...
end VECTOR_USE;
```

In particular, vector arithmetic may be used to specify a package
that provides matrix arithmetic (cf. Klatte et al. 1985).

The package VECTOR_ARITHMETIC can be parameterized, e.g. by
making COMPONENT a generic formal floating point type. In this case, the
functions declared within the generic package specification remain non-
generic, of course. Therefore their bodies can be implemented in another
language via pragma INTERFACE; alternatively, they can be realized within the

generic package body by employing machine code insertions. This is interesting in that the generic package body, being nothing but a template, may contain code statements. (In general, there will be as many different code sequences for the same algorithm in the generic body as there are different floating point machine data types to be supported. Upon instantiation the appropriate piece of code will be selected.)

The above-mentioned facilities and additional packages dealing with other issues such as logical vector/matrix operations or vector/matrix comparison complete a tool that should belong to any future APSE supporting vector processors.

CONCLUSION AND PROSPECTS

The goal of this paper has been the presentation of one solution to the problem of executing high level Ada code on a special vector processor by exploiting its hardware architecture extensively. Ada does not provide language constructs that support vector processing directly. However, in contrast to many other languages, it offers several facilities that help implement vector operations. First of all, Ada allows for defining new operators, overloading their names and using them by infix notation; thus, it provides the appropriate abstraction level. The solution proposed here relies on the fact that specifications and bodies can be separated: the vector operations are specified in the normal "high level" way, and the corresponding bodies are implemented by resorting to low-level features which invoke hardware vector instructions. The definitions of vector operations are encapsulated in a package, on which application programs can then be based. To some (limited) extent, generics may be employed.

In detail, there are many problems to be considered. The implementation defined attributes X'DISP, X'X_REG and X'BASE_REG, which return adress information about an arbitrary object X and which are applied within code statements, are difficult to implement on a machine with sliced memory. Moreover, if they are dynamic, their use will be inefficient. Instead of implementing machine code insertions, one may resort to the use of pragma INTERFACE.

Further considerations should deal with the problem of serialization. There ought to be as much parallelism as possible to speed up program execution versus as much serialization as necessary to run a program deterministicly. In addition to this there should be extensions of all operator implementations in order to work on vectors or matrices containing more than 1024 components.

Further issues of interest (which cannot be discussed here for space reasons) deal with the question of portability, with exception handling, and with the fact that the VP 200 instructions take operands no matter whether they are of a floating point type or not.

Computing vector or matrix operations is only a small part of all the operations on data types provided by Ada. Vectorized algorithms of data types as for example lists, trees or graphs are usually handmade today (cf. Brandes 1986) and should be generated by an auto vectorizing Ada compiler containing a knowledge based system within its synthesizing part in the future.

The work described here is being partially supported by the Commission of the European Communities under its Multi-Annual Data-Processing Programme.

REFERENCES
Bohlender, G. , Grüner, K. , Kaucher, E. , Klatte, R. , Krämer, W. , Kulisch, U. , Miranker, W. L., Rump, S. M., Ullrich, C., Wolff von Gudenberg, J. & Böhm, H. (1982): MATRIX PASCAL. IBM. Yorktown Heights. NY. Res. Rep. RC 9577 (42297)
Brandes, Th. (1986): Vektorisierung für High-Level-Languages. Research Report. University of Marburg. Germany. Jan 1986
Ehlich, H. (1984): PASCALV. from Series 'Bochumer Schriften zur parallelen Datenverarbeitung'. Rechenzentrum der Ruhr Universität Bochum. Germany
Fujitsu Limited (1984): FACOM VP SYSTEM General Description
Hibbard, P. A. , Hisgen, A. , Rosenberg, J. , Shaw, M. & Sherman, M. (1981): Studies in Ada Style. Springer-Verlag New York
Klatte, R. , Ullrich, Chr. & Wolff von Gudenberg, J. (1985): Arithmetic Specification for Scientific Computation in ADA. IEEE Transactions on Computers. Vol. C-34. NO 11, 996-1005
Kowalik, S. J. (Editor) (1984): High Speed Computation. Springer Verlag New York Heidelberg Berlin Tokyo. Series F: Computer and Systems Sciences. Vol. 7. Part 1L
Lamport, L. (1974): The Parallel Execution of DO Loops. In: Communications of the ACM. Vol. 17. No. 2. February 1974
Li, K. C. & Schwetman, H. (1985): VectorC. from 'Journal of Parallel and Distributed Computing'. Vol. 2. Number 2. Academic Press. Inc. N.Y. 10003
Reference Manual of the Ada Programming Language (1983): ANSI/MIL-STD 1815A
Schonberg, E. & Schonberg, E. (1985): Highly Parallel Ada - Ada on an Ultracomputer. in: Barnes, Fisher: Ada in Use. pp. 58 - 71. Cambridge University Press
Siemens (1985): System 7.800 Hardware Principles of Operation

THE IMPLICATIONS OF ADA FOR CONFIGURATION MANAGEMENT AND
PROJECT SUPPORT ENVIRONMENTS : TOWARDS ADEQUATE SUPPORT

G. M. Wilson

Plessey Research and Technology (Roke Manor), Romsey,
Hampshire, SO5 0ZN, U.K.

D. P. Youll

Plessey Research and Technology (Roke Manor), Romsey,
Hampshire, SO5 0ZN, U.K.

Abstract. This paper describes the work carried out in
investigating the implications of Ada for software
configuration management. Particular emphasis has been placed
on the discussion and understanding of the technical issues
involved. Satisfying the requirements identified as a
consequence of this discussion, a conceptual model of a
database supporting configuration management of Ada code
is presented on which is based a limited demonstrator; the
implementation of this demonstrator is also described.

1   INTRODUCTION

In support of a major Ada Research Programme (Selwood 1985)
undertaken by the Plessey Company U.K., a number of projects are being
carried out to study key aspects of developing Ada software. One of these
projects concerns the discipline of software configuration management and
the particular impact that Ada will have in this area.

In order to be sure of the real requirements of the user for
adequate automated support, initial emphasis has been placed on
identifying and discussing the technical issues involved in the transition
to Ada in this area. We discuss these issues in-depth, and consequently
identify these requirements. In the course of this discussion, we have
made use of a number of configuration management terms. In view of the
little standardisation of terminology used in texts on this subject, we
first supply definitions of these terms.

To gain some practical experience of some of the technical
issues involved, it was decided to develop a limited, demonstrable
configuration management system. We describe the form of this demonstrator
and discuss the complications involved in extending its functionality.

The ultimate goal of this work is to identify a migration path
towards adequate configuration management support for Ada. In view of
this, we are currently evaluating a number of specialised configuration

management tools and support environments. It is hoped to that we will be able to present the findings of this work in a future paper.

2   DEFINITIONS OF TERMS USED

We now present definitions of the configuration management terminology used in the following sections.

2.1   Components

In the course of a software development project, numerous documents are created to serve many different purposes (e.g. requirements expression, system-level design document, module specification, etc.) together with a multitude of software modules in various representations (e.g. source code, object code, etc.). These uniquely identifiable entities are termed components and are embodied in one or more incarnations.

2.2   Configuration Items (CIs)

Some of these incarnations are distinct and indivisible, whilst others are created by positioning and linking together existing incarnations. An incarnation of the latter type is said to have been configured and is therefore termed a configuration. The incarnations of a component are termed configuration items (CIs) because they have the potential to become components of a configuration.

2.3   Versions

If a CI is regarded as inadequate (e.g. due to imperfect or slow operation) a new CI is created to replace it. A CI created for such a purpose is termed a version. A version and its successor possess a common physical interface and share the same functional and performance specifications. It is possible, however, for a new version to possess a functional specification that encompasses that of its predecessor.

2.4   Variants

Occasionally, a CI is derived from an existing CI with the new CI retaining many of its characteristics but differing in minor respects. Unlike a version, the resultant CI is not intended as a replacement for the CI from which it was derived. A CI derived in this way and its successors are collectively termed a variant and are normally associated with the same component. It is therefore possible for a number of variants to co-exist and be maintained in parallel for each component.

When a new piece of software is created which is functionally identical to an existing set of versions but which employs a different algorithm, a new variant is derived from one of these versions (e.g. a new sort routine is based on an existing sort routine). Variants are also derived to show some logical association between different version sets (e.g. they may be used as replacements in different system configurations intended for different customers).

3 THE ISSUES INVOLVED IN THE CONFIGURATION MANAGEMENT OF ADA-BASED SYSTEMS

We now discuss the issues perceived as being involved in the configuration management of Ada-based systems.

3.1 The need for a fully integrated configuration management system

The major shortcoming of currently commercially-available Ada compilation environments is their general lack of support for version and variant control of the outputs of the compiler. This fact can be partly attributed to the Ada LRM (Ichbiah et al. 1983) whose specification of the program library manager is satisfied by these "minimum implementations". On the other hand, many of the proposed project support enviroments have being designed to provide full support for configuration management, including version and variant control of components in general.

Current Ada compilation environments can be improved by extending the scope of the configuration management facilities of a support environment to control the contents of the Ada program library and the Ada compilation process. To achieve this, the configuration management facilities must be integrated with the Ada compilation environment. There are two degrees to which these components can be integrated.

A configuration management system integrated to the first degree is one in which the Ada compiler and its program library manager is given access to the contents of the configuration management system but which is only able to control those CIs submitted by the user.

The ideal is a system that is integrated to the second degree in which the configuration management facilities are able to "oversee" the entire development process. This is achieved by tightly coupling the

configuration management facilities to the development facilities of the
support environment (including the Ada compilation environment). A system
integrated to this degree is termed a fully integrated configuration
management system and has the following advantages:

   (i) the user no longer needs to submit a component CI to be placed
      under the control of the configuration management system, since
      each version becomes visible to, and under the control of, the
      system automatically at creation-time;

  (ii) one no longer needs to recompile source code submitted for quality
      approval acceptance in order to ensure that it corresponds to the
      object code CI and CIs of the compilation units upon which it is
      supposed to depend;

(iii) its visibility of the development process CIs enables it to
      automatically record history attribute information as called for
      by "Stoneman" (Buxton 1980);

 (iv) support can be provided for the compilation and linking processes
      (see below).

3.2 Support for the compilation and linking processes in an integrated system

The concept of an integrated configuration management system
and Ada compilation environment is not new (e.g. the MCHAPSE development,
U.K. Ada Study (1981) and the ECLIPSE environment, Pierce (1985)).
However, we feel that the need for support of the compilation and linking
processes in an integrated system can be made more effective. By this we
mean the task of placing into a program library, those files whose
presence is required for the successful compilation of a given compilation
unit or the linking of a specified program configuration.

To make use of the multiple versions and variants of Ada code
recorded by an integrated system in the compilation and linking processes,
it should be possible for the user to enter the CIs of those files
required into the desired program library. To assist in this task, the
user should be provided with at least the following convenient defaults
options for the selection of those CIs required:

(i) use the specified version;

(ii) use the versions currently in the program library;

(iii) use the latest versions available for use in the project;

(iv) use the latest versions approved for inter-project reuse;

(v) use the versions from a particular baseline.

In the case of "with" dependencies, which are explicitly written into the source code, the user should be able to use one of the above options in the context clause to select the particular CI(s) to be imported. The source code would then have to be pre-processed before compilation and the specified file(s) entered into the library automatically.

3.3 Storage of compilation dependencies

The recording of the compilation dependencies which exist between the component CIs generated by the compiler is essential to the support of the compilation and linking processes. We now consider how best to record these dependencies.

As recognised by Pierce (1985), the types of files generated and used by an Ada compiler is dependent upon a number of factors. These factors include the type of compilation unit being compiled, the implementation of the compiler and the context in which the compilation is done (e.g. the qualifiers used with the compile command).

Taking into account the above factors, it is logical to store compilation dependencies between the collective of the source code CI and the outputs from its compilation. This collective is termed a compilation and should be allowed to exist as a number of CIs. To further assist compilation support, the system should also record details of each program library and its current contents in terms of compilation CIs.

The need for support of multiple versions and variants has been recognised (e.g. the ECLIPSE environment (Pierce 1985) and the Telesoft/Telelogic Library Manager (LM) (Narfelt & Schefstrom 1985)). These developments do not support the versioning of "compilations" (or a similar construct), but record versions of the contents of the program library itself, the user choosing when to create a new program library version. In the integrated system of ECLIPSE, each program library version is recorded explicitly, whereas with the Telesoft LM, a program library is constructed from ordered layers (or sublibraries) which can be used to represent its versions and variants.

The major drawback of these approaches is that the user is only able to recall those program configurations chosen to be recorded; unless care is taken, these may include inconsistent program states. With our approach, the user can compose program configurations (subject, of course, to consistency with the compilation dependencies) from compilation CIs which can be easily interchanged with others under the control of the configuration management system.

4   A CONCEPTUAL MODEL OF A DATABASE SUPPORTING CONFIGURATION
    MANAGEMENT OF ADA CODE

As a consequence of the discussion in the preceding section, a number of data-handling requirements were identified for adequate support of configuration management of Ada developments. We now present a subset of a conceptual model designed to satisfy these requirements. This we have chosen to represent as an entity-relational model (Chen 1976) because of its simplicity and its wide familiarity.

The subset of the model (as shown in figure 1) shows only the entity and relationship types; their attributes are not shown for the sake of conciseness. We now describe the entity and relationship types chosen to represent the various forms of Ada code.

The concept of a compilation CI was defined in 3.3. The relationships: imports, has_bodies, subunit_of and expands_inline are introduced to model "with" dependencies, specification/body dependencies, dependencies between subunits and their parent units, and dependencies introduced by use of the INLINE pragma, respectively. A compilation CI is has the relationships: has_source, has_listings, etc. A source text CI corresponds to a source code file which may contain the source of many compilation units and hence may generate many compilation CIs. Also, one may compile a given source text CI more than once.

To record the current contents of the program libraries being used (in terms of resident compilation CIs), the program library entity type is introduced with its relationship, contains.

The entity type, executable image CI, and the relationship, linked_into, allow us to record the mapping of object code CIs to executable image CIs.

Figure 1 - A conceptual model of a database supporting CM of
Ada code

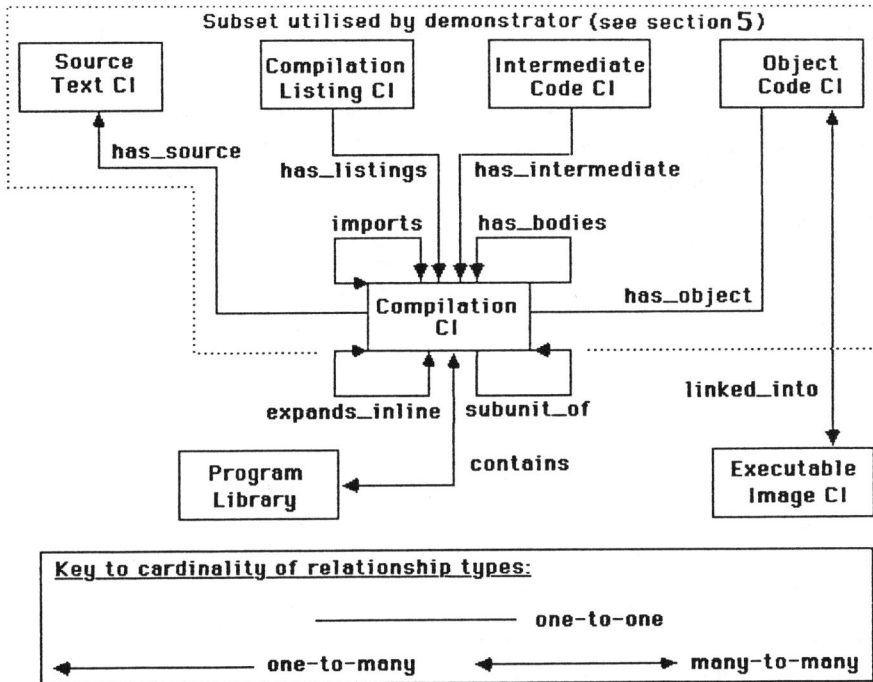

```
┌──────────────────────────────────────────────────────────────────────────┐
:          Subset utilised by demonstrator (see section 5)                  :
: ┌─────────┐   ┌───────────┐      ┌────────────┐        ┌─────────┐         :
: │ Source  │   │Compilation│      │Intermediate│        │ Object  │         :
: │ Text CI │   │ Listing CI│      │  Code CI   │        │ Code CI │         :
: └─────────┘   └───────────┘      └────────────┘        └─────────┘         :
:      │   has_source                                                        :
:      │         has_listings      has_intermediate                         :
:      │                                                                     :
:      │          imports     has_bodies                                     :
:      │         ┌─────────────────┐                                         :
:      │         │  Compilation    │      has_object                         :
:      └─────────│      CI         │────────────────                         :
:                └─────────────────┘                                         :
└──────────────────────────────────────────────────────────────────────────┘
       expands_inline │ subunit_of          linked_into
   ┌─────────┐              contains    ┌─────────────┐
   │ Program │◄─────────────────────    │ Executable  │
   │ Library │                          │  Image CI   │
   └─────────┘                          └─────────────┘
```

```
┌──────────────────────────────────────────────────────────────────────┐
│ Key to cardinality of relationship types:                             │
│                          ──────────────── one-to-one                   │
│  ◄───────────── one-to-many    ◄────────► many-to-many                 │
└──────────────────────────────────────────────────────────────────────┘
```

Figure 2 - Example of an illegal program configuration

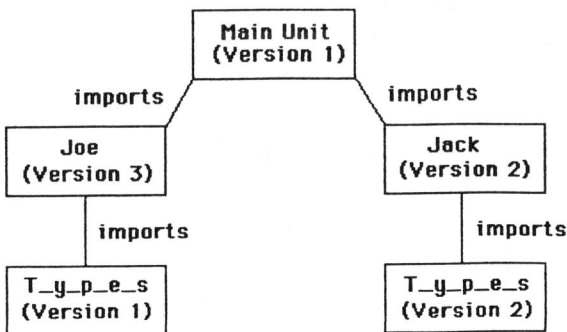

```
                    ┌──────────────┐
                    │  Main Unit   │
                    │ (Version 1)  │
                    └──────────────┘
           imports   ╱          ╲   imports
      ┌──────────────┐        ┌──────────────┐
      │     Joe      │        │     Jack     │
      │ (Version 3)  │        │ (Version 2)  │
      └──────────────┘        └──────────────┘
           │  imports              │  imports
      ┌──────────────┐        ┌──────────────┐
      │   T_y_p_e_s  │        │   T_y_p_e_s  │
      │ (Version 1)  │        │ (Version 2)  │
      └──────────────┘        └──────────────┘
```

5 THE DEVELOPMENT OF A LIMITED, DEMONSTRABLE CONFIGURATION
   MANAGEMENT SYSTEM

To demonstrate the principle of fully integrating an Ada
compilation environment with a configuration management system, and to
improve upon our understanding of the technical issues involved, it was
decided to develop a configuration management system limited to the
support of version and variant control of compilations.

The conceptual model was implemented on a binary relational
database management system which serves as the underlying data repository
for the demonstrator. The Ada compilation environment used is the DEC Ada
implementation which includes the Ada Compilation System (ACS).

Three basic facilities were regarded as the minimum necessary
to demonstrate the principle of "integration". We now briefly describe
these facilities.

5.1 Demonstrator facilities

5.1.1 Compile and save facility. The first of these facilities is
referred to as the 'compile and save' facility. This facility works in
much the same way as DEC's ADA compile command, which is used to compile
the contents of a specified file, but differs in two respects. The primary
difference is that every compilation CI created by use of this facility is
automatically placed under the control of the configuration management
system; the user has the option of specifying that a compilation CI is to
become a member of a variant.

To simplify the implementation of the demonstrator, all
compilations are performed in the context of a single program library
whose whereabouts in the directory structure are not made known to the
user, thereby reducing the risk of library corruption by the user
circumventing the demonstrator. To prevent compilation CIs from being
overwritten in the event of their recompilation, they are stored in
dynamically created program libraries which "hang" from the main library.

As can be seen in figure 1, only the 'imports' dependencies
and 'has_bodies' dependencies are recorded; the compilation of subunits
and generic units is not supported. This limitation is due to the fact
that ACS only makes the latter two dependency types visible to the user;
the other dependency types are encoded in a specially formatted file.

5.1.2 General Query Facility. The second facility developed was a general query facility. This was provided to enable the user to ascertain which compilation CIs have been compiled and saved by use of the above facility. When invoked, this facility outputs an alphabetically-ordered list of the compilation units, the versions compiled so far (in their variants), and their compilation dependencies. The facility also indicates which versions and variants are currently entered in the library.

5.1.3 <u>Re-enter Facility</u>. The third facility provided enables the user to select a currently withdrawn version of a compilation to be placed into the library.

Since it is possible for a compilation CI of a specification to possess several compilation CIs of its corresponding body, the demonstrator ensures that in the event of the compilation CI of a body being re-entered, the corresponding version of its specification is also entered. In the reverse case, the demonstrator automatically removes any corresponding body CI currently resident. In a more practical configuration management system, one would be able to select the compilation CI of a body by a default such as those listed in 3.2.

5.2   <u>Additional facilities considered for implementation</u>

A number of other facilities in addition to those described above were identified as being necessary in a practical configuration management system. The provision of these facilities and the complications involved in their implementation are discussed below.

5.2.1 <u>Re-enter compilation closure facility</u>. To borrow a definition used by DEC, the total set of compilation units that a given unit depends upon, both directly and indirectly, is called the compilation closure of the given unit. As an extension to the re-enter facility described above, a facility to re-enter the compilation closure of a specified compilation version is thought to be useful.

Unfortunately, the meaning of the term 'compilation closure' becomes unclear in cases where a compilation CI of a specification possesses several CIs of its body. There should therefore be a number of selection options made available to the user such as those listed in 3.2.

5.2.2 <u>Equivalents of the ACS COMPILE and RECOMPILE commands</u>. ACS provides two powerful compile commands which act on the compilation closure of a specified compilation unit as opposed to a single compilation unit. The former recompiles (compiles from copied source) any unit in the closure that needs to be made current, whilst the latter does this and also compiles those units whose source has changed. The provision of equivalents of these two commands was considered but we found that we were faced with the same complication as described in 5.2.1.

5.2.3 <u>Linking facility</u>. In a practical configuration management system, a linking facility should allow the user to specify a particular version of the main program unit. However, in programs that contain compilation CIs of specifications which possess multiple compilation CIs of its body, the above information is insufficient to identify the compilation closure. Therefore, a number of options, such as those listed in 3.2, should be made available to enable the user to select those body CIs required.

Although it is not possible to link the object code of more than one compilation CI of a compilation unit into an executable image CI, it may still be possible to compile several compilation CIs of a compilation unit into the same program (see example in figure 2) if adequate controls do not exist. Not only does this practice contravene the rules of Ada (Ichbiah et al. 1983), it may also lead to serious run-time errors if one is allowed to link a program configuration that is inconsistent with the compilation dependencies recorded. Ideally, an integrated system should detect, and disallow, such a practice at compile-time. Failing this, it should check the compilation dependencies at link-time and disallow the link.

6   Conclusions

The need for a fully integrated configuration management system and Ada compilation environment was identified and justified. The integrated nature of support environments aimed at supporting Ada developments will make it possible to satisfy this need. Indeed, this has been been recognised in a number of recently proposed developments. Some of these developments have advocated the approach of recording versions of the contents of the program library. We have proposed an alternative approach of recording versions of the collective of the source code and its associated compiler outputs which can be treated as an interchangeable component of a program. It is argued that this approach, coupled with a suitable set of selection options for retrieving these collectives, is

more flexible in its support of the compilation and linking processes.
In describing a limited configuration management system developed to
demonstrate our approach, we have identified a number of controls which
are required to prevent the user from composing program configurations
which are either illegal or inconsistent with the compilation dependencies
recorded by the system.

7 Acknowledgements
        The authors would like to thank the Plessey company for their
financial support of this project and J. R. Hunt for his assistance in
this work.

Reference List
Buxton, J. (1980) Department of Defense Requirements for Ada Programming
        Support Environments "STONEMAN", U.S. Department of Defense.
Chen, P. P. S. (1976) The entity-relationship model - towards a unified
        view of data. ACM Trans. Database Systems, 1,1 Mar., 936.
Ichbiah, J. D. et al (1983). Reference Manual for the Ada Programming
        Language. ANSI-MIL-STD-1815A-1983, U.S Department of Defense.
Narfelt, K. H. & Schefstrom D. (1985). Extending the Scope of the Program
        Library. Ada in Use: Proceedings of the Ada International
        Conference, 1985, 25,40.
Pierce, R. H. (1985). Ada in the ECLIPSE Project Support Environment. Ada
        in Use: Proceedings of the Ada International Conference, 1985,
        309,320.
Selwood, M. (1985). Practical Experiences of the Ada Language for
        real-time embedded systems development for the Defence-Related
        Market. Proceedings of the 4th Annual National Conference on
        Ada Technology.
U.K. Ada Study (1981). Final Technical Report Volume 2. K3-2-2.

Part III Reusability

UNDERSTANDING Ada[R] SOFTWARE REUSABILITY ISSUES FOR THE TRANSITION
OF MISSION CRITICAL COMPUTER RESOURCE APPLICATIONS

A. Gargaro
Computer Sciences Corporation, Moorestown, NJ 08057, USA

T. Pappas
Computer Sciences Corporation, Moorestown, NJ 08057, USA

Abstract. This paper identifies fundamental issues relevant to the
successful reuse of Ada software in Mission Critical Computer
Resource (MCCR) applications. The reusability of an Ada program is
defined in the context of three criteria for evaluating the degree to
which Ada software is reusable. These criteria are important to
writing reusable software for the timely transition of MCCR systems
to the Ada Language.

PROLOGUE

A central idea in the design of the Ada language (Department of
Defense 1983) is to assemble a program from independently produced software
components. Therefore, the reusability of Ada software components (STARS 1985)
is viewed as the cornerstone in reducing the cost of developing Mission Critical
Computer Resource (MCCR) systems. If the promise of reusing Ada software
components is fulfilled, the reduction in cost is expected to be significant
(Anderson 1985).

There is little practical experience in reusing Ada software
components for MCCR applications. In the initial transitions to the Ada language
the reuse of software components may be adversely affected by fundamental issues
that affect the writing of reusable components. Understanding these issues is
necessary to managing the transition if the potential costs and benefits of Ada
software reusability are to be predicted.

APPROACH

Several studies have reported on transitioning currently deployed
MCCR systems to the Ada language (Friedman 1985). These studies have focused on
evaluating the adequacy of the Ada language to meet existing performance
efficiency requirements and do not specifically consider the reuse of
transitioned software among different MCCR applications.

The results from the studies indicate that in transitioning to the
Ada language, rigid performance requirements upon the run-time environment will
necessitate the use of Ada constructs where their level of abstraction may be

compromised by explicit and implicit dependencies upon the run-time environment. Consequently, developing Ada software that is both reusable and meets the performance requirements of MCCR applications presents a conflict. The conflict is exacerbated by programming practices that have exploited idiosyncracies of the execution environment. These practices have resulted in application specific techniques that are efficient but reduce the level of abstraction essential for software reuse.

For example, one requirement that pervades MCCR applications is the facility for periodic control of both concurrent and serial processing. Traditionally this requirement has been satisfied by variations of the Cyclic Executive which has become the classical paradigm for examining the efficacy of using the Ada language for real-time programming (Hood 1985; MacLaren 1980; Phillips & Stevenson 1984). Often the adaptation of the Cyclic Executive to provide efficient use of processing resources can lead to dependencies by the application software on programming techniques that are nonreusable. These techniques may persist after the transition depending upon the implementation of the Ada Run-Time System (RTS). In understanding the issues of software reuse, the ramifications of such techniques must be understood to perform tradeoff analysis between efficiency and reuse when transitioning to the Ada language.

To understand the reuse of Ada software components an approach must address, at a minimum, the issues of writing efficient code that is reusable in different run-time environments. Particular emphasis should be given to: performance efficiency requirements of MCCR applications as they affect software reuse, program composition features of the Ada language that facilitate the creation and use of reusable components, and the implementation options of the Ada RTS that may compromise software reuse. In this paper, the technical foci is directed towards the latter two topics.

Ada SOFTWARE REUSABILITY

Software reusability comprises the concept to execute a program in an execution environment different from that in which it was originally developed, i.e., transportability, and the concept to combine components from different programs in the development of a new program, i.e., reusability. The comprehensive support of the Ada language for modern software engineering principles, viz., abstraction, composition, encapsulation, and instantiation, provide a framework for writing reusable software. The distinction made in this paper between the concepts of reusability and transportability of Ada software is discussed in the following paragraphs. This distinction partially resolves the inherent ambiguity of these two concepts and is consistent with the notion of both reusability "in the large" and "in the small" (Lubars 1986).

Program Transportability

The transportability of an Ada program is defined as the ability of a program to complete functionally equivalent execution in different environments consistent with the Ada language. Transportability is measured by the degree this execution can be achieved without modifying the source code. This definition is derived from an earlier one (Oberndorf et al 1982) and work that has been previously reported (Nissen & Wallis 1984; Pappas 1985). The stipulation for equivalent execution rather than identical execution recognizes that the processing capacity of the execution environment and the sophistication of the compiling system may affect the execution behavior of the program within the semantics of the Ada Reference Manual (RM) (Volz et al 1986). For example, the number of times a loop body is performed may vary because the source code invites compiler optimization. In addition, it does not exclude the use of representation specifications to influence execution since their use is perceived as essential to most MCCR applications.

Program Reusability

The reusability of an Ada program is defined as the ability of one or more of its components to execute with identical functionality in the construction of a new program. Reusability is measured in the degree that different components of the program can be used to construct new programs in the same and different execution environments. This definition is more stringent than the one recently proposed for developing reusability guidelines (Braun et al 1985) since three important criteria for evaluating program reusability are mandated: the transportability of the program, the orthogonality, i.e., functional independence, of its composition, and its freedom from dependencies on a specific implementation of the Ada Run-Time System (RTS). The definition does not discriminate between writing reusable components and programs where their constituent components can be reused.

A necessary first step to reusing components in different execution environments is to achieve the transportability of the program. When only the program is to be reused, the distinction between reusability and transportability is the fidelity of execution, i.e, equivalent or identical. When a component is to be reused in different programs, e.g., an Ada generic unit, the transportability criteria ensures a context for validating execution.

<u>Composition Orthogonality</u>. In discussing composition orthogonality,
it is convenient to introduce degrees of reusability. A component whose
potential for reuse is low is said to be weakly reusable, while a component
whose potential for reuse is high is said to be strongly reusable. These
represent the extremes of reusability. Source modifications and limited
applicability are expected with weak reusability, while with strong reusability
no source modifications and potentially frequent applicability are expected. An
effectively reusable component differs from a strongly reusable component only
in that some source modifications may be required due to Ada language rules. In
practice weak reusability is to be avoided, strong reusability strived for,
with effective reusability actually obtained.

The orthogonality of a program's composition is an attribute of the
program which reflects the independence of its components from the enclosing
context. The stronger a component's dependence on its context, the less likely
its potential for reuse since more of the context must be transported with it,
i.e., weak reusability is more likely. Conversely, the weaker a component's
dependence on its context, the greater the potential for the component's reuse
since little, if any, of the surrounding context need be transported with it,
i.e., strong reusability is more likely. When coupled with programming for
generality, striving for context independence will yield effectively reusable,
if not strongly reusable, software components.

Composition orthogonality is not an issue in program transportability
since the entire context of each program component is transported to the new
execution environment. It is only when a component is extracted from its context
that composition orthogonality becomes an issue. The exception to this is a
program whose main subprogram has parameters. But in this situation, the context
dependency is on the execution context and not the application context.
Therefore, the issue is one of transportability rather than reusability.

Degrees of reusability are illustrated in Example 1, where two
versions of a binary search are shown. Example 1.a, which is typical of binary
searches used in practice, is weakly reusable for several reasons. First, it has
several context dependencies. Reuse of this example requires providing three
entities in the new context: a named number, Max_Table_Elements, a type named
Element_Type, and an array named Table with the structure shown. If these entity
names or the array structure are not appropriate in the new context, then the
component must be modified. A second problem with this example is its lack of
generality. In addition to only providing a binary search for a particular
array, it strongly depends on the array index subtype being a subtype of

Positive. This dependency is explicit in the Mid_Point calculation and in the calculations of the left and right end points. The dependency is implicit in the use of zero to indicate that the element is not found in the Table. The result subtype of the Binary_Search function, Natural, extends the array index subtype by one value to allow it to serve a dual purpose — return the array index upon a successful search and indicate failure upon an unsuccessful search.

Example 1.a - Weak Reusability

```
Table : array (1 .. Max_Table_Elements) of Element_Type;
. . .
function Binary_Search (Element : in Element_Type) return Natural is
   Left_Point  : Positive := 1;
   Right_Point : Positive := Max_Table_Elements;
   Mid_Point   : Positive;
begin
   while Left_Point <= Right_Point loop
      Mid_Point := (Left_Point + Right_Point) / 2;
      if Element < Table (Mid_Point) then
         Right_Point := Mid_Point - 1;
      elsif Table (Mid_Point) < Element then
         Left_Point  := Mid_Point + 1;
      else
         return Mid_Point;
      end if;
   end loop;
   return 0;
end Binary_Search;
```

Example 1.b illustrates a strongly reusable version of the binary search. Here, the function has been encapsulated within a generic package. Through the use of generic formal parameters, all context dependencies have been removed. In addition, the parameterization in Example 1.b encompasses all possible generalizations of this binary search that do not change its functionality.

While there is no difference between effective reusability and strong reusability in Example 1.b, there are situations where a difference may occur. For example, consider a generic subprogram implementing a numerical algorithm such that the algorithm requires a real type. The "real" type is a generic formal parameter of the generic subprogram. If only standard mathematical operations are required for this type, then a private type can be used. The mathematical operations would be generic formal function parameters, with appropriate defaults, to the generic subprogram. If, however, accuracy demands necessitate the use of floating point or fixed point attributes, then two versions of the generic subprogram are needed: one for floating point types and

one for fixed point types. In this case there is a difference between effective
reusability and strong reusability. Both versions are effectively reusable but
neither is strongly reusable.

Example 1.b - Strong Reusability

```
generic
   type Element_Type is private;
   type Index_Type   is (<>);
   type Table_Type   is array (Index_Type range <>) of Element_Type;
   with function "<" (Left, Right : Element_Type) return Boolean is <>;
package Binary_Search_Package_Template is
   function Binary_Search (Table: Table_Type; Element: Element_Type)
                         return Index_Type;
   Not_Found : exception;
end Binary_Search_Package_Template;

package body Binary_Search_Package_Template is
   function Binary_Search (Table: Table_Type; Element: Element_Type)
                         return Index_Type is
      Left_End  : Index_Type := Table'First;
      Right_End : Index_Type := Table'Last;
      Mid_Point : Index_Type;
   begin
      if Table'Last < Table'First then
         raise Not_Found;
      else
         while Left_End < Right_End loop
            Mid_Point := Index_Type'Val (Index_Type'Pos (Left_End)
                                       + Index_Type'Pos (Right_End) / 2);
            if Element < Table (Mid_Point) then
               Right_End := Index_Type'Pred (Mid_Point);
            elsif Table (Mid_Point) < Element then
               Left_End  := Index_Type'Succ (Mid_Point);
            else
               return Mid_Point;
            end if;
         end loop;
         if Left_End = Right_End and then Element = Table (Left_End) then
            return Left_End;
         else
            raise Not_Found;
         end if;
      end if;
   end Binary_Search;
end Binary_Search_Package_Template;
```

One strongly reusable version could be written that would necessitate
using a private "real" type. Several additional generic formal subprograms
would need to be included as generic parameters, but rather than providing the
user with any real benefit, these subprograms would simply serve to isolate
floating point and fixed point attribute dependencies, perform type conversions,

etc. While this version might satisfy the strong reusability notion of this paper, in reality, users would not be likely to use a generic component requiring generic actual parameters merely to comply with Ada's language rules.

Components that are effectively or strongly reusable seem to be consistent with good programming style so, ideally, all program components should be written in this manner. This would maximize the reusability of the program's components. In reality, this is not likely to occur since MCCR performance issues may dictate otherwise. While the binary search in Example 1.b may be strongly reusable, program tuning may require a weakly reusable version. In particular, the distributed binary search due to Knuth (Bentley 1982) may be needed in the tuned program. Since the distributed search could be produced by a program generator it may still be correct to view it as strongly reusable, but at the level of a program generator.

RTS Dependencies. The potential for RTS dependencies to affect the reuse of Ada program units can be appreciated by reviewing a specific example that presents a dependency on a particular implementation of task scheduling. This dependency does not necessarily prevent program execution from meeting the transportability criterion when the dependency is not satisfied in the environment to which the program is transported for reuse. However, successful reuse of the program unit that includes the dependency cannot be guaranteed in the new environment.

The example is contrived to expedite a straightforward discussion and the referenced code does not represent recommended use of the language or a dependency that cannot be mitigated in some other way. The example originated from a revision to a program from the Ada Fair benchmark suite (Bardin et al 1985). The original program included packages designed to control access to a shared variable as a means of evaluating the integrity of the task scheduler. In the revised version, the access control task has been modified to service concurrent reader and writer tasks where the access protocol is biased in favor of writer tasks to simulate real-time updating of the shared variable. The shared variable is of a composite type and may be read concurrently by more than one task providing no task has been granted write access. Furthermore, writing must be serialized and outstanding writes should be serviced before a task is granted read access, since writer tasks are assigned highest priority.

The two code fragments to be examined are shown in Example 2. The first fragment is the select statement enclosed by the task that grants read/write access. The second fragment is the timed entry statement enclosed by the procedure that is called by the writer tasks. The dependency is associated with the use of the COUNT attribute in the iteration scheme of the while-loop that is designed to service all outstanding write requests before a new read is accepted.

. Example 2 - Implicit RTS Dependence

```
— Task controlling read/write access to shared variable
  task body RW_Control is
  . . .
  select
  — Activate new reader if no writer is waiting
    when Start_Write'COUNT = 0 =>
         accept Start_Read;
         Active_Readers := Active_Readers + 1;
  or
  — Activate writer if no active readers
    when Active_Readers   = 0 =>
         accept Start_Write;
         accept Stop_Write;
  or
  — Wait for active read to complete
         accept Stop_Read;
         Active_Readers := Active_readers - 1;
         if Active_Readers = 0 then
  — Activate and serialize waiting writers
            while Start_Write'COUNT > 0 loop
  — >>> Implicit dependency on stability of COUNT
                accept Start_Write;
                accept Stop_Write;
            end loop;
         end if;
  or
     terminate;
  end select;
     . . .
  end RW_Control;
```

```
— procedure called by writer tasks

  . . .
  select
     RW_Control.Start_Write;
  — Update shared variable with actual parameter from call
  or
     delay Write_Time_Limit;
     RW_Control.Start_Write;
  — Update shared variable to indicate that the writer was late
  end select;
```

The RM cautions against the use of the COUNT attribute because its value is not stable. In this instance sufficient stability is only required to ensure that the Start_Write entry queue is not decremented prior to accepting the Start_Write entry. This depends upon a class of First-In-First-Out (FIFO) task scheduling that prevents interruption of control task execution until it is blocked by the Stop_Write entry even in the presence of an expired timed entry statement. The dependency requires that expiration of the delay does not result in run-time action, viz., changing the state of the delayed writer task, until the executing task is blocked and a new task has to be executed.

This dependency does not preclude successful execution in a different environment where task scheduling is not guaranteed to maintain the stability of the value of the COUNT attribute. For instance, an RTS that implements a preemptive class of task scheduling may result in the value being decremented after the evaluation of the while-loop but prior to accepting the Start_Write entry. However, because of the priority of the writer tasks and the Start_Write entry statement following the expired delay, the number of queued requests cannot decrease. Consequently, program transportability is achieved since execution is functionally equivalent in both environments.

When the above implicit dependency is not clearly stipulated, the control task may be mistakenly considered to be strongly reusable in the new environment on the basis of program transportability. An attempt to reuse the control task with a different procedure for writer tasks can have aberrant execution behavior in an environment that does not guarantee the stability of the COUNT attribute. A simple change to the timed entry statement that removes the Start_Write following the delay can cause the entry queue count to reach zero. The control task is now forced to unexpectedly wait at the Start_Write resulting in disruption to performance since the reader tasks are dependent for execution on a write request. This is contrary to the guard specification of the enclosing select statement. In a worst case situation, when no further writes are requested, the control task is blocked indefinitely from execution.

EPILOGUE

This paper has presented a refinement to the concept of reusability. This refinement provides insight into understanding issues in writing reusable Ada software components for MCCR applications. Composition orthogonality and independence from the Ada RTS implementation are identified as useful criteria for assessing program reusability. Understanding these criteria will allow varying degrees of program reusability to be specified in transitioning MCCR applications to the Ada language. Composition orthogonality is important because many Ada features that facilitate program reusability have been avoided or unavailable in past MCCR application software that have commonly relied upon simple constructs with predictable performance efficiency (Bassman et al 1985). In addition, dependencies on the implementation of the Ada RTS to imitate low-level control of processing resources can thwart strong reusability achieved through composition orthogonality.

In managing the transition, software reuse should be safeguarded by balancing program reusability with performance during the design phase. Furthermore, reusable Ada software components will be facilitated by language implementations that are guided by the specification of classes of Ada Virtual Machines for MCCR applications and practical restrictions on Appendix-F of the Ada RM. This would increase the likelihood of formally certifying the degree of reuse for software components (Cohen 1985).

REFERENCES

Anderson, C.M. (1985). Reusable Software - A Mission Critical Case Study.
    AIAA Computers in Aerospace V Conference, pp 136-139.
Bardin, B. et al (1985). Report on the L.A. AdaTEC Ada Fair'84: Compiler Test
    Results. ACM SIGAda Ada Letters 4, No. 4, pp 52-58.
Bassman, M. J. et al (1985). Evaluating the Performance Efficiency of Ada
    Compilers. ACM DC SIGAda Washington Ada Symposium.
Bentley, J. L. (1982). Writing Efficient Programs: Prentice-Hall.
Braun, C. et al (1985). Ada Reusability Guidelines. SofTech Inc., 3285-2-208/2.
Cohen, N. H. (1985). Verified Ada: A Key to Reliable Software. AIAA Computers
    in Aerospace V Conference.
Department of Defense (1983). Reference Manual for the Ada Programming Language,
    ANSI/MIL-STD-1815A.
Friedman, F. (1985). Issues Affecting Software Productivity due to the
    Introduction of Ada. Computer Sciences Corp., TR No. SP-IRD 4.
Hood, P. (1985). Cyclic Executives: Pros, Cons, and Relation to Ada.
    SofTech Inc., Working Paper 1123-WP1.
Lubars, M.D. (1986). Code Reusability in the Large versus Code Reusability
    in the Small. ACM SIGSOFT SEN 11, No. 1, pp 21-28.
MacLaren, L. (1980). Evolving Toward Ada in Real-Time Systems. ACM SIGPLAN
    Notices 15, No. 11, pp 146-155.
Nissen, J. & Wallis, P. (1984). Portability and Style in Ada: Cambridge
    University Press.
Oberndorf, P. et al (1982). KAPSE Interface Team: Public Report Vol. 1.
    Naval Ocean Systems Center Technical Document 509.
Pappas, T. (1985). Ada Portability Guidelines. SofTech Inc., ESD-TR-85-141.
Philips, S. & Stevenson, P. (1984). The Role of Ada in Real-Time Embedded
    Applications. ACM SIGAda Ada Letters 3, No. 4, pp 99-111.
STARS (1985). STARS Workshop on Reusable Components of Application Software.
    Naval Research Laboratory.
Volz, R. et al. (1986). Toward Real-Time Performance Benchmarks for Ada.
    University of Michigan.

SOFTWARE METHODOLOGY AND
THE AIE PROGRAM LIBRARY

David Carney
Intermetrics, Inc.
Cambridge, MA 02138
USA

INTRODUCTION

The role of the Program Library in Ada environments has received
less attention than other elements of the language. Ada's linguistic features - tasking, generics, and the like - are perhaps more riveting to the newcomer; Ada's
difficulties, especially in compiler design, have certainly received greater publicity.
But at least one other contributing element is the fact that the Library, as the
cornerstone of any true Ada environment, could emerge only when compilers
reached genuine maturity. Now that we are nearing this goal, we are also witness-
ing the appearance of Library Management Systems written entirely in Ada, and
playing a part in Ada environments no less vital than does the real-world library
play in the real-world University.

The Ada Integrated Environment (AIE) is sponsored by the United
States Air Force and includes an optimizing compiler along with various environ-
mental and support tools. The project, written entirely in Ada, was developed on
an IBM 3083 using a Universal Time-Sharing system. The project made use of an
interim Program Library until the full AIE library was phased in during November,
1985.

This paper will describe the Program Library system of the AIE. It
will also describe both typical library experiences and those specific to a complex library management tool, all of these encountered in writing a large software project
in Ada.

DEFINITION OF THE PROGRAM LIBRARY

The Ada Language Reference Manual (LRM) specifies very little about the Program Library. It requires only that the language rules of Ada be enforced "in the same manner for a program consisting of several compilation units... as for a program submitted as a single compilation". Otherwise, the Program Library is simply described as a means whereby

> information on the compilation units ... must be maintained by the compiler or compiling environment ... The possible existence of different program libraries and the means by which they are named are ... concerns of the programming environment.
>
> (LRM 10.4)

This statement implies that the Library have a close relation with the compiler, and that it deal specifically with compiled units. For this reason, even though the term 'program library' has sometimes referred to libraries of source files only (Broido, Leavitt), such collections, however valuable, are not Program Libraries in the Ada sense.

Presuming that the library mechanism does fulfil the LRM's requirements, there is obviously a wide range of possibilities for its design. These points are critical:

1. The repository of compiled units can be seen to be either public or private; i.e., autonomous users with separate libraries, or a system-wide pool of available units;

2. The library can be construed to be strictly the compiled units, or can also include the source files which generated them.

3. The question of software reusability will have a considerable influence on the overall design.

Problems in Library Design

If the public/private views are regarded as extremes, clearly neither is desirable. The totally private concept will result in no sharing whatsoever, and in numerous redundant compilations. The unconstrained public view is simply too unwieldly, at least in a large environment. All users are vulnerable to a single error; such practical details as package naming conventions would be chaotic.

The matter of whether or not to manage source files presents equally difficult choices. If other users' source files are not available by some means, then software sharing becomes a dead issue. But the inclusion of source files in the library imposes the necessity of a dependable tracking mechanism between the source and the generated objects. In a large environment, where a typical package may have many revisions, this soon becomes a configuration management nightmare.

Common to both of these points is the question of software reuse. If it is a genuine goal of the environment, then the library tool, whatever its implementation, will be a significant factor in achieving that goal.

IMPLEMENTATIONS OF THE PROGRAM LIBRARY

Implementors have dealt with the above points in various ways. Since the Program Library is typically a portion of a large Ada environment, it generally reflects the bias of that particular system. One such system, the Ada Language System (ALS), emphasizes management of source files and their revisions. The Program Library in the ALS is defined as "a collection of directories and revisions in one subtree ... There is one Program Library for each variation of an executable program". (Thall) Another large system, the Distributed Software Engineering Control Process (DCP), places the Program Library at the center of a database management system which also includes a Dictionary and an Encyclopedia; the Library is "one of several objects carried in a non-RDBMS portion of the overall database". (Dempsey)

The AIE Program Library

The AIE differs from these systems in two critical areas. First, the AIE Program Library is primarily concerned with compiled units, not with the source/object pair. Second, most library activities take place not with compilation units themselves but in terms of a construct called a Catalog.

Catalogs and Collections

A user's Program Library is an organization of program units which have successfully compiled. (LRM.10.3: "If any error is detected [during compilation] ... it has no effect whatsoever on the program library.") Units exist in three forms: an abstract syntax tree (AST) suitable for automatic recompilation; a Diana form used for type checking at compile time; and an Object Module containing generated code. These units are contained within the framework both of a Catalog and of a Collection. A Catalog is analogous to a real-world library catalog: it identifies its constituent units in every significant detail. A Collection is a holding place for the compiled units ("Objects") and for the Catalogs which identify these Objects.

Membership in a Catalog is intended to reflect some natural relationship: a group of mutually dependent utility packages is a typical example. Membership in a Catalog also results in visibility of that Catalog's other compilation units.

Resource Catalogs and Catalog Links

The Catalog, or Primary Catalog as it is properly called, is the user's principal sphere of activity. At any point, a Primary Catalog may be Promoted. This action freezes its units; they may not be altered after promotion. The new structure is called a Resource Catalog, and its units are available for use ('withing') by any other user in the system. All Resource Catalogs are potentially available to all other users. The agency for this is a Catalog Link, which is made from a Primary Catalog to a Resource Catalog; the link makes the units in the target Resource Catalog visible to the units in the linking Primary Catalog. Links are transitive, and the constellation of a Primary Catalog together with its linked-to Resource Catalogs thus forms a single conceptual Program Library.

Resource Catalogs are also subdivided into two kinds, Interface and Implementation. This division roughly corresponds to the Ada distinction between specification and body. An Interface Catalog can have multiple Implementations, allowing for different instances of a package body. Also, a Resource Catalog can exist in several Revisions; the structure is more properly called a Resource Catalog Set. Revisions to a Resource Set are accomplished by "deriving" from the Resource Catalog Set. The derived catalog is then writable, and its units may be changed until the catalog is repromoted to be a new revision of the Resource Set.

Program Library Manager

The compiler installs the compiled units into a user's Collection and makes the appropriate entries into the Catalog. From that point on, all Library operations are performed through the interactive Program Library Manager (PLM). This tool allows several classes of operations. These primarily include listing, linking, creation and deletion, and updating. Listing operations include the display of the units in a catalog, the up-to-date condition of a unit, and the like. Linking operations manage the establishment and severing of links between catalogs. Creation operations bring new Catalogs and Collections into existence; deletions remove them, along with whatever units they contain. Finally, the PLM can update a Catalog's links, can bring a given unit up-to-date, or can bring an entire Catalog up-to-date. The PLM validates its operations: when an illegal action is attempted, i.e., a link to two different revisions of a Resource Set, the illegal situation is reported and the link rejected.

The PLM uses a command language which is modelled on Ada. Some small deviations in syntax are present, but the commands largely resemble Ada aggregate notation. For example, the command to link one catalog to another is:

```
Link primary => my_catalog,
      resource => (name => his_catalog,
                   collection => his_collection)
```

Source Files

Source is not currently kept in the AIE Program Library. Source is available through source reconstruction, which operates on either the AST or Diana forms. This simplifies the tracking mechanism between source and object, since the source which generated a unit is implicit in its Diana.

EXPERIENCE USING AN ADA ENVIRONMENT

Since the entire AIE is written in Ada, experiences with a Program Library were coincident with its construction. Some of these experiences pertain only to the AIE, but many others could have occurred in any true Ada environment. Of all experiences directly related to the Program Library, those dealing with dependency and recompilation are the most telling.

There is no difficulty in understanding the concept of dependency. But a user can be thoroughly unprepared for the rigour that Ada's dependency rule imposes. For example, it is a common tendency when one begins to write in Ada, to let intuition guide the packaging of code. A frequent practice is to collect all of the needed data structures into a single package. This is intellectually satisfying, naming conventions will be consistent, and a great deal about a project can be inferred from such a package.

But this particular intuition has two flaws. It leads to bad Ada, since the packaging of data, in fact Ada packaging in general, should subscribe to the overall principle of information hiding. (Nissen & Wallis) In addition, given the context of a Program Library, this intuition can be a treacherous one. Because while a single data package is very neat, far too many other packages will depend on it. And if even one array range must be changed, then all dependent packages will need recompilation. Perhaps such occasions should never arise, and proper design should obviate them. But they seem to happen, all the same.

Practical Solutions

The effect of even one such experience will likely have practical results. First and most important, a general software principle, information hiding, will be realized by individual users in their daily work. This will result in packaging designs being subjected to much closer scrutiny than had seemed obvious. In the above case, data structures will be more safely defined only where their visibility is needed.

Second, frequent rechecking will be done to be sure that all dependencies are genuine. It is not uncommon to find 'with' statements in specifications even if they are only needed in the body. Nor is it rare to see a 'with' statement that has become obsolete due to some later design change. Such unneeded statements can cause a staggering amount of recompilation.

Third, software conventions themselves can be altered to minimize recompilations. One such tactic concerns specification constants. At least in the development stage, constants are susceptible to change; any change will then trigger recompilation of all dependent packages. If the constant is replaced, however, by a function which returns the needed type, then the value can itself reside in the package body, where a change is cheaply made. A simple strategy, but one which can save significant millions of CPU cycles.

Experiences Specific to the AIE

Many other experiences are particular to the specific design of the AIE. Perhaps the most immediate one was the realization that dealing with Catalogs was vastly different from dealing with single compilation units. Promotion of a Catalog, for instance, is imperative when its units are needed by many other users. But it is sometimes difficult to insure that all of a Catalog's units are equally ready for promotion, especially if several programmers are working in tandem on the Catalog.

But the overall design has proven sound. Catalog links, reaching through dozens of Resource Catalogs, demonstrate that large numbers of packages can be shared by large numbers of users. The Program Library Manager has been invaluable in its ability to manipulate entire libraries flexibly and quickly. One minor but consistent problem has been the PLM command language. Users have found it awkward, since Ada's aggregate notation is cumbersome in interactive use.

The most profound experience for a user of the AIE is that sooner or later he undergoes a conversion to a belief in 'reusable software'. It is one thing merely to understand the term; it is quite another to let the concept inform and shape the code that one is actually writing. Old habits die hard, after all, and few programmers will suddenly write code with an eye toward future reuse. Yet there are innumerable ways that code can be generalized with no real loss of specificity for the job at hand. Not all problems need once-only solutions, and many packages, with only a small amount of reshaping, can be generalized and reused several times. A conversion to this view, however, presupposes an environment which encourages it. Without such encouragement, an individual's conversions will hardly be swift.

CONCLUSION

In sum, the experiences with the AIE library produced changes in habit on a quite different plane than that of language per se. Users at every level realized the interconnections between portions of the project, and the changes brought about by the AIE are properly in the domain of software engineering.

The Program Library will confront any user of Ada: the language is simply not separable from it. Ada is more than its syntax, and is more than tasks and generics. It is a powerful language whose design goals include flexible and efficient software environments; these in turn revolve around their program libraries. Management systems such as the AIE are equally powerful instruments for making Ada's goals a practical reality.

REFERENCES

Broido, M. & Burton, B. (1986). Development of an Ada Package Library. Presentation at the 4th Annual National Conference on Ada Technology. March, 1986. Atlanta, Georgia.

Dempsey, J. (1984). The Distributed Software Engineering Control Process/ An Ada Development. In Proceedings of the 1st Annual Washington Ada Symposium, ed. Joseph P. Johnson, pp. 31-36. New York: ACM.

Leavitt, R. (1985). Some Practical Experience in the Organization of a Library of Reusable Ada Units. In Annual National Conference on Ada Technology, pp. 68-71. Fort Monmouth, NJ: Center for Tactical Computer Systems.

Nissen, J. & Wallis, P. (1984). Portability and Style in Ada. Cambridge: Cambridge University Press.

Reference Manual for the Ada Programming Language. (1983). ANSI/MIL-STD 1815A.

Thall, R. (1984). Configuration Management with the Ada Language System. In Proceedings of the 2nd Annual Conference of Ada Technology, pp. 11-24. Fort Monmouth, NJ: Center for Tactical Computer Systems.

REUSABILITY OF SOFTWARE COMPONENTS IN THE BUILDING OF SYNTAX-DRIVEN SOFTWARE TOOLS WRITTEN IN Ada.

Ch. Genillard
Department of Mathematics, Swiss Federal Institute of Technology, CH
1015 Lausanne

N.Ebel
Department of Mathematics, Swiss Federal Institute of Technology, CH
1015 Lausanne

Abstract. We are currently engaged in a research project in which we are
building a set of syntax-driven software tools. These tools range from a
language oriented editor, pretty printer, data collector for metrics,
filters, source transformer, to an intelligent browser.
The kernel of this project involves the use of BNF grammars. For each
specific application the grammar is "painted" with so-called actions. At
the same time, the programmer also writes Ada packages which
encapsulate these intended actions.
The whole project is written in Ada, and, after a year of research we
claim that the choice of Ada as a programming language for such a
project has shown a high reusability factor for software components. We
feel that this would not have been possible using any other currently
available language.
First we will present our motivations to build software tools in Ada and
an overview of the architecture of the GRAMACT project. Next we will
present some of our reusable low-level software components and justify
some choices made. Finally, we will give some practical advice to writers
of basic components and discuss how the choice of Ada can lead to build
reusable components.

1. MOTIVATION

The work started 5 years ago with the construction of a program editor
which does syntax check of sources. This editor, called EDIS, offers a character as
well as a token approach to editing, in which travelling goes through a lexical
analyser. Its knowledge of the language is limited to indentation of constructs and to
syntactic verification.

EDIS is now widely used on campus and at various others institutions. It
is written in Pascal, and implemented on UCSD, MS-DOS, Unix and VMS. It was first
tailored to check entities written in Pascal, but it soon became evident that many
others languages could be verified by EDIS. As the syntactic check is table driven, it
was quite simple to also write grammars for Modula-2, LISP, Ada, and even FORTRAN.

The difficulty resided in the maintenance of a 5000 line monolithic
program for five different operating systems using five different dialects of Pascal
(UCSD II, IV, MS-DOS, VMS and Berkeley Unix).

2.   THE GRAMACT PROJECT

2.1 *Presentation*

At the beginning of the year 1984, we initiated the design of a project building software tools for a programming environment. These tools range from a language oriented editor, a filter, a pretty printer, an interactive source browser and zoomer to a preprocessor for building interfaces between relational data bases and the Ada language. Every such application plugs itself into a prewritten grammar for the target language.

The project furnishes a table-driven syntax analyser capable of calling specified actions (procedures). These actions must be specified at certain places in the grammar. Furthermore, the builder of such a tool must furnish a detailed package containing these actions. A general overview is shown on the next figure.

General Overview of GRAMACT

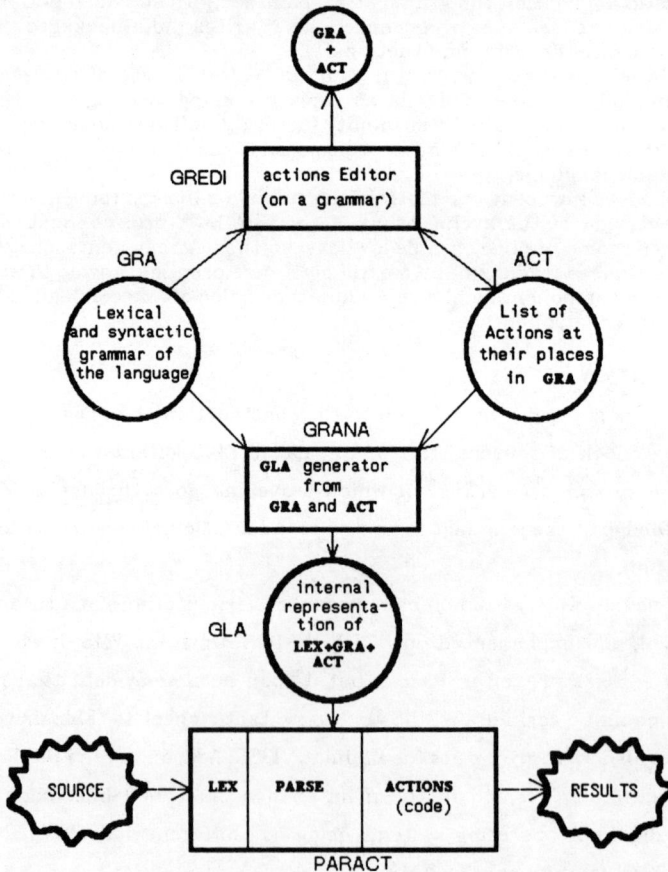

The grammar is in the GRA file, and the actions are in the ACT file. At the top of the figure we see a file GRA + ACT furnished by the GREDI editor. It is simply a listing of the grammar with the actions in place. It is necessary to have the editor GREDI so that specific grammars remain untouched by the (application) writers. GREDI inputs a grammar and edits and updates actions, which are kept in a separate file. GRANA is the compiler which checks grammatical properties and builds a binary file containing the lexical and syntactical grammar used by the parser.

At the bottom of the figure we see an application of PARACT which is built from three building blocks: Lex and Parse, which are furnished as packages to the programmer who builds the application and Actions which the programmer must write himself. All of these packages are written in Ada. This bundle forms a table driven parser which can be a program by itself or which could be part of a bigger program. (eg. the syntax checker included in the editor).

Our project is different from Yacc and Lex in Unix. These programs help build C programs for any specified language, but it is impossible to switch in the same Yacc program from one language to another. In GRAMACT this is possible as the program is table-driven.

2.2 Reusability of the whole project

We can speak of reusability for the whole project: modularity and separate compilation of Ada allows us to offer a ready-to-use PARACT machine. The user does not have the burden of writing a lexical and a syntactical parser. He can concentrate on his specific application. He writes the code for the Actions, for which the specification is already predefined. The actions will then be called by the parser according to their presence in the grammar. For a specific application it could also be necessary to rewrite the body of some other units, as for example the I/O or parts of the main procedure. We can see that every new application reuses an important part of the PARACT machine.

3.   REUSABILITY OF LOW-LEVEL SOFTWARE COMPONENTS.

We have been able to develop several packages which have been reused several times. We will shortly list these packages here, then we will discuss extensively the first four of them.

3.1 General overview of our reusable components

DYNAMIC_STRING_G: A package which handles variable-length strings, generic for the maximum length.

QUEUE_G: A package which implements queues (FIFO list) of objects of any limited type, also generic for the type of the objects.

SET_G, GENSET_G: Two packages which implement sets, one for objects on a discrete type and the other for objects of any limited type. They are generic for the type of the object.

STACK_G: A package which implements stacks (LIFO list) of objects of any limited type. This package is very similar to the Queue_G. It has been used in the lexical analyser for stacks of characters and states (to allow backtracking) and in the syntax part to implement a stack of tables of identifiers. Some user of GRAMACT also use stacks for their application, i.e. stacks of block names in a Pretty-Printer.

TABLE_G: A package which implements associative tables; it is generic for limited types *key* and *item*. This package allows one to create tables of elements accessed by a key. These kinds of tables are used extensively in the GRANA program to implement a table of terminals, non-terminals and actions.

BINARY_TREES_G: A package which implements balanced binary trees. It is generic for the type of objects to be stored in the tree, and also for a relational function "<" between objects of this type. This package has been used to implement the package Table_G and Genset_G. It is also used in another project to implement some kind of structure called Magmas which is more complicated than Queues and Stacks.

3.2 Package Dynamic_String_G

The package Dynamic_String_G has been built to cover the absence of built-in routines for handling variable-length dynamic strings in Ada. The package exports a type D_STRING, the maximum length being the generic parameter. Here is a part of the specification of this package:

```
with TEXT_IO; use TEXT_IO;
generic
    MAX_LENGTH : POSITIVE;
    -- Give the maximum length of variable length strings

package DYNAMIC_STRING_G is
------------------------

    type D_STRING is private;

    MAX_D_STRING_LENGTH : constant POSITIVE := MAX_LENGTH;

    EMPTY_D_STRING : constant D_STRING;

    function TO_D_STRING(SOURCE : CHARACTER) return D_STRING;
    function TO_D_STRING(SOURCE : STRING) return D_STRING;
    function TO_D_STRING(SOURCE : INTEGER) return D_STRING;
    -- Raise D_STRING_LENGTH_ERROR if the D_STRING returned would have more
```

-- than MAX_LENGTH characters.

function TO_CHARACTER(SOURCE : D_STRING; POS : POSITIVE := 1) return CHARACTER;
-- Raise D_STRING_POS_ERROR if POS is > LENGTH(SOURCE).

function TO_STRING (SOURCE : D_STRING) return STRING;

function TO_INTEGER (SOURCE : D_STRING) return INTEGER;

function LENGTH(SOURCE : D_STRING) return NATURAL;

function "&" (LEFT : D_STRING; RIGHT : D_STRING) return D_STRING;
...   -- Overloading of "&" for D_STRING, STRING and CHARCTER.
-- Raise D_STRING_LENGTH_ERROR if the D_STRING returned would have more
-- than MAX_LENGTH characters.

function "<" (LEFT, RIGHT : D_STRING) return BOOLEAN;
...   -- Overloading of relational operators for D_STRING.

function SUBSTR(SOURCE : D_STRING; POS : POSITIVE; SIZE : NATURAL) return D_STRING;
-- Extract a substring of SIZE characters long, starting at position POS in SOURCE;
-- if SIZE is greater than the length of the substring starting at POS and ending
-- at the end of SOURCE, then this substring will be returned.
-- Raise D_STRING_POS_ERROR if POS is > LENGTH(SOURCE).

procedure DELETE(DESTINATION : in out D_STRING; POS : POSITIVE; SIZE : NATURAL);
-- Delete SIZE characters from DESTINATION starting at position POS; if
-- SIZE is greater than the number of characters from POS to the end of
-- DESTINATION, then these characters will be deleted.
-- Raise D_STRING_POS_ERROR if POS is > LENGTH(DESTINATION).

procedure TRUNCATE(DESTINATION : in out D_STRING; SIZE : NATURAL);
-- Truncate DESTINATION at a length of SIZE characters; if SIZE is greater
-- than the length of DESTINATION, then no character will be deleted.

procedure INSERT(SOURCE : D_STRING; DESTINATION : in out D_STRING; POS : POSITIVE);
...   -- Overloaded for SOURCE of type STRING and CHARACTER
-- Insert SOURCE into DESTINATION starting at position POS.
-- Raise D_STRING_LENGTH_ERROR if LENGTH(DESTINATION) would be > MAX_LENGTH.
-- Raise D_STRING_POS_ERROR if POS is > LENGTH(SOURCE)+1.

procedure REPLACE(SOURCE : D_STRING; DESTINATION : in out D_STRING; POS : POSITIVE);
...   -- Overloaded for SOURCE of type STRING and CHARACTER
-- Replace by SOURCE a part of DESTINATION which starts at position POS, if
-- SOURCE is too long then DESTINATION is extended.
-- Raise D_STRING_LENGTH_ERROR if LENGTH(DESTINATION) would be > MAX_LENGTH.
-- Raise D_STRING_POS_ERROR if POS is > LENGTH(SOURCE)+1.

function UPPER_CASE(SOURCE : D_STRING) return D_STRING;
-- Convert lower-case characters of SOURCE into upper-case.

function LOWER_CASE(SOURCE : D_STRING) return D_STRING;
-- Convert upper-case characters of SOURCE into lower-case.

function POS(PATTERN : D_STRING; SOURCE : D_STRING; START : POSITIVE := 1)
      return NATURAL;
function POS(PATTERN : STRING; SOURCE : D_STRING; START : POSITIVE := 1)
      return NATURAL;
function POS(PATTERN : CHARACTER; SOURCE : D_STRING; START : POSITIVE := 1;
      SAME   : BOOLEAN := TRUE) return NATURAL;
-- Return the position of the first occurrence of PATTERN in SOURCE after position
-- START (return 0 if not found), for a PATTERN of type CHARACTER, SAME allows
-- (if FALSE) to search the position of the first CHARACTER different from PATTERN.

procedure GET(DESTINATION : out D_STRING;LENGTH : NATURAL);
procedure GET(FILE : FILE_TYPE;DESTINATION : out D_STRING;LENGTH : NATURAL);
-- Overloading of TEXT_IO.GET for D_STRING.
-- Raise D_STRING_LENGTH_ERROR if LENGTH is > MAX_LENGTH.

procedure GET_LINE(DESTINATION : out D_STRING);
procedure GET_LINE(FILE : FILE_TYPE; DESTINATION : out D_STRING);
-- Overloading of TEXT_IO.GET_LINE for D_STRING.

```
...     -- Overloading of TEXT_IO.PUT & TEXT_IO.PUT_LINE for D_STRING.

D_STRING_LENGTH_ERROR : exception;
-- Raised when a D_STRING of more than MAX_D_STRING_LENGTH characters
-- is attempted to be built.

D_STRING_POS_ERROR : exception;
-- Raised when a position (parameter POS) attempts access outside of a D_STRING.

private

    ...

end DYNAMIC_STRING_G;
```

We will now discuss some particular points of this specification:

-     To avoid the compatibility problem between different instantiations of this package, a standard instantation is used:

```
with DYNAMIC_STRING_G;
package DYNAMIC_STRING is new DYNAMIC_STRING_G(MAX_LENGTH => 255);
```

Other instantiations for several maximum lengths are reserved for certain particular applications.

-     The type of a variable-length string is *private* rather than *limited*, because it is pleasant to use the assignement for objects of that type (users appreciate the analogy with the type STRING). We use a *generic parameter* for the maximum length rather than a *discriminant* of the type D_STRING (as in DOD (1983) pp. 7-13) because our type is *private*. A *private* type with discriminant would have allowed to declare objects with different maximum length, but they would then be incompatible.

-     We have tried to offer many low-level operations on these strings, overloading many routines for the types D_STRING, STRING and CHARACTER to assure more flexibility.

-     We offer further higher level functions UPPER_CASE, LOWER_CASE or POS, which render such a package more attractive for a user.

-     Finally the I/O procedures for STRING from TEXT_IO have been overloaded for the type D_STRING. This is a case where the fixed length strings of Ada are not comfortable to use in an interactive way.

The package DYNAMIC_STRING has been reused many times in several packages and also as type for declaring identifiers in our lexical analyser and in most I/O text routines.

3.3 Package QUEUE_G

Queue_G has been created to implement lists with First-In First-Out (FIFO) managment. It is generic for the type of the elements of the queue. Here is the specification of this package:

```
generic
    type ITEM is limited private;
    with procedure ASSIGN (DESTINATION : in out ITEM; SOURCE : in ITEM);
    with function "=" (LEFT,RIGHT : ITEM) return BOOLEAN is <>;
package QUEUE_G is

    type QUEUE is limited private;

    procedure INSERT (Q : in out QUEUE; X : in ITEM);
    --+ OVERVIEW : Inserts the item X into the queue Q as the last item.

    procedure REMOVE (Q : in out QUEUE; X : in out ITEM);
    --+ OVERVIEW : Removes the first item X from the queue Q.
    --+ ERROR    : If Q is empty then EMPTY_QUEUE_ERROR is raised.

    procedure DESTROY (Q : in out QUEUE);
    --+ OVERVIEW : Empties the  queue Q.

    function FIRST (Q : QUEUE) return ITEM;
    --+ OVERVIEW : Returns the first item of the queue Q.
    --+ ERROR    : If Q is empty then EMPTY_QUEUE_ERROR is raised.

    function EMPTY (Q : QUEUE) return BOOLEAN;
    --+ OVERVIEW : Returns true if the queue Q is empty.

    function SIZE (Q : QUEUE) return NATURAL;
    --+ OVERVIEW : Returns the number of items in the queue Q.

    function "=" (LEFT,RIGHT : QUEUE) return BOOLEAN;

    procedure ASSIGN (DESTINATION : in out QUEUE; SOURCE : in QUEUE);
    --+ OVERVIEW : DESTROY (DESTINATION); Copies SOURCE into DESTINATION.

    generic
        with procedure ACT_ON_ITEM (X : in ITEM;ORDER_NUMBER : in POSITIVE);
    procedure TRAVERSE_G (Q : in QUEUE);
    --+ OVERVIEW :
    --+   Applies procedure ACT_ON_ITEM on each item X of the queue Q.
    --+   ORDER_NUMBER is the order of X within Q.

    EMPTY_QUEUE_ERROR : exception;

--------------------------------------------------------------------------------
--+ STORAGE CONSIDERATIONS :
--+   The following variable and procedure are needed if the user has any problems
--+   with the memory size (STORAGE_ERROR).

--+ ALGORITHM :
--+   The queues are implemented with linked lists. An internal free list is used to avoid
--+   returning each free item (coming from REMOVE or DESTROY) to the system, provided
--+   that the length of the internal list does not exceed MAX_FREE_LIST_SIZE,
--+   in which case the free item is unconditionally returned to the system. When a new item
--+   is asked for (by procedure INSERT) it first consults the internal free list,
--+   and asks for a new item from the system (only if the free list is empty).

MAX_FREE_LIST_SIZE : NATURAL := NATURAL'LAST;

procedure RELEASE_FREE_LIST;
--+ OVERVIEW :
--+ Releases all items of the internal free list. All items containted
--+ in this list are returned to the system.
--------------------------------------------------------------------------------

private

    ...

end QUEUE_G ;
```

We will now discuss some particular points of this specification:

-     The generic formal part contains the *limited type* ITEM and also a procedure ASSIGN and a function "=". We chose this solution rather than having only one generic parameter which would have been *type ITEM is private*. We find that it is more general and allows one to instantiate the package with any limited type having a procedure ASSIGN and a function "=". For example it is possible to build queues of stacks, sets or even queues !

-     The procedure ASSIGN of the generic formal part is specified with mode *in out* for the parameter DESTINATION. This allows certain implementations with type access to destroy the old structure refered by DESTINATION before creating a new one. For instantation with any actual non limited (non dynamic) type, we provide a generic procedure ASSIGN:

```
generic
    type ITEM is private;
    procedure ASSIGN(DESTINATION: in out ITEM; SOURCE : ITEM);
```

which simply implements the statement DESTINATION := SOURCE. So instantating QUEUE_G with a non-limited type can be made in two declarations and is not too tedious.

-     The procedure TRAVERSE_G is useful to act on every element of a queue. It replaces a construction like: "for X in Queue loop". It is also used for debugging purpose. In this way one can have a look at the content of the queue.

-     The storage consideration part is provided to ensure reusability of the package when some memory problems occur. But we must recall that providing this control of memory is not compulsory to any particular implementation. On a particular system with a garbage collector it is possible to suppress the free list; in this case the procedure RELEASE_FREE_LIST and the variable MAX_FREE_LIST_SIZE would not have any effect and the package could let the system do the memory management.

3.4 Packages SET_G, GENSET_G

Here we will present two packages which implement sets. SET_G allows one to create sets of elements of discrete type. This kind of set is usually found in other programming languages and were proposed in several books (Barnes (1984), Booch (1983), ...). Here is the first part of the specification:

```
generic
    type ITEM is (<>);
    package SET_G is
    type SET is private;
    ...
```

GENSET_G allows one to create sets of elements of any type with certain operators:

```
with BINARY_TREE_G;
generic
    type ITEM is limited private;
    with procedure ASSIGN (DESTINATION : in out ITEM; SOURCE : in ITEM);
    with function "<" (LEFT,RIGHT : ITEM) return BOOLEAN is <>;
    with function "=" (LEFT,RIGHT : ITEM) return BOOLEAN is <>;
package GENSET_G is
    type SET is limited private;
    ...
```

We have found it necessary to provide two different specifications. SET_G offers a *private type* SET, which allows assignement. With the generic formal type ITEM being discrete, it is possible to offer more features (complement, constant full-set, ...) and to implement this kind of set very efficiently.

In the package GENSET_G, the type SET is *limited*. It is therefore not so easy to use but it can define sets of any kinds of objects. Pratically, the two packages were necessary in our project. SET_G was used to define sets of characters, and sets of states in an automata. On the other hand, GENSET_G was necessary for defining sets of classes of characters, i.e. sets of sets. We note that GENSET_G is realized with the package BINARY_TREE_G.

4.   SOME GENERAL ADVICE ON WRITING REUSABLE UNITS.

We will try now to list some general advice from our experience with reusable units. It is important to note that our practice mainly concerns abstract data types and doesn't involve parallel programming.

Type Compatibilities. When writing a reusable package that defines a new *private type*, be aware of certain kind of discriminant with this type (see D_STRING in 3.2). For exemple, you could be unable to assign one variable-length string to another only because their maximum lengths (their discriminant field) are different.

Generic Parameters. In the case of a type for a generic parameter, we found that it was more general to have a limited formal parameter (see 3.3) rather than a private one. In this case a procedure ASSIGN and a function "=" can always be provided as we have seen in section 3.3.

Limited Type. When a package defines a limited type, try to provide, if possible, a procedure ASSIGN and a function "=" with the specification and implementation corresponding to the use mentionned in the previous paragraph.

Strorage management. If you work with an access type, take care of problems that occur with storage management without a garbage collector. We have proposed a solution in the specification of Queue_G (3.3).

Operators and Procedures. Try to offer a large scale of low-level procedures, using overloading and default values for parameters (see DYNAMIC_STRING_G). Problems often occur with more complicated routines for which the semantics is not obvious. For exemple in the package QUEUE_G we decided not to provide a procedure APPEND for two queues as it is not clear if the appended queue must be destroyed or not. On the other hand we feel that these "high level" routines can easily be built with the intended semantics using the "low-level" routines INSERT and REMOVE or TRAVERSE_G.

5.   *REUSABILITY PROPERTIES OF Ada (compared to other languages)*

We will compare here the programming practice that we used to realize EDIS in Pascal and GRAMACT in Ada. Then we will show which concepts of Ada have allowed high reusability factors, which we did not reach with other languages (Pascal, Modula-2).

In the building of EDIS, when someone had written a unit (module) and told the others of the interest of this unit, it was generaly found that some minor change (type representation, parameters of a procedure, ...) had to be brought to adapt it to his specific needs. The unit therefore could not be used without change. The source code was copied, adapted and had finally nothing to do with the original one.

When we built GRAMACT using Ada, the practice dramatically changed: we defined a library to store reusable units. When someone needed a specific unit, he could look in the library for a specification which hopefully matched his needs. If found, it was easy to understand the precise functionality by simply reading the specification. If not, he could propose a specification for the new unit to the other member of the team. The specification was then discussed and generalized to satisfy the particular needs of everyone. Here, it is mainly the concepts of genericity and private type which allow the unit to be generalized. Finally the author built the body of the units and introduced it in the library.

We often made some minor changes to the specification when using a unit for the second or third time, but by overloading an existing procedure or by creating a new one it was generaly possible to adapt the units to all specific needs.

With Ada it was possible to write some reusable components (listed in 3.1) for our project, that had not been possible before, e.g. during the building of EDIS. We feel that five concepts of Ada mainly allowed us to build reusable units:
-    private types,
-    overloading of subprograms,

- generic units,
- separate compilation units with strong distinction between specification and body,
- the existence of a library.

These five concepts are not available together in any other language.

6.   PROBLEMS WITH Ada

We will now make a short list of problems and negative effects that we have encountered when we switched to Ada.

At the beginning we had problems to find a good Ada compiler. The first Ada compilers were not bug-free, even if they had been validated.

Another problem is the time it takes to learn Ada well. We think that many people underestimate this time. This problem is increased by an academic environment as students work only for a short period on our project.

We also had problems with the resources necessary to program in Ada. As Ada is a very powerfull language, it also needs a lot of time and space.

Finally, as we noticed in section 5, the library is an important concept of Ada, especially for reusability; but we haven't yet found an implementation with all the functions that we would like. For example when one works on a big project, it would be necessary to use many libraries and to have links between them. One would also want to know for a specified unit when it is used by other units.

7.   CONCLUSION.

As we have tried to show, it is now possible to write reusable components. The detailed caracteristics needed by a reusable unit are still difficult to list. But by following some practical advice and by accepting some minor changes, it is often possible to reuse some units. We have showed that Ada offers the concepts necessary to write reusable units. Using Ada, we feel that we are no more obliged to write every component again and again. We are still far of the software shop hoped by Barnes (1983) but now it is possible to own a stock of reusable building blocks for some projects.

References.

Aho, A.V. & Ullman J.D. (1977). Principles of Compiler Design. Addison Wesley.
Barnes, J.G.P. (1984). Programming in Ada. Addison Wesley.
Booch G., (1983). Software Engineering with Ada. Benjamin Cummings.
DOD. (1983). Ada Programming Language. ANSI/MIL-STD 1815A.
Hibbard, P. & Hisgen, A. & Rosenberg, J. & Shaw, M. & Sherman, M. (1981).
           Studies in Ada Style. Springer Verlag.
Wirth, N. (1976). Algorithms + Data Structures = Programs. Prentice Hall.

Part IV   Experience in Application

Experiences in using Ada with DBMS Applications

M McNickle & A Reedy
PRC Government Information Systems, McLean, VA 22102, U.S.A.

The final version of this paper was not received in time
for inclusion in these proceedings.

A PROCESS SIMULATION PACKAGE CONCEALING MULTI-TASKING

Sarah A. Steele
Richard Beeby
Ada and Software Engineering Technology
59 George Square, Edinburgh, EH8 9JU

Abstract. The paper describes a general purpose simulation
package, written in Ada, which makes use of the language's
tasking model. It emphasises the suitability of Ada as a
language for simulation and highlights the aspects of Ada
which made a general discrete event simulation package feasible.
The ability to effectively extend the language using general
purpose library packages of this kind is seen as one of the
benefits of the transition to Ada. The problems encountered
in formulating such a package are described, along with
their solutions.

INTRODUCTION

This discrete event simulation Ada package is based on the
process interaction method of simulation (Franta, 1977). Under this
method, the system being modelled is decomposed into processes, each of
which describes the behaviour of a specific activity in the real system
that evolves concurrently with other activities (see Bruno, 1984).

The package allows the modeller to create three kinds of
entity: processes, queues and resources. The queues are represented by
lists; resources are also represented by lists with header records
defining the maximum and currently available amounts of the resource;
and processes are represented by tasks. None of these implementation
details are visible to the package user. In particular, the tasking
element is completely hidden behind a procedural interface:

```
package Process_Simulation is
   type PROCESS_IDENTITY  is private;
   function Anonymous return PROCESS_IDENTITY;

   generic
      type SIM_TIME    is delta <>;
      type MODEL_ITEMS is (<>);
      with procedure Model_Actions(Model : in MODEL_ITEMS;
                                   Ref   : in PROCESS_IDENTITY);
   package Model_Simulation is
      function  Current_Time return SIM_TIME;
      procedure Set_Current_Time(To : in SIM_TIME);

      function  New_Process(Of_Kind : MODEL_ITEMS;
                  Activate_At : SIM_TIME        := Current_Time;
                  Creator     : PROCESS_IDENTITY := Anonymous)
         return PROCESS_IDENTITY;
```

```
type      QUEUE_IDENTITY is private;
function  New_Queue return QUEUE_IDENTITY;
function  Queue_For (Name : PROCESS_IDENTITY)
   return QUEUE_IDENTITY;
      -- plus other subprograms for manipulating queues

type PRIORITY is range 0 .. INTEGER'Last;
      -- higher values have higher priority
type RESOURCE_IDENTITY is private;

function  New_Resource(Max_Quantity : POSITIVE)
   return RESOURCE_IDENTITY;
procedure Seize  (Name     : in RESOURCE_IDENTITY;
                  Caller   : in PROCESS_IDENTITY;
                  Quantity : in POSITIVE;
                  Urgency  : in PRIORITY := 0);
procedure Release(Name     : in RESOURCE_IDENTITY;
                  Caller   : in PROCESS_IDENTITY;
                  Quantity : in POSITIVE);

procedure Wait_For_Service(Caller,
                           Server : in PROCESS_IDENTITY);
procedure Hold(Name     : in PROCESS_IDENTITY;
               Interval  : in SIM_TIME);
procedure Deactivate(Name : in PROCESS_IDENTITY);
procedure Activate  (Name : in PROCESS_IDENTITY);
function  Is_Idle   (Name : PROCESS_IDENTITY)
   return BOOLEAN;
function  Random_For(Entity : PROCESS_IDENTITY)
   return FLOAT;
procedure Simulate;

generic
   with procedure Output_Requirements;
procedure Reset_Simulation;

private
   ...  -- QUEUE_IDENTITY and RESOURCE_IDENTITY
end Model_Simulation;
private
   ...  -- representation of PROCESS_IDENTITY
end Process_Simulation;
```

Resource packages in a concurrent environment should generally present a procedural interface (Burns, 1985) and this has the considerable advantage, in this case, that the modeller is not required to know anything about the Ada tasking model (though see later for a complication). Previous process oriented simulation packages by Bruno (1982, 1984) and by Sheppard *et al* (1984; Friel & Sheppard, 1985; based on Bryant, 1982) export tasks visibly, as does a library of packages supporting discrete event modelling in Ada by Downes & Tellaeche Bosch (1984); we feel that the present approach is likely to look less unfamiliar, and less open to misuse.

Ada is a large language that includes many features, the tasking model included, that will be unfamiliar to most software users with experience of other languages. Where possible, it is clearly desirable that users wishing to take advantage of previously written modules should not themselves require high levels of Ada expertise. A simple interface to a module makes for a more easily used unit, whatever the level of experience the user has.

It is also likely that the more conventional interface will facilitate the transfer of existing simulations in other languages over to Ada. GPSS, Simscript II.5 and Simula have simulation supporting features which are process oriented, with the ability to define both processes and resources. While acknowledging our superficial knowledge of these languages, some preliminary research would appear to support the view that simulations written in these languages could be translated into Ada using the primitives exported by this simulation package, for many applications, almost statement for statement.

These same advantages arise from simply taking non-parallel discrete-event simulation implementations, such as that of the Demos package in Simula (Birtwistle, 1979), and implementing them directly in Ada, as in Lomow and Unger (1982; Inkster et al., 1984). Such an approach, avoiding the use of the concurrency features of Ada, gives a more efficient implementation on existing monoprocessor systems, but at the cost of losing the ability to express true parallelism with potential future gains on multi-processor/distributed systems.

BENEFITS OF USING ADA
We believe that the benefits of using Ada for simulation purposes are very large. Existing first-choice languages for simulation, whatever their merits, do not posses Ada´s real-time features, and simulation packages written in them cannot generally be slotted into real-time production systems for such purposes as performance evaluation. The importance of such a facility has been emphasised by Bruno (1984). The potential for use of simulation in design performance management is well illustrated by Gaither (1985).

The use of Ada means, then, that the same language can be used to both control and simulate a system. That is to say, it is possible to test the logical correctness of the actual code for a system, or part of a system, on a simulation model of the system. The possibility of embedding simulation models of critical activities into the real-time management of a system means, we believe, that facilities of the kind offered in a preliminary way by this package should be available in any APSE or IPSE.

THE USE OF Ada CONSTRUCTS
It is worth emphasising here the degree to which the following Ada constructs facilitated the production of a general purpose package:

Generics
Without generic program units, a general purpose module is only possible by providing low level primitives for the user to incorporate into his program. When a concurrent package is being considered, an understanding of Ada´s tasking model is clearly required. While the present package does not eliminate the need for the package user to write what will often be a considerable amount of code, the bulk of this will be in a subprogram which is passed as a parameter to the inner generic package. Concurrency is then handled without involving

the user directly (a potential problem here is that the user is effectively able to introduce code into the package, and so potentially undermine its security: see below).

The main package, Process_Simulation, is not generic, but exports a generic package, Model_Simulation, which the user is required to instantiate. There are three formal parameters to this generic package: the first, SIM_TIME, is a fixed point type, allowing the user to specify the absolute accuracy of time measurements and arithmetic; the second is a discrete type, MODEL_ITEMS, the values of which represent the kinds of processes to be modelled; and a procedure, Model_Actions, which encapsulates actions appropriate to each of the values of MODEL_ITEMS. The idea is that the actual subprogram parameter is essentially a case statement which selects for execution the alternative specified by the value of the subprogram's first parameter.

...with tasks as processes

The instantiation of Model_Simulation makes available a function, New_Process, one of the parameters to which is of the discrete type MODEL_ITEMS. A call to this function will (invisibly to the user) create a task, of type PROCESS_TASK, to represent the process (various housekeeping records are also created). The task type specification, hidden in the body of the package, has the form:

```
task type PROCESS_TASK is
    entry Initialise (Model : in MODEL_ITEMS; ...);
    entry Go;
    entry Hold;
    entry Wake_Up;
    entry Shut_Down;
    entry Start_Again;
    entry Service_Completed;
end PROCESS_TASK;
```

Each task is advised of the type of process it is representing through its Initialise entry, so that the correct section of the procedure Model_Actions will be executed by the task.

```
task body PROCESS_TASK is
    My_Type    : MODEL_ITEMS;
    My_Name    : PROCESS_IDENTITY;
    My_Details : REF_ENTITY_RECORD;  -- pointer to record
    ...  -- other declarations
begin
    ...
    accept Initialise (Model   : in MODEL_ITEMS;
                       Name    : in PROCESS_IDENTITY;
                       Details : in REF_ENTITY_RECORD) do
        My_Type    := Model;
        My_Name    := Name;
        My_Details := Details;
    end Initialise;
    ...
    Model_Actions(My_Type,My_Name);
    ...
end PROCESS_TASK;
```

This circumvents the problem that Friel and Sheppard (1985) had of queues only being able to contain processes of one type (requiring that there be as many queue types as modelled process types), since in the present package all processes are associated with a single task type.

Downes & Tellaeche Bosch (1984) did not have the access to a compiler supporting generics when they developed their simulation library and hence had to adopt the technique of using a special task type, with just two entries SIGNAL and WAIT, to sit in the queue instead of the actual process. The drawback of this method is that there is then no way of ascertaining which particular processes are in a queue and no way, therefore, of accessing information about them held in their process-records; nor of aborting these tasks, if necessary, when the simulation ends. Downes & Tellaeche Bosch (1984) left it to the programmer to make sure that all tasks were terminated or aborted once the simulation had come to an end.

Private types

The ability to specify abstract data types is now widely accepted as an essential feature of any programming language for use in large-scale programming. Ada supports such types by private and limited private types, which restrict the available operations to those specified by the user (and, in the former case, to assignment and testing for (in)equality). In the present package, the entities QUEUE_IDENTITY, RESOURCE_IDENTITY, and PROCESS_IDENTITY are all private types, with their representation hidden from the user program. This provides a clean and secure user interface. Appropriate operations for these types are provided, and the user can additionally specify the behaviour of the processes he/she wishes to create.

PROBLEMS ENCOUNTERED

Creating a simulation package that makes use of Ada's multi-tasking model did introduce several problems. For many of these problems, the solutions found have been very satisfactory while others have been less elegantly dealt with.

Scheduling

In existing discrete event simulations, only a single process is active at a time. Process activation involves releasing that process currently at the head of the events list, and updating the simulation time accordingly. The next process is activated whenever the released process returns to the list or terminates.

As Sheppard et al (1984) point out, a multi-tasking implementation implies that all processes with the same activation time are actually released together. This creates the problem that the simulation time cannot be advanced again until all currently executing processes have either been resuspended, or terminate. The solution adopted by Sheppard et al (to keep a count of the number of processes released, incrementing that count whenever a new process is created and decrementing it as processes complete, deactivate or reschedule themselves) has also been taken here, although it is not secure in the face of failure of any of the released processes (always a possibility, no matter how defensive our programming or powerful our exception handling facilities).

The solution adopted here, however, does simplify life for

the modeller relative to previous solutions:

        (a) the responsibility for keeping count is taken by the module, and is hidden from the user (cf. Sheppard *et al*,1984; Downes & Tellaeche Bosch, 1983)

        (b) there is no need to report the initial number of processes (cf. Bruno, 1984; Downes & Tellaeche Bosch, 1983; Sheppard *et al*, 1984)

        (c) the module imposes no limit on the maximum number of processes in the simulated system (cf. Bruno, 1984).

        The administration of these roles falls to a Scheduler task to which the package user has no access. The Scheduler manages the events list upon which processes are suspended to model the passage of time in the simulation. The body of the Scheduler is, in outline:

```
task body Scheduler is
   Active_Tasks : NATURAL := 0;
   ...    -- other declarations
begin
   ... -- start the simulation going
   select
      accept Start do
         -- set appropriate flag
      end Start;
   or
      terminate;
   end select;

   -- the simulation is finished if the (global)
   -- events list is empty
   while Is_Not_Empty (Event_List) loop

      ... -- update simulation time and release all processes
      ... -- having the the same activation time as that of the
      ... -- process at the head of the events list, keeping a
      ... -- count in Active_Tasks

      -- wait for all active tasks to complete,
      -- or reschedule
      while Active_Tasks > 0 loop
         select
            accept Increment do
               -- a new task is being created and
               -- activated immediately or a deactivated
               -- task is being reactivated
               Active_Tasks := Active_Tasks + 1;
            end Increment;
         or
            accept Decrement do
               -- a process is deactivating or joining a queue
               Active_Tasks := Active_Tasks - 1;
            end Decrement;
         or
            accept Reschedule
```

```
                    (Process  : in out REF_ENTITY_RECORD;
                     Interval : in     SIM_TIME) do
                    ... -- place the Process back in the
                    ... -- events list for activation at
                    ... -- (Current_Time + Interval)
                    Active_Tasks := Active_Tasks - 1;
                  end Reschedule;
              or
                  accept Stop(Name : in PROCESS_IDENTITY) do
                    -- a process has completed
                    Active_Tasks := Active_Tasks - 1;
                  end Stop;
                end select;
              end loop;
          end loop;
      end Scheduler;
```

The combination of a concurrent implementation with a central scheduler does create a potential bottleneck on systems with several processors available. The possibility of using distributed scheduling on the lines of Jefferson's (1983; Jefferson & Sowizral, 1983) *time warp* mechanism for implementing *virtual time* is under consideration.

Task Suspension and Resumption

Ada provides three ways of suspending processes without busy waiting. The first of these is the delay statement, which suspends a process for not less than a specified number of seconds. The other two are associated with interprocess communication. If a task issues an entry call on another task it is suspended until the call is accepted and completed. Similarly, if a task reaches an accept statement, and there are no outstanding calls on the entry concerned, it is suspended until such a call is received.

The use of the inbuilt delay statement in the language could not be used to suspend a process for a specified period of simulation time because of the impossibility of knowing what relationship between "real-time" and simulation time obtains for that particular process. Indefinite delays also require to be modelled.

To suspend a process for a definite or indefinite period of simulation time we used entry calls. Each delay involves (though the user is unaware of it) the "creation" of a task, which the process to be suspended calls. The created task is constructed so that it does not accept this call until it has accepted a call that releases it from a queue or wakes it up, depending on the kind of delay involved. In fact, because of the need to have processes of different types held on one queue, the synchronisation task created here is of the same type as the others - PROCESS_TASK - and is accessed via the process' ENTITY_RECORD via a special task-pointer field. The ENTITY_RECORD for each task records whether the task is acting as a synchronisaton task or simulating a process in a Boolean field called Waiting_Process.

```
      procedure Hold (Name           : in PROCESS_IDENTITY;
                      Delay_Interval : in SIM_TIME) is
        Actual_Record : REF_ENTITY_RECORD := ...;
        ... -- other declarations
```

```
begin
    -- create a synchronisation task, called Dummy,
    -- set the Waiting_Process field to True and
    -- initialise the task
    Dummy                      := New_Process_Task;
    Actual_Record.Waiting_Process := True;
    Actual_Record.Task_Pointer    := Dummy;
    Dummy.Initialise(Actual_Record.Process_Kind,
                     Name, Actual_Record);
    ...
        -- reschedule the ENTITY_RECORD that now points to the
        -- synchronisation task
    Scheduler.Reschedule(Actual_Record, Delay_Interval);
        -- hold up the main process by making a call on the
        -- synchronisation task
    Dummy.Hold;
        -- once this call has been accepted,
        -- reset relevant record fields and continue
    Actual_Record.Waiting_Process := False;
    Actual_Record.Task_Pointer    := null;
end Hold;

task body PROCESS_TASK is
    My_Details : REF_ENTITY_RECORD;
    ....
begin
        -- initialisation sequence
    select
        accept Go;
            -- from the scheduler
    or
        accept Service_Completed;
            -- from a server process that has finished servicing
    or
        accept Shut_Down do
                -- from the Deactivation procedure
            accept Wake_Up;
        end Shut_Down;
    or
        terminate;
    end select;

    if My_Details.Waiting_Process then
        -- this is a synchronisation task
        accept Hold do
            -- releases the main process task
            -- making the call
            ...
        end Hold;
        ...
    else
        Model_Actions(...);
    end if;
    ...
end PROCESS_TASK;
```

Process Identification

Since there are potentially several processes active concurrently, some or all of which may require the scheduler to specifically reschedule them on the events list, the scheduler must know which ENTITY_RECORD to reschedule. Due to the asymmetry of entry calls in Ada, the identity of a task calling the scheduler is not known. For this reason, each process task is told its identity on creation, and passes this as a parameter to the Scheduler, whenever they call it.

The parameters to the generic package include a subprogram, Model_Actions, which itself takes as a parameter the identity of a process (type PROCESS_IDENTITY). It is therefore clear that such an identity type cannot be exported by the generic package, for the PROCESS_IDENTITY definition must be in scope at the point the generic package is declared, and where it is instantiated. The generic package is thus declared in an enclosing package which also exports the process identity type.

The identification types for queues, resources and processes are private types, and the fact that integers were chosen to represent the values is of no relevance or use to the package user.

Resource Control

Resources, queues and processes are all internally uniquely identified by a number. There is an internal table relating identities to the ENTITY_RECORD representing them; an ENTITY_RECORD being a variant record with fields depending on whether it is representing a process, a queue or a resource.

A resource is actually implemented as a queue, with the header record containing fields for the maximum and current quantities of the resource. Two procedures are provided, Seize and Release, which are parameterised by the kind of resource requested, the amount requested, and the identity of the requesting process. In addition, the Seize procedure has a parameter for specifying the priority of the request (set by default to the lowest value).

Seize will release the process immediately if enough of the resource is available; if not, the process will be deactivated and queued. The queue is ordered on priority, with the priority of a suspended process increasing with time (unless/until it has the highest possible priority). Note that the problems of resource management in Ada, arising out of the resource manager being unable to deactivate calling processes (Wellings et al, 1984), are avoided in this package.

At present, there is no facility for seizing different resources simultaneously. We are currently looking into the feasibility of implementing such a facility.

Shared Variables

The problem of shared variables is an interesting one - the more so as the user, since he is unaware of the underlying tasking model, will also be unaware that any variables he declares as global variables are potential shared variables.

The problem does not arise with variables of type PROCESS_IDENTITY, QUEUE_IDENTITY, or RESOURCE_IDENTITY, created using the provided operations, as the package automatically assigns mutual exclusion tasks to protect them. User declared global variables of other types are a problem, however. The only solution to this that

avoids alerting the user to the underlying tasking model (so forcing him
to program with concurrency in mind) is to preprocess the user code,
attaching mutual exclusion tasks to all global variables and inserting
the code to call these tasks wherever the variables are accessed. As
any problematic calls will occur in the procedure which is the actual
parameter associated with Model_Actions, the amount of work the
preprocessor is required to do will generally not be excessive.

Memory Management

The user of the module may declare a new process at any
point in his/her simulation. The package, for this and other reasons,
creates task dynamically during execution. As the language definition
requires that memory allocated to dynamically created tasks cannot be
explicitly returned by the user program to the system (through the use
of a suitable instantiation of Unchecked-Deallocation, for instance),
the tasks are constructed so that, when a particular activation is
complete, they do not terminate but return themselves to a pool for
reuse (see also Burns, 1985). Tasks are withdrawn from this pool by the
internal subprogram New_Process_Task, and created by the language **new**
operator only if the pool is empty at the time of the call (and the user
program has not reached its system-dependent maximum memory allocation).
Without such a pool, the program would eventually, for a long
simulation, run out of memory.

```
task body PROCESS_TASK is
   My_Details : REF_ENTITY_RECORD;
   ...
begin
   loop
      ...   -- initialisation sequence
      ...   -- activation sequence
      if My_Details.Waiting_Process then
         select
            accept Hold do
               Return_A_Process_Task(My_Details.Task_Pointer);
            end Hold;
         or
            terminate;
         end select;
      else
         Model_Actions(...);
         Scheduler.Stop(My_Name);
         Return_A_Process_Task(My_Details.Task_Pointer);
      end if;
      ...
   end loop;
end PROCESS_TASK;
```

Determinancy - Repeating Simulations

The major problem with using a multi-tasking model for a
simulation package concerns the allocation of processor time to tasks on
successive runs of a given simulation. This cannot be explicitly
programmed in Ada, and so such runs may result in a different sequence
of task activations for each execution of a simulation. As Friel and
Sheppard (1985) discuss, this creates problems when, as in virtually all

simulations, a pseudo-random number generator is used, for the order in
which processes call the generator, and hence the number they receive,
will differ from one run to another. This precludes repeating a
simulation, as a level of indeterminancy is admitted into each run.
Friel and Sheppard resolve this problem by giving each process its
own random number generator. As processes do not share the generator in
this approach, the problem is avoided. Good pseudo-random number
generators have long cycle lengths, and are not auto-correlated. It
seems likely, therefore, that if such a generator is available, the
solution adopted is a sensible one.
We experimented in this package with an alternative
solution, which imposes an additional load on the program, but enables
all processes to share the same generator. This involves keeping a
record of the numbers allocated to different processes, and retaining
this information over successive runs. This ensures that the same
sequence of numbers is received by each process, whatever the order of
the requests is. It may be more statistically sensible not to retain
the numbers themselves, but the order in which processes call the
generator. It is for repeating simulations that the subprogram,
New_Process, has a parameter, Creator, which records the identity of the
parent of a given process. The function Anonymous is provided so that
first generation processes can be dealt with, and for use in simulations
which will run only once.

Statistics Collection
There are currently two schools of thought about statistics
collection. One opinion is that statistics collection and reporting
should be automatic, as this is an aid to the programmer and more
efficient. The other opinion is that automatic statistics collection
and reporting is an unnecessary burden on the run-time of the
simulation, and that it should be left to the user to do his/her own.
At present, our module exports certain facilities for the
user to gain access to statistical information - such as queue lengths
etc. However, we are considering the introduction of some basic
automatic statistics collection, for the convenience of the user.

IMPLEMENTATION
The work described was performed on a Data General MV4000,
using the validated DG/Rolm Ada Compiler (version 2.20 and latterly,
2.30). The availability of a powerful source code debugger was
invaluable throughout the development of the package. All of the
previous simulation packages we have referred to were hampered by the
lack of complete compiler implementations of Ada.

SUMMARY
A general purpose simulation module, requiring of the
modeller no knowledge of the advanced features of the Ada tasking model,
has been described. The powerful abstraction facilties in the language
have been exploited to provide a clean and relatively simple interface
to the package user.
The package uses multi-tasking in its representation of
processes, and we recognise the inherent inefficiencies of such a
multi-tasking package on existing monoprocessor implementations. The
representation of an active entity by a task is otherwise sound
abstraction, and will be beneficial if future multi-processor

implementations allow true parallelism and are efficient (see, for
example, Schonberg & Schonberg, 1985).

   The introduction of parallelism, by its very nature, reduces
determinancy (see Kuck, 1978), and this has been most strongly seen with
the problem of repeating simulations when pseudo-random numbers are
required.

   Acknowledgements. We are grateful to Rob Pooley for helpful
discussions and comments on an earlier draft. We thank a number of
anonymous reviewers for comments on an extended abstract of this paper.

References
Birtwistle, G. (1979). DEMOS - A System for Discrete Event Modelling in
      Simula. New York : Macmillan.
Bruno, G. (1984). Rationale of the introduction of discrete simulation
      primitives in Ada. In Simulation in Strongly Typed Languages:
      Ada, Pascal, Simula. 13, no.2, 10-15.
Bryant, R.M. (1982). Discrete system simulation in Ada. Simulation 39,
      111-121.
Burns, A. (1985). Concurrent Programming in Ada. Cambridge: Cambridge
      University Press.
Downes, V.A. & Tellaeche Bosch, R. (1984). Discrete event modelling
      in Ada: Implementation and application. In Proceedings
      of the Third Joint Ada Europe/AdaTEC Conference, ed. J. Teller,
      pp. 53-63. Cambridge: Cambridge University Press.
Franta, W.R. (1977). The Process View of Simulation. New York: North
      Holland.
Friel, P. & Sheppard, S. (1985). Implications of the Ada environment
      for simulation studies. Simuletter 16, 14-26.
Gaither, B. (1985). The role of simulation in management of
      architecture performance. Proceedings of the 13th Simula
      Users Conference, University of Calgary, Alberta.
Inkster, J., Lomow, G.A. & Unger, B.W. (1984). Combined discrete and
      continuous simulation in Ada. In Simulation in
      Strongly Typed Languages 13, no.2, 16-21.
Jefferson, D. (1983). Virtual time. Computer Science Department,
      University of Southern California, Technical Report TR-83-213.
Jefferson, D. & Sowizral, H. (1983). Fast concurrent simulation using
      the time warp mechanism. Part I: Local control. The Rand
      Corporation, Santa Monica, California, Technical Report,
      June 1983.
Kuck, D. (1978). The Structure of Computers and Computations. 1.
      New York: John Wiley & Sons.
Lomow, G.A. & Unger, B.W. (1982). The process view of simulation
      in Ada. Proceedings of the 1982 Winter Simulation
      Conference. 77-86.
Schonberg, E. & Schonberg, E. (1985). Highly parallel Ada - Ada on
      an ultracomputer. In Ada in Use, ed. J.G. Barnes &
      G.A. Fisher, Jr., pp 58-71. Cambridge: Cambridge
      University Press.
Sheppard, S., Friel, P. & Reese, D. (1984). Simulation in Ada:
      implementation of two world views. In Simulation in Strongly
      Typed Languages: Ada, Pascal, Simula. 13, no.2, 3-9.
Wellings, A.J., Keeffe, D. & Tomlinson, G.M. (1984). A problem with
      Ada and resource allocation. Ada Letters 3, 112-124.

TRANSITION TOWARD EMBEDDED REAL-TIME APPLICATIONS IN ADA

R. Bayan, C.Bonnet, A. Kung
Tecsi-Software, 29 rue des Pyramides, F-75001 Paris,
France

W. Kirchgassner, R. Landwehr, B. Schwarz
GMD Karlsruhe, Haid und Neu Str.7, D-7500 Karlsruhe,
Germany

Abstract. The Ada language was originally designed
for embedded real-time applications. We study in
this paper the characteristics and requirements of
real-time applications, show some problems that Ada
will introduce in those applications and the
requirements that Ada execution systems will have
to meet. We finally propose an approach in which a
standardized Ada multitasking Kernel is used to
facilitate the transition toward the use of Ada for
industrial embedded real-time applications.

Keywords: Real-time applications, Embedded
systems, Ada tasking, Run-time, Executive.

This work is partially funded by the European
Communities under the Multi-Annual Programme
(project ASTERIX 765)

1. EMBEDDED REAL-TIME APPLICATIONS

Real-time applications are often characterized as
programs which have to meet some predetermined timing
constraints. These constraints are particularly severe in
embedded applications, for which slower, "ruggedized" hardware
is often used for reliability reasons, thus preventing the use
of sophisticated fast hardware. Overall, highly efficient
programs have to be written. Even though they concern a wide
spectrum of applications, embedded systems are similar in
their main characteristics, in the programming model which
they use and in their functional needs.

1.1 *Characteristics*

Embedded real-time systems are mainly concerned with the control of external events of the physical world (e.g. robot control, missile control...). They generally show the following characteristics:

- Ability to handle <u>asynchronous</u> events.
- Support of some predetermined workload and timing constraints.
- Communication with external events is typically done through hardware interrupts.
- Use of compact and sometimes slower hardware to optimize space occupation, increase reliability, and sometimes to lower costs. Most of the time, memory space is limited.
- The overall size of the application including the run-time is small.

1.2 *Software programming model used for real-time applications*

One possible model for real-time applications consists of the implementation of a unique "polling" process which sequentially inspects all the external devices and acts accordingly. While this approach is quite efficient and often used for simple applications, it may lead to highly unstructured and hard to debug systems for complex applications. So the main programming model used is the **multitasking approach**. It simplifies the handling of asynchronous events by allowing the programming of sequential entities (i.e. tasks) to manipulate them. Actually, real-time applications use a very specific multitasking model in which interrupt routines must be supported as asynchronous software entities. Without this support it is possible to come up with restricted forms of multitasking like the coroutine model (Wegner 1969), used in many current Ada compilers. This model is not applicable to interrupts because of its synchronous deterministic nature.

The multitasking model must include a software component specialized in the **scheduling** of tasks. Several scheduling schemes may exist. Most of them are priority driven in which case they are either preemptive -the task with the highest priority in the ready state always runs- or non preemptive -a tasks owns the CPU until it releases it on purpose. None of these schemes are entirely satisfactory because they use information (i.e. priorities) which is indirectly related to the timing constraints of each task. This is why adhoc scheduling schemes are often used, for instance in avionic applications which generally consist of cyclic tasks.

Intertask communication support is another important aspect of multitasking. Facilities must be offered to allow for the communication of data between tasks, the use of synchronization points between tasks and mutual exclusion to resources.

1.3   *Functional needs*

The implementation of real-time applications is highly dependent on the availability of:

- a real-time operating system (i.e. an executive) based on the above model, to support multitasking.

- input-output facilities to handle external peripheral devices which are the essence of real-time systems. They may be provided by the run-time operating system or left as the responsability of the application. In either case these facilities rely on communication mechanisms between the software tasks and the interrupt routines provided by the executive. Asynchronous as well as synchronous IO should be available.

- multitasking debugging facilities running either concurrently with the application, or when the whole application (including the executive) is frozen.

- debugging and monitoring tools (probably hardware tools)

which operate without disturbing the target in order to test timing constraints.

2. *REAL-TIME APPLICATIONS WRITTEN IN ADA AND RELATED ISSUES*

We now analyse how Ada can be used for real-time applications. The following topics are considered: scheduling and priorities, synchronization primitives, interrupt handling, low level input-output, memory management, configurability, and debugging.

2.1 *Scheduling and priorities*

Ada adopts a tasking model with preemptive scheduling based on priorities which are statically specified through the PRIORITY PRAGMA. The only dynamic change takes place when two tasks are in a rendez-vous during which they get the same priority (the highest of the two).
We can see several issues in this approach. First of all, pragmas are not necessarily taken into account by compilers, secondly, priorities are associated with task types and not with task objects (so it is impossible to implement an array of tasks having different priorities), and finally the use of static priorities may make the tuning of an application difficult as one has to recompile a program in order to change a priority.

Ada also implicitly involves in its constructs dynamic scheduling points. This is the case of selective wait statements. We claim that they must be handled by the scheduler in a consistent manner (e.g. schedule the open entry with the pending task having the highest priority).

Finally, a major issue concerns the model used to map Ada tasks into the execution task entities. Ada tasks are likely to be overused (e.g. to implement other synchronization primitives), and probably not for their asynchronous properties. So one can argue whether a many-to-one rather than an one-to-one mapping should be considered.

2.2   *Synchronization primitives*

Ada implicitly includes in its programming constructs some synchronization mechanism (e.g. to activate tasks and to wait for the completion of dependent tasks), and proposes an explicit mechanism, the rendez-vous mechanism.

The synchronous nature of rendez-vous makes the implementation of asynchronous mechanisms such as asynchronous delays or supervizing tasks very cumbersome. While rendez-vous allow one to implement other types of primitives like semaphores, these implementations are not efficient (Habermann & Perry 1983) because they generally use tasking constructs. An issue is whether packages for such primitives including asynchronous primitives should be available to the applications. This would however go against the philosophy of Ada.

2.3   *Interrupts*

The support of interrupt handling is not imposed by the language and its implementation is system dependent. A model based upon rendez-vous is however provided which views interrupts as task entries. This model is quite consistent with the Ada tasking rendez-vous oriented philosophy and allows the writing of test programs which simulate interrupts by directly calling the interrupt entry.

Issues concerning this model are numerous and lead us to believe that some further maturation of the language is necessary. We can see three types of issues, having to do with efficiency, flexibility, and portability aspects:

One minor problem concerning **efficiency** is that some overhead is involved in the implementation of rendez-vous since it has to differentiate normal entry calls from interrupt entry calls. One major issue is that, due to timing constraints, complex interrupt routines may have to be written. Ada does not address this issue because interrupt routines are hidden.

Issues concerning lack of **flexibility** stem from the fact that it is not possible to associate an interrupt address clause with a task object instead of a task type (this prevents us from easily implementing arrays of task device drivers, handling for instance several terminals).

Issues concerning **portability** are obvious since the implementation of interrupts is system dependent. So interrupt intensive applications (that is most embedded systems) may not be portable from one compiler to another. This portability is further impaired by the fact that the address type is of type "system.address" which is not portable. Finally if the address specification clause is considered as the interrupt routine address, portability is also reduced and applications may need recompilation each time the hardware configuration is changed (often the case for embedded systems using evolving in-house hardware).

2.4 *Low level Input-Output*

Low level input-output is not part of the language and is left up to the application. The issue is that it is very difficult to implement asynchronous input-output primitives. This means that a system primitive allowing for asynchronous signals should be made available to the application in order to write efficient IO packages in Ada.

2.5 *Memory management*

Ada tasking imposes a model for memory management (i.e. cactus stack) allowing tasks to get visibility to the local data of some other tasks. Furthermore, dynamically allocated objects are always implicitly deallocated. The overall memory management is complex. In real-time applications, the main criteria for a model is efficiency. So it is not possible to use garbage collection algorithms having substantial or even impredictible overhead.

Implementation of virtual memory may be desirable,

but for protection only. Once again this would add much software and hardware overhead.

2.6   *Configuration of the run-time - Abortion*

Due to the limited resources of embedded systems, it is important to be able to configure the run-time. An application which does not use the file system should not include it in its configuration. Configurability may even contribute to efficiency. Abortion for example is unlikely to be used in those systems. It adds much complexity to the run-time, so the tasking run-time could be greatly optimized in configurations which do not include abortion.

2.7   *Debugging*

Since tasks are entities of the Ada language and since these are handled by the run-time executive, debuggers and monitoring tools will have to interface with it in order to get information (e.g. concerning entry queues). This makes such tools highly dependent on the run-time in use. The issue is that, if one is not careful, we may end up with the need for different debuggers for the same compiler, the same hardware but different run-times.

3.   *REQUIREMENTS FOR THE USE OF ADA IN REAL-TIME EMBEDDED SYSTEMS*

In the light of those issues we try in this section to derive some requirements that the compiler, the run-time and the language must meet to fully support real-time embedded systems.

3.1   *Concerning the compiler*

The compiler could optimize context switches in a variety of ways. Passive tasks are a category of tasks which do not need to be implemented as a process (Schauer 1982). For instance, the implementation of a semaphore in Ada requires the use of an intermediate task. An optimizing compiler could eliminate this by producing in-line procedural code to replace an entry call to that intermediate task. One could even go one step further and map groups of Ada tasks into one process of the run-time executive either automatically or through user provided directives (we prefer the latter approach which would make applications more portable, should the directives be standardized). Rendez-vous could be implemented so that the second task in the rendez-vous executes it (Habermann & Nassi 1980). This eliminates context switches, but may introduce some overhead in the memory management in the case where the caller executes the rendez-vous.

The code generator may have to include specific features (in addition to standard optimization). One specific feature could be the generation of position independent code, even after link-edition. This is a configuration requirement of many embedded systems.

3.2   *Concerning the run-time*

A multitasking executive supporting Ada tasking and interrupt handling should also optimize context switches. We saw above that this can also be done at the compiler level. The general requirement is that there should not be internal context switches. For instance, the activation of a set of tasks should be done in one shot (i.e. the activation should be atomic). This further ensures that after activation the next task to run will be the one with the highest priority.

Some synchronization primitives (e.g. semaphores) should also be made available to the applications, at least to allow for the efficient writing of asynchronous input-output. Standardized interfaces could be defined.

Interrupt handling primitives should be made directly available to the application, within the Ada model to allow for the writing of interrupt routines. Standardized interfaces could be defined.

Debugging support should be provided to allow for the full debugging of tasking. Standardized interfaces could be defined to make debugging tools independent of the run-time.

The run-time should also be configurable as mentioned previously.

3.3   *Concerning the language*

We think that further work should be carried out on the language specification concerning **task priorities** and **interrupt handling**. Task priorities should be associated with task objects instead of task types. The address clause should be associated with task objects instead of task types. The type of the address clause should not be system.address, but rather something general and standardized to improve portability. A mechanism should be specified to be able to program interrupt routines within the frame of the model to allow for efficient implementations.

In another area, Input-output system primitives allowing for asynchronous signals should be available to the application in order to write efficient IO packages in Ada. These primitives can either be part of the language or directly offered by the run-time.

4.   *MANAGING THE TRANSITION TOWARD EMBEDDED REAL-TIME APPLICATIONS IN ADA*

We saw in this paper some problems concerning the use of Ada for embedded real-time applications, and we derived some requirements that must be met in order to make such applications feasible. Current implementations do not fully meet those requirements so one may wonder whether an immediate solution toward real-time applications written in Ada does not simply consist in bypassing Ada tasking and in directly calling a conventional executive. The ASTERIX project (Bayan et al. 1985) aims at the study of an efficient implementation model of the run-time which remains within the framework of the language. ASTERIX only concentrates on the run-time aspects which are highly independent of any high-level optimizations done at the compiler level. It turns out (see Bayan et al. 1985 for more details) that a standardized specification of many aspects of the run-time can be proposed, allowing for the reusability of an efficient run-time. This run-time optimizes context switches, provides full support for interrupt handling, support of some asynchronous synchronization functions, and some support for tasking debugging. We conjecture that some standardization of internal interfaces, i.e. with the run-time executive and with some debugging facilities which must be provided along with the executive, may have to be carried out in order to favor the transition toward Ada real-time applications.

It is obvious that the overall performance of an application will still be highly dependent on the compiler and its code generator (e.g. optimizing passive tasks), and therefore much work has to be done in that direction in parallel with run-time optimization.

5. *CONCLUSION*

Ada will be effectively used for embedded systems if the run-time tasking provides adequate support for real-time programming. The ASTERIX project goes along those lines. Issues concerning distributed and multiprocessor systems have not been discussed in this paper. They are still immature topics (Cornhill 1984 and Roberts et al. 1981), so we do not think that Ada can presently be used in industry for those types of systems.

References

Bayan, R. & Bonnet, C. & Kung, A. & Kirchgassner, W. & Landwehr, R. & Schwarz, B. (february 1985). Requirements for a real-time Ada run-time kernel and proposed kernel interfaces. European Communities: ASTERIX MAP project 765 report.

Cornhill, D. (1984). Four approaches to partitioning Ada
    programs for Execution on Distributed Targets.
    Conf. Ada applications and Environments, St.Paul,
    Minn., Oct.84, pp. 153-162.
Habermann, A.N. & Nassi, I.R. (1980). Efficient Implementation
    of Ada Tasks. CMU-CS-80-103, Jan.80.
Habermann, A.N. & Perry, D.E. (1983). Ada For Experienced
    Programmers. Mass.: Addison-Wesley, Reading.
Roberts, E.S. & Evans Jr., A. & Morgan, C.R. & Clarke, E.M.
    (1981). Task management in Ada - A Critical
    Evaluation for Real-Time Multiprocessors. Software,
    Practice and Experience, Vol11, Oct.81,
    pp.1019-1051.
Schauer, J. (1982). Vereinfachung von Process - Systemen Durch
    Sequentialisierung. Dissertation,   Institut fur
    Informatik II, Karlsruhe university, Bericht 30/82.
Wegner, P. (1969). Programming languages, information
    structure and machine organization. Mac Graw-Hill.

DESIGNING AN INTERACTIVE, ADAPTIVE GRAPHICS SYSTEM USING ADA

Y.S. Eisa

High Integrity Systems Ltd., Sawbridgeworth, Herts., England

J.S. Page

High Integrity Systems Ltd., Sawbridgeworth, Herts., England

Abstract. In this paper, the authors describe their experience of
using Ada in the development of a novel, interactive medical
imaging system and the manner in which Ada helped in both the
design and implementation phases. The adaptive nature of the
system is outlined, illustrating how users could develop new image
processing features. Some abstractions of the tools developed to
allow users to create new system features are introduced. The
approach described employs an object-based viewpoint which was well
suited for coding in Ada. The implementation proved surprisingly
compact and consisted of 9300 lines of Ada. The programming
required one man-year of effort and involved two people. The paper
concludes that the use of Ada made it possible to follow the
object-oriented approach through to implementation, with the added
advantage that Ada allowed the design to be documented as it
evolved.

Introduction

As consultants, it is the authors' privilege to be involved in projects
which have a high degree of complexity and novelty. In the case of the
project discussed in this paper, the authors were asked to assist in
developing a Medical Information System which could handle patient
information. The system was required to provide storage and retrieval
of both data and video images and also to act as an investigative and
diagnostic tool in a clinical environment. This was a novel application
in the sense that although much research had taken place in this general
area, the use of such facilities on a day to day basis in a working
hospital had little precedent (Constable 1985). Many aspects of
introducing powerful image processing systems into the clinical
environment remained unclear. For example, how could complex image

processing features be presented to medical practitioners in a user
friendly way? Of what value were individual techniques, and how would
they be used?

Broadly, the target system had to have the following characteristics:

Ease of use -   It needed to be used by a variety of people with
                   different skills, interests, and levels of computer
                   literacy.

Adaptability -   It needed to adapt and acquire new facilities, and to
                   encourage users to become involved and to build their
                   own tools suited to their clinical environment.

Interactivity -   It needed to provide a very friendly interface,
                   employing known design principles of effective
                   man-machine interaction (Foley & Wallace 1974)

Sophistication -   It needed to control real world devices with the
                   concurrency and multi-tasking that this involved, and
                   to deal with the complexities of imaging processing
                   and graphics.

Open-endedness -   It had to be proof against changes in technology, to
                   be able to take advantage of developments such as
                   multiprocessor architectures and to be expandable
                   without fundamental changes to the software.

The main concern of the interactive system design was how to establish a
relationship between the user and the system. Rather than present a
user with an array of input devices, it was decided that a digitising
tablet would provide all of the forms of input needed either by means of
a touch on the tablet with the stylus or by moving the stylus over the
tablet. Where text entry predominated it was felt that a keyboard would
be more acceptable, and this was retained as a secondary input and as

the system console. The primary task of the project was the building of
a user friendly interface using the digitising tablet for input.

During discussions with potential users, it became evident that at each
installation of the system the way of working would be governed by the
particular clinical methods and specialisations involved. Skilled users
at each site would determine the day to day procedures and the commands
needed by the less skilled users.

Since neither the facilities (eg. image manipulation tools) nor the way
in which they would be used could be identified with any certainty, it
was necessary to make the interface adaptive in the sense that users
could build the features of the system from the basic facilities
offered. As it was not clear how user friendliness could best be
interpreted for this group of users, the control of the system also
needed to be adaptable.

In order to provide long term viability and maintainability of the
software, Ada was selected as the implementation language. The support
of Ada for abstraction was seen as advantageous for the evolution of the
software design as more operational experience was gained. Another
reason for selecting Ada was to allow the system to be portable to other
target hardware.

Overview of the Design

At first the design requirements could not easily be determined. To
overcome this difficulty, a set of desired target system features was
conceived by abstracting the use of a digitising tablet. By viewing the
digitising tablet as a part of a plane which served as a large control
panel, the active surface of the tablet could be mapped into the plane
at any of a number of positions by means of overlays. A library of such
overlays could be provided for the needs of each clinical and research
environment. Each overlay was divided into regions whose size and
position could be defined by the user. An overlay was defined as an
array of regions which were in turn defined as variant records of

type BUTTON using the type VOCABULARY as the discriminant:

```
type VOCABULARY is        -- an active region
          (NOUN,          -- used to specify things to which commands
                          -- apply, eg. a video tape recorder VTR
          ADJECTIVE,      -- modifies the meaning of a noun, eg. TWO
          VERB,           -- an action to be applied, eg. move FORWARD
          ADVERB,         -- modifies the action, eg. FAST
               -- a typical 'phrase' might be VTR TWO FORWARD FAST using
               -- four regions defined as above, and which can be input
               -- by touching the regions in sequence.
          ASCII_CODE,     -- a soft keyboard for alphanumeric input
          SUPER,          -- a region defined as a whole phrase or series
                          -- of phrases
          GRAPHIC,        -- a region used in mouse or digitising mode
          SPECIAL,        -- a control region common to all overlays
               -- for example to 'assign' a phrase (eg. VTR TWO FORWARD
               -- FAST, see above) to a SUPER button
          URGENT);        -- a special region for commands having an
                          -- immediate effect, eg. controlling the system.
```

Sequences of button touches (ie. phrases) could be assigned to SUPER
buttons and a phrase or sequence of phrases from one overlay could be
reassigned to a SUPER button on another overlay. This allowed a user
who was skilled in the application of the system to start from an
initial overlay containing primitive buttons (ie. not SUPER) and define
complex commands as SUPER buttons. Then an unskilled user could invoke
these commands literally at the touch of a button.

The above illustrates the way in which overlays were defined for a
user's needs. Physical overlays, in the form of printed plastic sheets
onto which readily recognisable symbols were drawn, conveyed the meaning
of the regions of an overlay. However, this meaning also needed to be
conveyed to the system. For this purpose each valid phrase was
interpreted as a semantic token by means of a tree structure made up

from records as follows:

```
type NODE is
    record
        UP        : NODE_PT; -- pointer to preceding NODE
        IDENTITY  : INPUT.BUTTON_INDEX; -- pointer to BUTTON definition
        ACROSS    : NODE_PT; -- next node of this type
        DOWN      : NODE_PT; -- next node type
        SEQUENCE  : SEQUENCE_ID := 0; -- points to a leaf in an array
                                      -- of leaves
    end record;
```

As each phrase was input, it was parsed and used to search the tree. A
tree constructed from elements of the type NODE could be scanned easily
and the same scanning process was used both for storing and for building
the tree. A leaf selected a list of one or more elements of type TOKEN
(see below), which allowed the basic facilities of the system to be
invoked. A SUPER button selected a list of elements of type TOKEN
directly.

To give substance to the tokens, the system was viewed as a collection
of real and abstract components on which actions were carried out. Each
action affected the state of these components in a consistent way, even
if an error was encountered. These actions were the fundamental
functions provided with the system. They included VTR control, frame
grab, false colouring, image manipulation, storage operations and so
on. These actions were held in a global array indexed by subtype
OPERATION_RANGE. The token selected when a leaf was reached on the tree
determined the action to be taken by the system:

```
type TOKEN(JOB : JOB_TYPE := NORMAL) is
    record
        MASK : STATUS; -- used in conditional testing with status
                       -- and return codes
        NEXT_OPERATION : TOKEN_POINTER; -- next TOKEN in list at leaf
```

```
        case JOB is
            when NORMAL =>
                OPERATION : OPERATION_RANGE; -- the action to be done
            when SPECIAL =>
                SPECIAL_OPERATION : SPECIAL_OPERATION_RANGE;
                                -- control statement identifier
            when MACRO =>
                MACRO_START: SEQUENCE_ID; -- points to start of macro
            end case;
        end record;
```

Once a token was selected as a consequence of a phrase being entered,
parsed and validated, it was passed to routines within an application
executive package. This executive invoked the specified action or
sequence of actions.

As an example of the process of abstracting ways of working with the
system, the abstraction employed to derive the application executive was
that of a punched card reader (a token being the equivalent of a card)
and a job control language using SPECIAL_OPERATION_RANGE to provide the
control functions. The stack of cards to be fed in (a token or a list
of tokens) was selected by the leaf found by parsing the phrase, and the
application executive then executed the job control statement given by
each card (a token). By analogy with such practices in the batch
operation of data processing systems, this was a manageable way of
putting together quite complex operations made up from sequences of the
basic functions of the system.

The features provided by the system were determined partly by the low
level actions (OPERATION_RANGE in NODE) and partly by the adaptive
nature of the system which had the ability to define new buttons and new
phrases, and to associate phrases with tokens. New tokens could be
defined as sequences of the low level actions.

An indication of the success of the design was that some of the earliest
overlays to be defined were those which allowed buttons, phrases,

tokens, etc. to be defined to the system. The actions provided for
these overlays were those which updated or changed this data. These
helped considerably with the debugging of the system.

The Approach taken on the Project

The lack of firm requirements made it hard to see how to carry out the
project effectively. With a small team (not more then three people of
whom only two would be writing Ada) and a limited budget, the prospect
of trial implementations followed by rewrites did not seem viable. A
set of prototyping tools was needed to make this process simple and
quick to carry out. As it happened, this proved to be a similar
requirement to that of making the system adaptive for users.

As the design was based on abstractions, the programming team were able
to exploit these concepts in the implementation. Each of the
significant abstractions provided a tool to make the system adaptable
and these were readily interpreted as having creation, management and
other operations over a relevant data type. Thus for the parsing tree,
the following were provided:

```
        procedure SEARCH_TREE  -- publicly declared
-- SEARCH_TREE includes the following procedures
        procedure ADD_NEW_BRANCH -- adds new information to the tree when
                                 -- the search failed during definition
        procedure EXECUTE_LEAF -- passes the token to the application
                               -- executive package
-- in addition two recursive operations are provided within the body
        function CLIMB_TO_LEAF( .. )  -- go down tree till farmost leaf is
                                      -- reached
        procedure TRAVERSE_TREE( .. ) -- climb back up to next higher level
                                   -- move sideways and climb to farmost leaf
-- together with management functions
        procedure SAVE_TREE( .. ) -- saves the tree data
        procedure RESTORE_TREE( .. ) -- restores the tree
-- the root node is created when a new overlay is defined
```

Implementation in Ada

As noted above, Ada was originally proposed for the project in an
attempt to give the software some longevity in the face of system,
processor or specification changes. At the time the project was being
set up there were few Ada compilers and even fewer target systems on
which the software could be run. The project was fortunate in having
access to both of these. The target system used initially contained a
tightly coupled microprocessor system for which an Ada compiler was
available. Although not validated, this compiler provided most features
of Ada including tasking and generics. The system was implemented in a
board set for Multibus I and consequently a range of I/O boards was
available, including video and frame store boards for the imaging
facilities.

The informal starting point for the object-based design led to the
establishment of tasks and packages. Thus common declarations were
grouped into packages, operations became procedures and interfaces
between concurrent activities became entries whilst the activities
became tasks. Such structuring tended to be retained as the design
evolved unless a major change occurred in the design concepts. By
grouping declarations together within a few packages, for example, the
maintenance of the design was kept to a minimum.

Although the design expressed in Ada eventually acquired some formality,
initially Ada gave little more than an orderly way of writing down the
design in natural English. However, Ada was helpful in limiting the
vocabulary used for the design and also allowed it to retain a measure
of flexibility. Some topics in the design did need to be formally
defined before the associated objects and operations could be written
down in Ada.

It is a characteristic of a good design methodology that it begins to
play an active part in the design process and to inspire more elegant
solutions. This occurred whilst using Ada and it is considered that it
resulted from having good, early documentation of the design so that

common features could be identified. Additionally, the ability to
compile the design brought to light inconsistencies and omissions, and
facilitated the testing of ideas and strategies early on. One example
of this support was the introduction of a simple substitute for the
token interface that allowed the development and testing of the overlay,
button and tree concepts. A user was able to work and experiment with
this part of the system and provide valuable feedback to the design team.

In its initial form, the implementation was surprisingly compact and
consisted of 9300 lines of Ada. There were 19 packages included in the
system. The programming required one man-year of effort and involved
two people. For much of the time, the work was split so that work
proceeded in parallel on the input sections of the system and on the
application executive sections. The interface between these two areas
of work was provided by the type TOKEN and its associated operations.
Additional design effort of about three man-months was provided and
included experience in object-based design. The programming staff each
received training of about one man-month each.

Experience Gained with Ada

The programming staff assigned to the project were new to Ada, and their
progress highlighted the significant differences between Ada and other
languages. Teaching design staff to work with an object-based approach
seemed to be a prerequisite for successfully using Ada, and this notion
has been reinforced on other projects. It appeared that whilst Ada
allowed explicit structuring and separation of concerns, the use of
these attributes could only be effective if the design was viewed in the
same way. Objects seemed to provide the necessary conceptual framework
to allow this.

Many of the structures that accommodated the complexity of an adaptive
system were readily implemented in Ada by means of variant records and
access types. These were particularly useful in creating and modifying
such structures as lists and trees when defining new features. The use
of the dot notation was helpful in generating the code and proved to be

an asset for maintaining and understanding the code later.

Some difficulties were experienced with the use of Ada. For example, it was found that performance deteriorated as the number of tasks was increased. Consequently, the number of tasks was optimised to utilise the multiprocessor configuration efficiently without undue overhead. Another problem which was experienced concerned the need to avoid interleaved I/O. To resolve this, I/O was managed within the main Ada routines and the basic I/O operations were provided as an essentially sequential activity.

Overall, the use of Ada was very beneficial. It is believed that a design might not have been realised within the constraints given, if it were not for the ability of Ada to support abstractions so readily and clearly. Furthermore, the use of Ada to provide continuous documentation of the design from the outset proved to be of considerable value in terms of project management and productivity.

The success achieved in following the dictates of software engineering principles (Ross et al 1975) was not only due to Ada's ability to enforce good coding discipline and consistency, but also to its capacity to support the design process. Ada has helped to create a much better understanding of the underlying problems, has allowed an object-based approach to be followed and, most importantly, has allowed the design to be documented as it evolved.

References

Constable, T.B. (1985). Filmless Feasibility. The British
        Journal of Health Computing, vol 2, No 3, pp 23 - 25
Foley, J.D. & Wallace, V.L. (1974). The Art of Natural Graphic
        Man-Machine Conversation, Proc. IEEE, April 1974
Ross, D.T. et al. (1975). Software Egineering: Process, Principles, and
        Goals. Computer, May 1975, p. 66.

SOFTWARE COMPONENT LIBRARY

T.O. Hulkkonen
NOKIA, PL 780, SF-00101 HELSINKI, FINLAND

V.M. Kehä
NOKIA, PL 780, SF-00101 HELSINKI, FINLAND

Abstract. This paper presents some of the experiences and future plans concerning development of a software component library in an Ada environment. User needs were assessed by interviews. Existing Ada programs at Nokia were surveyed. Quality criteria were defined and design guidelines for components were produced. Possible sources of components were surveyed. A prototype was implemented to study automated component library access. The users were informed and trained. The component usage is being monitored. According to our judgement, significant reuse of components can be achieved only through careful consideration of all relevant technical, psychological, and managerial factors.

INTRODUCTION

Ada programs have been written at Nokia since 1981. These include a full scale operating system, a relational data base management system, utility programs, and banking applications. The number of software engineers is now about 80 and the total number of lines of Ada code produced is about 1 500 000.

When programming with Ada began, programs were written in much the same way as before with other languages. There were no observable changes in software productivity. Compilation time increased but testing and debugging times decreased.

The effects of using Ada have been evident in features that are unavailable in most block-structured languages, such as exceptions and tasks. The use of exceptions has varied depending on how well the particular programmer has understood this language feature. The use of tasks has made the writing of real-time programs simpler but has produced inefficient code.

In the beginning of 1985 we concluded that the use of Ada had not significantly improved software production. Therefore we started a project with the goal of improving code reusability by all possible means.

A central issue has been the establishment of a *Software Component Library (SCL)*. We want to achieve a situation where 80% of new program source code comes from library components and only 20% is written from scratch. At the moment we fall badly short of this goal.

ASSESSMENT OF NEED

During June and July of 1985 we interviewed a sample group of 13 Ada programmers and project managers. We wanted to determine the extent of reuse in software development. We also asked their opinions of how SCL could be of help to them. The results indicated that software reuse was restricted to within project teams with no information interchange between teams. A typical project group consists of 3 to 5 members. No information existed about available SW components except within projects.

To be able to decide on reusing a component, the user must have the following information: the package specification, an abstract, and short application notes. There are various access methods for finding the right component for a particular purpose. Interactive access via terminal was considered best. Specification listings and abstracts were also considered useful. However, there were few really reusable components. The sample group felt that components are not produced automatically. In project work the focus is in meeting the schedule, and there is no time for considering the reusability of the produced code. The interviewees said that they would eagerly use components if any existed. The programmers had a positive attitude towards reuse but, due to reasons mentioned above, components were not being reused.

According to the interviewees, components should be available in the following software domains: string manipulation, file handling, user interface, data transformation, error messages, sorting, lists, queues, stacks, buffers, mathematical functions, dynamic data types, and handling dates and weekdays.

The conclusion was that we need a centralized method for collecting, producing, storing, and delivering components. An effective way of informing about components and their applications is also required. The organization must have a person, an SCL administrator, in charge of the above tasks.

EXISTING COMPONENTS

We performed a literature survey to find reusable Ada components. Literature about components is so far scarce, except articles in magazines and conference proceedings. The survey resulted in only a few components that can be used in an Ada environment without major changes. The most useful of these was a sorting package. It has been used e.g. in training and demonstration programs.

We bought a sample of commercial GRACE sotfware components. These components are suitable to the SCL without modification.

We retrieved public domain Ada programs from the Ada Repository through ARPANET. The quality and coverage of the components in the ARPANET is variable. Some of these programs were used in testing of our Ada compiler. We announced a contest in the MPS 10 community to find the best string manipulation package ever. Eight different collections of operations were found. Using these ideas we have written a string handling package specification. This package will be included in the SCL.

All Ada software currently in use at Nokia was scanned using a tool program created for this purpose. Existing Ada software contains a considerable amount of redundant code. The project team members do not know about programs written in other projects. Coding practice has been very varying because of lack of standards and guidelines. The quality of documentation is variable. Due to reasons mentioned above there are no packages in the existing software that could be readily used as components. Instead, there are packages that can be refined to components and inserted in the SCL.

GOOD AND BAD COMPONENTS

A component is a program that can be reused in contexts other than the original design context. Subsystems, which are used in various applications to perform their original task, are not components. A component can be an independent compilation unit or a piece of code that can be inserted in the user program. Often components are generic.

The following attributes of components represent opinions of many experienced software engineers, and they are not based on scientific studies. In our opinion, however, they are very relevant.

Good components are easy to use. Good components are large enough that using them is easier than coding them anew. A good component has a clear, simple caller interface. A good component implements an abstraction, that is, a high level description of an object. When calling a good component there is no need for type conversion or dummy variables.

A poor component has a complex name. A poor component has poor comments. A poor component does not conform with programming standards. A poor component takes with it many other packages.

Only good components should be included in the SCL because the use of a poor component causes difficulties that ruin the users' willingness to use components. It also causes extra work both for the SCL users and for the SCL administrator.

COMPONENT POLICY

New components are selected as follows: When a sufficient number of component candidates that pertain to certain subject has been found, all the different variations are evaluated and the best one is selected and possibly modified. The component then goes through a quality assurance procedure before release. There are, however, many packages of different nature available in the same domain.

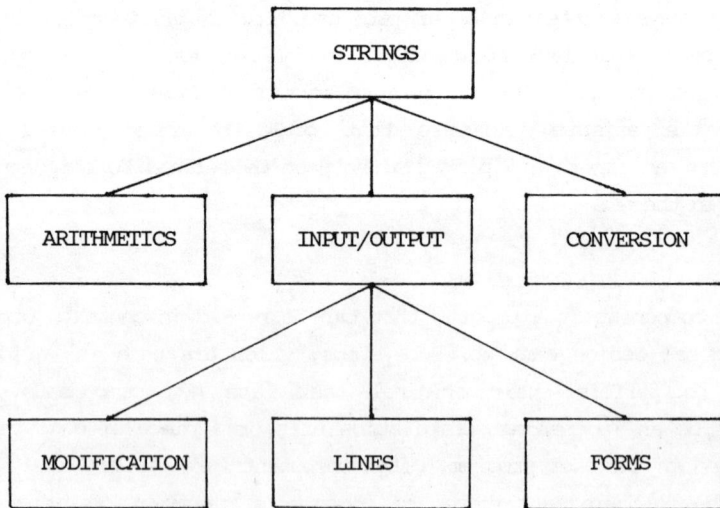

Figure 1. Classification of string components

Components have been classified for easy access. We were not able to find a suitable classification system through the literature survey mentioned above. Therefore, a classification system of our own was designed in which components are classified by their nature and purpose of use. As an example, a part of our classification of components by purpose is sketched in Fig. 1. It is related to string handling components. At the moment we also use the taxonomy designed by Grady Booch. This taxonomy describes the nature of the components by their time and space requirements.

QUALITY CRITERIA

We designed a "Quality Criteria for Software Components" guide to be used in component design and quality evaluation. The guide defines what should be included in the component source code. It gives practical guidelines on comments, naming, using parameters and exceptions, error handling, and efficiency. There is also a description of properties required of component specification and body. These properties include among others completeness, understandability, consistency, reusability, portability, consistent error handling, reliability, and efficiency. The guide contains examples of components and the full source text of a small component. In addition, there are guidelines on testing. This guide is not sufficient alone. The component designer must also have insight in reusability and how it should be applied.

Several sources are used to find components. Our aim is to find the best possible components for our library. High quality is a prerequisite for components that are frequently used in varying applications.

PRODUCING COMPONENTS

Some components are produced in cooperation with the University of Helsinki and the Tampere University of Technology. These components have been designed according to the guide mentioned above. The components completed so far include: string package, list, queue, stack, set and mathematics package. Components for handling dates and nets are currently being designed.

At the moment the SCL contains components covering the following domains: mathematics, bit manipulation, string manipulation, conversions, timers, random number generator, date handling, data structures, index structures, file handling, file name handling, input/output support, and user interface. The data structures include lists, queues, stacks, sets, and AVL-trees.

Producing reusable components requires motivation. In our opinion, there is no such motivation without special actions. In order to be able to produce components, the organization must allocate resources for this purpose. Actual component production of our own has not yet started because of lack of resources.

TOOLS

We made an analyzer tool program to scan most of our Ada source code. This tool scans source files of an application and outputs three different kinds of listings. The module listing lists names and types of compilation units in each file. The abstract listing lists comments contained in the header part of a compilation unit. The subprogram listing lists names of functions and procedures in a compilation unit. Our analysis revealed a set of packages that can be refined to reusable components. It also revealed considerable redundancy of existing software.

The goal right from the start of the project was for the SCL to be user-friendly. Therefore we built a prototype Ada editor to find out the problems concerning the simultaneous use of a text editor and library search routines. There are features supporting Ada programming in this prototype, even though it is not a real syntax-driven editor. In addition there is a feature for searching information about the library components via menus or by keywords. The component's source code or subprogram call template can easily be copied to the program being edited. The comments from pilot users were very encouraging. The implementation of the actual tool is going on.

TRAINING AND INFORMATION

The existence of components does not in itself guarantee their large scale reuse. Therefore, management support is essential to increase the extent of component reuse. The users have been taught to use components and the library by examples in short informative lectures. Personal consulting has also been given when needed. The next effort is to arrange a course on using components for all Ada programmers. The course concentrates on using the library and related tools. A course on component design is arranged for selected programmers.

The whole user community is informed of new components so that they can be readily exploited. We have introduced a series of information letters. These letters contain component release notes and other relevant information concerning SCL. Until now we have published 7 information letters. We have also published working examples of applications using components.

FOLLOW-UP

We plan on building a tool for monitoring component usage in our software production. The tool will provide valuable information about the actual benefits achieved in our organization.

In connection with the quality assurance sessions, the software products will also be evaluated based on the rate of component usage. This feedback is important to determine what kind of components are really needed. The management has been informed about component usage.

Statistics are gathered concerning errors in components. The users are informed about errors detected. The interviews described earlier will be made again in order to determine the changes in attitudes and working practices.

CONCLUSION

Ada provides features that encourage reusability. Using Ada as a programming language does not, however, in itself guarantee the birth of a new kind of software culture. With Ada one can write programs just as one did before with COBOL or PASCAL.

Large scale software reuse can be achieved only after a large collection of high quality software components becomes available. This requires determined and continuous component survey, development, and quality control. Other important factors are easy component access and active information and training that covers the whole software development community. The management must actively encourage using components.

BIBLIOGRAPHY

Bowles, K. (1983). Software components industry. *In* Ada-Europe/AdaTEC
    Joint Conference on Ada. Brussels, Belgium: Comm. Eur.
    Communities.
Bron, C. (1983). On reusable software. *In* Ada-Europe/AdaTEC Joint
    Conference on Ada, pp. 26/1-9. Brussels, Belgium: Comm. Eur.
    Communities.
Horowitz, E. & Munson, J.B. (1984). An Expansive View of Reusable
    Software. IEEE Trans. Software Eng., *SE-10*, no.5, pp. 477-487.
Lahtinen, P. (1984). Guidelines for Software Component Specification.
    Tampere, Finland: Oy Softplan Ab.
Lanergan, R.G. & Grasso, C.A. (1984). Software Engineering with Reusable
    Designs and Code. IEEE Trans. Software Eng., *SE-10*, no.5, pp.
    498-501.
Mendal, G.O.(1984). Micro Issues in Reuse from a Real Project. Ada
    Technology Support Lab. Sunnyvale, CA: Lockheed Missiles and
    Space Company, Inc.
Nissen, J. & Wallis, P.J.L. (1984). Portability and Style in Ada.
    Cambridge: Cambridge University Press.
Symm, G.T. & Wichmann, B.A. & Kok, J. & Winter, D.T. (1984). Guidelines
    for the design of large modular scientific libraries in Ada.
    Report DITC 37/84. Teddington, England: National Physics
    Laboratory.

INTEGRATING ADA IN AN EXISTING ENVIRONMENT -
THE ARCS EXAMPLE

Dick Schefstrom
TeleLOGIC AB
Regnbagsallen 4,
S-951 87 Lulea, Sweden

ABSTRACT

Undertaking the transition to Ada today will to most of us not
mean using a full APSE, [DOD80, BUX80], tailored for this purpose. Instead, this transition must be made by using an existing environment, incrementally integrating its proven tools and
concepts in the realm of Ada.

This paper describes one effort taking this approach, where the
UNIX revision control tool RCS, [TIC85], is integrated with an
Ada program library, using a UNIX style library interface.

1. Introduction

    Even at the beginning of the development of Ada, the importance of
the programming environment was pointed out, and a number of ambitious
projects and investigations were initiated, [DOI81, THA82, INT82,
KIT84].   However, today few APSE's of this spirit are available for
production use, and even if they were, existing environments could be
chosen for a number of reasons: such as that they are proven and people
know how to use them.

    It can therefore be argued, [ICH85], that we, at least for the
moment, should take a bottom-up approach to tools and environments, and
make the effort to carefully integrate existing operating systems and
the Ada-world. To make it convenient to use Ada in an existing environments, the interfacing to the Ada utilities should be carried out in
the spirit of the host environment, and its tools should be reused in
the Ada context whenever possible.

    The **Arcs** program, described here, is an example of an attempt to
do this for the UNIX programming environment.

2. Revision Control in an Ada Environment

    Revision and configuration management was given a very important
role in the requirements of the APSE, [DOD80], and has consequently
been given much thought in different APSE-efforts. Still there are
tools, such as RCS, widely in use for such purposes today, which could
be reused very neatly in the context of Ada if suitable measures are
taken.

    The Ada program library is very important to notice in this case,
since it will always be there (in one form or another), describing the
user's world of Ada units, and their relationships to each other. It is
likely that these program libraries will be a main focus of interest,
just like file directories are today. Examples of such program
libraries are [DDC84], [DEC85], [NAR85a], [VER85], [SOF85]. But, at
the same time, users will still want to keep track of successive revisions of source code located in files, using tools like RCS [TIC85],
SCCS [ROC75], or CMS [DEC84].

If these two tools, the program library and the revision control tool, don't know about each other, we will experience a number of difficulties using the system:

*   Which revisions/versions of a program unit are actually present in the program library?

*   What is the name of a unit: the Ada unit name as present in the library or the filename as when dealing with RCS?

*   For a particular unit in the program library: where is its "RCS-file"? Is the unit under revision control or not? Has its source code been checked in since it was last modified?

*   How do we interpret concepts defined in the context of program libraries when using RCS, and vice versa. For example, can we check in a whole Ada program, (as defined by the program library)? Check it out?

The problem is really that we will have two uncoordinated representations of the program; leading to unwanted redundancy and confusion.

Typical revision control tools, such as RCS, are good at keeping successive revisions of a single file together. However, they are not that good at describing system structure and relationships between different units. On the other hand, an Ada program library explicitly represents relationships between separately compiled units. It catches more of the semantics of what is being stored, but usually does no tracking of successive revisions. So, by combining the two we can get the best out of both tools.

The examples given in this paper will be UNIX specific, but the basic ideas are not UNIX dependent in any way. Infact, a version for VMS, and its revision control tool CMS, is currently under development.

3. **The Program Library**

The work described here is the initial result of an attempt to integrate the UNIX revision control tool RCS with the TeleSoft Ada program Library, [NAR85a], [NAR85b], [SCH85a], [SCH85b]. To give the necessary background, a short discussion of the properties of the program library is appropriate. For a more detailed investigation see the references given above.

The full typechecking between separately compiled units, as required by the Ada language, implies a close interaction between the compiler and the environment. It leads to the introduction of a file, or "database", holding the descriptions of which units have been compiled earlier, what services they provide, and how they relate to each other. Although each compilation must be performed in the context of a program library, the Ada language definition does not prescribe its functioning in any detail, but regards it as part of the environment. At this point we also get implications for "programming-in-the-large" and software engineering. Interesting criticism has been presented on this subject by some researchers, [BUX85], arguing that Ada maybe went to far into environment issues in its separate compilation mechanism, thereby failing to make a clear separation between the language and the environment.

Since a lot of information about the software is automatically collected in the program library, in a form suitable for mechanic manipulation, there is a big potential for building new tools utilizing

that information. Among the more obvious is an alternative, or substitute, for Unix/Make [FEL79], system structure, or cross-reference,
-generators, and configuration and version management tools. In another
paper, [NAR85a], the author argues that the "environment database"
envisioned by the original APSE requirements, is best approached as an
outgrowth of the program library.

The implementation of an Ada program library used here, the
TeleSoft Ada program library, is composed out of a freely constructable
sequence of sublibraries, together constituting a full library. Each
sublibrary includes a datamodel, a directed graph where the edges are
typed and the nodes may have arbitrary attributes. Besides being nodes
in a typed directed graph, the nodes are, within a sublibrary, arranged
in a hierarchy to allow for local namespaces. Although every node may
be part of the directed graph, every node must be part of the hierarchy, and nodes are named by giving the path from the root node. In the
following figures, if no name is attached to a connection between two
nodes, it represents a relationship within the hierarchy.

The library is extensible in the sense that new nodes, edges,
types of edges, and attributes may be introduced dynamically. Further,
procedures to do this are available as Ada package specifications, making it possible for different organizations to tailor their own bridges
between the world of Ada and their existing environments. We believe
that such extensibility is very important for a smooth transition to
Ada.

As an example, a package specification for a package "pack_a" is
represented by a node with the same name. To distinguish the specification from its body, (which in Ada has the same name, but is a different
compilation unit), it is the child of a special node called "lib",
(while the body is the child of a node called "sec"):

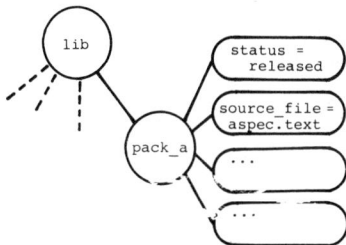

To fully name a node, one must specify its path from the root of
its sublibrary, so the unit above would be called "/lib/pack_a". The
rectangular boxes attached to the node represent attributes, which may
arbitrarily be attached to any node. The text inside the attribute symbols always has the format <attr_name>=<attr_value>.

The graph of a small system is illustrated below.

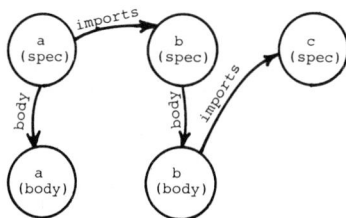

The different labels of the arcs could be viewed as a typing, or categorization, of the corresponding relationships. Different tools, (most frequently the compiler), introduce different types of edges between nodes.

It is a main point that different programming-in-the-large concepts, like consistency levels, configurations, and releases, can be defined in terms of the datamodel used [NAR85a], and this is explored in the integration with RCS which is described in the following.

Edges may also span between sublibraries, so that what we get could be viewed as a "layered graph". Different layers, (sublibraries), may be used to hold different subsystems, versions, or act as a means for sharing of objects between many programmers [NAR85a].

4. Basic Concepts of Arcs

A program library may contain lots of attributes and many different types of edges between nodes. At any single moment, a user is probably not interested in all of that, but rather a subset of the information important for the task at hand: there is a need for an ability to define views. However, since the library is extensible, one cannot restrict listings to a predefined format. Extensibility of the program library calls for extensibility of the presentation tool.

In **Arcs**, the basic library listing command, ("l"), takes a list of attribute names, (each signalled by an initial flip, "'"), a list of edge type-names, (each signalled by an initial colon, ":"), and a list of node, (or unit-), names. The given attributes are listed, if present, for each unit reachable by starting at a given unit following edges of any given type, as far as possible. Such a reachable graph may be described to each command of Arcs, with the effect of repeating the command for each node in the resulting graph.

The command...

    l 'time_stamp 'unit_kind :body /lib/

...would therefore list the values of the attributes "time_stamp" and "unit_kind" for all library units, (the ending "/" generates a list of all child units), and for each of these, all units reachable along edges of kind "body". This happens in this case to result in graphs of exactly two units, each containing a specification and its body.

Another example: the command...

    l 'state :imports :body :subunit main

...would list all units needed for the execution of main, and for each such unit, the value of its "state" attribute. (Each listing also points out units which are out-of-date, or missing completely, so that the command can also work as a consistency check).

This facility acts as a basic mechanism for specifying views: the user has complete freedom to operate on, or see, an arbitrary subset of the program library contents. To make it convenient to use such views, the alias facility may be used: instead of explicitly giving every attribute and edge type-name, the user could issue the command...

    alias my_view 'state :imports :body :subunit

...reducing the previous command to...

    1 my_view main

Arbitrary many aliases may be defined, and each may represent a different view of the program library.

Arcs contains lots of commands, and for each command there may be many options and variables affecting its detailed functioning. Commands are also available to inspect or edit sources, (or sets of sources if a "graph" is specified), and to select which tool in the environment to use for this task.

Arbitrary Arcs-commands, such as alias definitions, settings of variables, and opening of a default library, may be put in a ".arcsrc" file, so that these commands are automatically performed at each invocation of "arcs".

5. Coordinating with the Revision Control Tool

When we successfully compile a unit, a node with the same name as that unit, and some associated attributes, is created, or updated, in the program library. As an example, if we have the source of a package spec called "pack_a" located in a file "pack_a_spec", the following would be created...

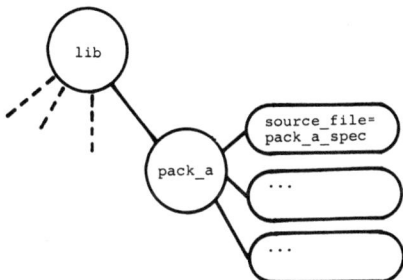

Typically, the user is not satisfied with "pack_a" just because it was compiled without errors, so he will repeatedly edit and compile the file "pack_a_spec". However, at some point in time he feels that the current state of "pack_a" spec is something of a milestone, and should be put under more formal control.

So, the units in a program library are of two kinds...

(1) **Milestones**, which are revisions considered important and complete, and whose source has been stored using a tool like RCS.

(2) **Editions**, which are in a state of development and whose source is not saved.

Working under UNIX, RCS [TIC85] might now be used, "checking in" the file "pack_a_spec" resulting in a new revision, stored in an "rcs-file" called "pack_a_spec,v". However, this is normally not reflected in the program library.

If the program library is to be a central information storage, activities like checking in and checking out must be made to affect it, in a more or less automatic way. To achieve this all the commands of RCS can be given from within Arcs, which let us talk about software in

terms of the compilation units and configurations of the program
library, and also makes it possible to reflect in the program library
what revision control actions have been performed. These commands take
the usual rcs-parameter flags as a subset, (prefixed by "-"), but does
also take Arcs-specific flags, (prefixed by "+").

A check-in of the current version of pack_a's spec now changes
from "ci pack_a_spec" to...

   ci pack_a

The program looks in the current library for a unit "pack_a",
takes the file described by the "source_file" attribute and calls "ci"
to check it in to an RCS-file.

To register that what is now in the library is a unit under revision control, a "version_nr" attribute is associated with pack_a,
resulting in the following node in the program library graph...

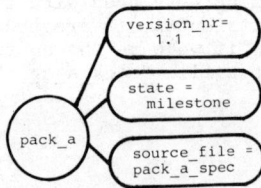

We can now see from the attribute "version_nr" that the unit is
under revision control and what version number it has. The "state"
attribute tells us that it is the checked-in 1.1, and not an edition of
it. A subsequent compilation of pack_a changes the state to "edition"...

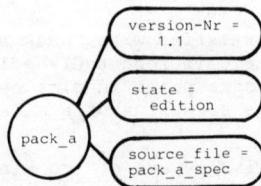

As a way of increasing reliability, the check-in program also
checks that the source file has not been changed since it was compiled
into the program library, and issues a warning if necessary.

So, by putting some other software around the check-in program we
can, in the program library, maintain an explicit distinction between
the different states of compilation units, and get a more homogeneous
environment with the program library as a main entry into different
services.

As discussed earlier, we allow different versions of the same unit to coexist in the environment if they belong to different sublibraries. This makes it possible to make full use of both versions without checking in or out, and without any need for recompilations when using another version. However, although these versions can be treated as independent units, there are good reasons for letting them share a single RCS-file:

(1) We get a description of how the different versions relate to each other historically.

(2) The sources can be stored space-efficiently.

The question that now arises is: how do we locate that common RCS-file? As a general rule, a system should not force a user to any particular methodology but should provide convenient defaults. In the case of RCS-files this implies that the user is allowed to provide the name of the directory where the RCS-file is to be located. A typical check-in would then look like...

    ci +d/u0/proj_a/rev pack_a

That is, the user tells the system that the source of the library unit pack_a is to be checked in at the directory /u0/proj_a/rev. This is also registered in the program library, resulting in the following...

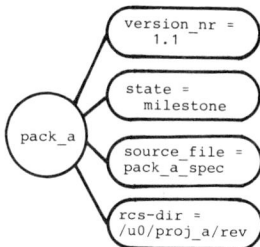

```
                    ┌─────────────────┐
                    │ version_nr =    │
                    │    1.1          │
                    └─────────────────┘
                    ┌─────────────────┐
                    │ state =         │
                    │   milestone     │
        ┌────────┐  └─────────────────┘
        │ pack_a │  ┌─────────────────┐
        └────────┘  │ source_file =   │
                    │ pack_a_spec     │
                    └─────────────────┘
                    ┌─────────────────┐
                    │ rcs-dir =       │
                    │ /u0/proj_a/rev  │
                    └─────────────────┘
```

Once a unit has been assigned an RCS-directory, the check-in program looks in the program library for the name of the RCS-file during subsequent check-in's, providing a natural default. So, the user has to decide on the location of the RCS-file only at the creation of the first revision of a unit.

Some information in the program library is now in the form of file names, referring to files in the host file system. To enable the tools to act "intelligently", one must agree on an interpretation of these file names.

Filenames can be of two kinds, absolute or relative. Absolute filenames are no problem to process: they can be interpreted in only one way, Relative filenames make it easier to move files between directories, but require some rule for translating a relative filename into an absolute.

The UNIX way of using a current directory does not always work in the context of sublibraries. A sublibrary may exist in the same directory for a long time, while users change their current directories and continue to use the sublibrary. To make up for this, the library tools treat relative filenames as relative to the directory of the sublibrary where the names are stored.

Using this idea, the RCS-file is located in the same directory as the sublibrary of the compilation unit, if not explicitly provided.

To automatically repeat the check in operation for a whole set of units, "reachable graphs" can be used. For example, a complete executable Ada program is defined by starting at the "main" unit and following arcs of type "imports", "body", "parent", and "subunit". Using this in the check in command...

    ci :imports :body :subunit main

...would repeat the check in for each unit in this reachable graph which "need to be checked in". A unit is said to need to be checked in if it has been compiled since the last check in, (state = edition).

Of course, the long list of relation names may be replaced by an alias.

The check-out command works in a similar way. It can be used for single units by giving the name of a compilation unit as in the command...

    co -r2.1 /sec/pack_a

...which would try to localize the rcs-file of the body of "pack_a" and check out revision 2.1 into the current directory, (the "/sec/" prefix talls it is the body of pack_a that is meant).

Assuming "prog" is alias for the necessary set of edge type names, the following command...

    co prog main

...would check out, for each unit in the given reachable graph, the latest version on the trunk.

A reachable graph can be thought of as a configuration, where each unit is of a particular version, (as described by the "version_nr" attribute). To be able to, for each unit in a reachable graph, check out the source corresponding to that particular version, substitutors are available so that the correct revision numbers are submitted to the "co" program. Besides such program library specific methods, the usual RCS ways of identifying a revision, (for example symbolic), can be used.

6. Automatic recompilation

As is shown in [NAR85a], the order of the necessary recompilations after a change are very easily computed using the high-level graph-manipulation operations provided by the TeleSoft Ada program library.

However, if the compiler only can compile whole files, the compilation of a unit must be done by compiling the whole file it is located in, possibly generating side-effects because of other units in that same file. It can be argued that the user should not put several units in the same file, if he expects things to work smoothly, but this is in reality too hard a restriction: although the "file" is not suitable as the unit of compilation, it may be a suitable unit of editing, since there may still be users out there having small screens and single window editors.

Instead we make the compiler take not only a file and a library as a parameter, but also a list of unit-names. In the following example...

    ada -u/sec/pack_a pack_a.text

...both the spec and body of "pack_a" are located in the file "pack_a.text", but because of the "-u" parameter, all units in the given file, except the body of "pack_a", are skipped by the compiler.

At any moment the program library contains zero or more units from the same "revision-family", (units whose source is stored on the same rcs-file), and these "representants" act as entries into that revision-family. If some member of a revision family is present in a library, we say that the family is "represented" in that library. If one wants to compile into the library another member of a represented revision family, it can be done by using the "ada" command...

    ada -r2.3 /sec/database

...which, in the example above, would check out revision 2.3 of "/sec/database" and try to compile it into the library. Sometimes this doesn't work, however, since the desired revision "withs" other versions, or other units, than are present in the library. Where the "ada" command fails, the "tli" command can be used instead...

    tli -r2.3 /sec/database

...resulting not in a full compilation, but making the relationships of "2.3" to its environment visible in the library. This gives a convenient way of observing the separate compilation structure of "2.3", thereby pointing out what kind of environment is needed to perform a full compilation. In practice, this program is just a special version of the Ada compiler front end.

Finally, the ada command can also be used to automatically carry out the necessary recompilations after a change in one or more units of a system. As an example, the command...

    ada +c /sec/database

...would recompile /sec/database, (if needed), and before that, all the units needed before /sec/database could be compiled. Instead of giving the "+c" flag, which tells Arcs to do the necessary work before the given unit can be compiled. We could also have given the "+e" flag, causing all the compilations necessary to make the unit executable.

7. Further Development

Overview is crucial to most activities in software development and maintenance. Without it, we can hardly understand a system good enough to undertake any changes except the most local ones. While the separate compilation structure of an Ada program can provide some of this overview, it must be presented in a good way to be of any interest.

In Arcs, the initial system presentation facility was based on printing a program graph by listing adjacent nodes together, using indentation to show the direction of the connecting edge. The following program...

```
with A, B;
procedure MAIN is
  ...

package A is
  ...

with B;
package body A is
  ...

with C;
package B is
  ...

package body B is
  ...
```

...would by the command "l :body :imports main" be presented as follows (the << >> brackets are used to mark revisited nodes);

```
        MAIN
         :imports A
          :body A
            :imports B
             :imports C
            :body B
         :imports << B >>
```

There are several drawbacks with this simple technique. First, it doesn't look like a graph. A much better overview would result if a more picture-like layout was used. Second, it is batch oriented. The user first specifies the root and some relation names, and then has the complete structure listed. A better approach would be to let the user expand the graph interactively, in the directions he want to explore at the moment. This would also solve the problem of "not interesting subsystems": If for example TEXT_IO was imported by some package above, its internal structure would be presented although it is probably not of interest.

To overcome these problems, we are developing a screen oriented mode of Arcs, where the user walks around in the program graph, expanding it in the directions he wants, using the current cursor position to denote the unit to be acted upon.

In the screen oriented mode, the user first enters a flat program library, (the cursor position is underlined):

```
        MAIN
        A
        B
        C
```

The user may now start to explore the program graph, for example by asking for expansion of "imports" edges in one step starting at MAIN:

```
         |-imports-> A
MAIN-|
         |-imports-> B
```

The cursor may now be moved to any of the other nodes, and expansion may continue from, for example, A:

```
         |-imports-> A -body-> A -imports-> B
         |
MAIN-|
         |-imports-> B
```

Different commands, such as source inspection, checking in or out, attribute listing etc. may be given at any time, using the node currently pointed to as the target.

The Arcs screen mode is first developed for a conventional alphanumeric terminal, although the potential of program viewing user interfaces could be much more developed using bit mapped graphics.

Similar ideas have been in use in other systems for a while, of which one example is the STRIX program development environment, [STR85].

8. Conclusion

During the beginning of the Ada project, there was a lot of emphasis put on the "APSE", the programming support environment, which should accompany the pure language implementation. This APSE was often thought of as something to a large extent built from scratch, using new paradigms, and including new advanced tools.

What is described in this paper is an example of a more incremental/evolutionary approach, where an existing, proven successful, tool, is taken advantage of, stepwisely including it into an Ada programming environment building on the UNIX system.

9. Acknowledgements

Mikael Beckman and Johnny Widen at the TeleLOGIC Lulea office made both conceptual contributions and carried out large parts of the implementation.

10. References

[BUX85]
     "Ada: The Language and its Environment", J.Buxton & D.A.Fischer, in Technology and Science of Informatics - Ada Special, North Oxford Academic, 1985.

[DDC84]
     "DDC Ada Compiler System Separate Compilation Handler, Functional Specification", Dansk Datamatik Center, Nov 1984.

[DEC84]
     "CMS Reference Manual", Digital Equipment Corporation, November 1984.

[DEC85]
     "Developing Ada Programs on VAX/VMS", Digital Equipment Corporation, February 1985.

[DOI81]
    "United Kingdom Ada Study: Final Technical Report", Department of
    Industry, London 1981.

[FEL79]
    "Make - A Program for Maintaining Computer Programs", S.Feldman,
    Software Practice & Experience, April 1979.

[ICH85]
    "Ada: Ready For Application", an interview with J.Ichbiah, pub-
    lished in Technology and Science of Informatics, Ada Special,
    North Oxford Academic 1985.

[INT82]
    "Computer Program Development Specification for Ada Integrated
    Environment", Intermetrics, Inc. Cambridge, MA, 1982.

[KIT84]
    Common Apse Interface Set, (CAIS)", proposed military standard,
    v1.4, Ada Joint Program Office, 1984.

[NAR85a]
    "Extending the Scope of the Program Library", K-H Narfelt & D.
    Schefstrom, in "Ada in Use: Proceedings of the 1985 International
    Ada Conference", Cambridge University Press 1985.

[NAR85b]
    "System Development Environments", K-H Narfelt, Licentiate Thesis,
    Department of Computer Science, Univ of Lulea, 951 87 Lulea,
    Sweden. 1985.

[ROC75]
    "The Source Code Control System", Marc J. Rochkind, IEEE Transac-
    tions on Software Engineering, Nov 1975.

[SCH85a]
    "Possibilities of Layered Graphs", D.Schefstrom, Memorandum, Dep
    of Computer Science, University of Lulea, 951 87 Lulea, Sweden.
    1985.

[SCH85b]
    On Data Organization in Programming Environments", D.Schefstrom,
    Licentiate Thesis, Dep of Computer Science, University of Lulea,
    951 87 Lulea, Sweden. 1985.

[SOF85]
    "ALS VAX/VMS Target Users Reference Manual", SOftech, January
    1985.

[STR85]
    "STRIX Reference Manual", September 1985, TeleLOGIC AB, 123 86
    Farsta, Sweden.

[VER85]
    "VADS Operations Manual - VADS Version 5.1", Verdix Corporation
    1985.

[THA82]
    "The KAPSE for the Ada Language System", R.M.Thall, ACM/AdaTEC
    Conference 1982.

[TIC85]
    "RCS - A System for Version Control", W.F. Tichy, Software - Prac-
    tice & Experience, Vol 15(7), July 1985.

Part V   Education

SOFTWARE ENGINEERING APPLIED TO Ada* CURRICULUM DEVELOPMENT

Putnam P. Texel, P.P. TEXEL & COMPANY, Inc.
and
Linda F. Blackmon, General Dynamics Corporation

ABSTRACT

This paper describes how a major defense contractor
combined in house capability and contractor support to develop a
software engineering curriculum to aid the transition to Ada.
Because the curriculum and its individual components are
considered as software, the courseware was developed using the
software development process following the principles of software
engineering.

1 INTRODUCTION

What does a large defense contractor do to facilitate transitioning
to Ada? There are many possibilities, which include

1. Ignore the problem and hope it goes away

2. Dedicate in house talent to address the issue

3. Contract outside

4. Use both in house and contractor talents

In the case of General Dynamics (GD) the decision was made to
combine in house capability with outside contractor support
acurriculum, base

In October 1984 General Dynamics contracted with P. P. TEXEL &
COMPANY, Inc. to address the corporation's transition to Ada.

2 PHILOSOPHY

Because of courseware will have a long life, but subjected to
frequent modifications, and be instructed by multiple individuals,
the decision was made to develop the courseware exactly like software
is developed. In addition to the life cycle model, the principles of
software engineering are being used throughout the project.

3 CURRICULUM DEFINITION

An in depth analysis of GD corporate needs was conducted. Determining these needs was complicated by the fact that General Dynamics has multiple operational divisions supporting various United States military services: the Electric Boat Division services the Navy; Land Systems Division services the Army; the Ft. Worth Division services the Air Force, and so on.

To determine each division's needs, P.P. TEXEL & COMPANY, Inc. visited every General Dynamics facility in the United States. An interview questionnaire was developed and used at each facility to drive the conversations in a directed fashion and to ensure that the same information was extracted at each site. Sample questions follow:

1.   What current Ada projects do you have?

2. What Ada projects do you anticipate?

3. How many individuals do you need trained, to what depth, and by when?

4. What training materials relevant training to this project do you currently have on hand?

Following this analysis, a curriculum was proposed to the corporation covering the entire software life cycle. The following parameters were identified and shaped the final curriculum: class time, costs, student background, development time, instructor availability, course material, sequencing of courses, primary customer, breadth of the curriculum, short term requirements, long term requirements were the primary parameters considered.

Figure 1 shows the projected curriculum as well as those courses that were identified as priority course to be developed immediately.

4 CURRICULUM IMPLEMENTATION

The following paragraphs describe the model used for the development of each course in the curriculum.

4.1 ANALYSIS

A Course Overview Form was developed and used to define the requirements of each course. A Course Overview Form requires the following be identified: the course name, length, goals, non-goals, projected audience, pre-requisite, pre-test, post-test, format

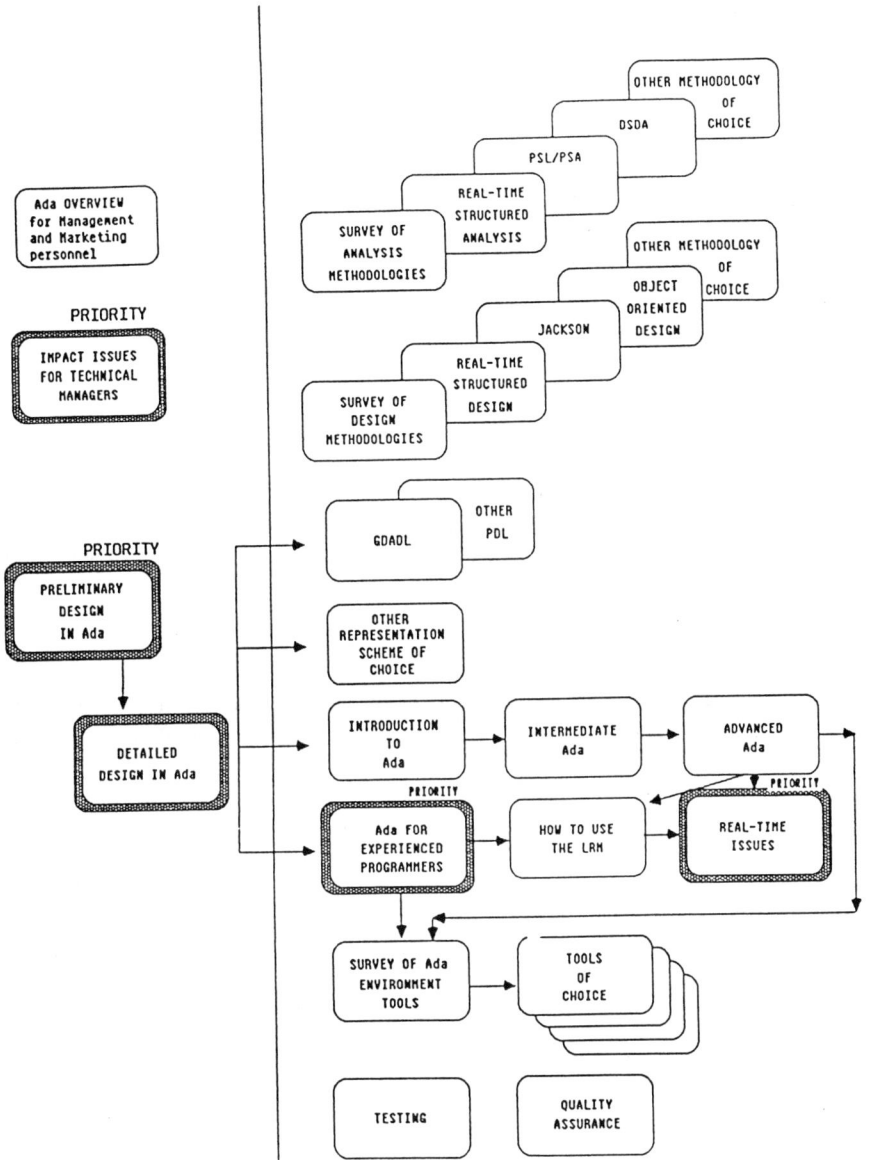

Figure 1: First Year Priorities

(lecture or hands on,), exercises (individual or group), handouts (papers, texts, lists, and so on), and next course.

4.2 PRELIMINARY DESIGN

During the preliminary design phase the following were used to drive the course design:

   o Level 1 Outline

   o Level 2 Outline

   o Time Map

   Level 1 and 2 outlines A Level 1 Outline specifies the major sections of the course and their order of presentation. The Level 2 outline adds the sub-sections for each of the sections identified in the Level 1 Outline.

   Time Map A Time Map Form is used to properly allocate time among the subsections. The Time Maps turned out to be very valuable during the actual implementation of the course because the course designer is constantly reminded of how much time has ben allocated for a specific subsectrion and does not include extraneous material in the course.

   A Preliminary Design Review (PDR) of the material is conducted, comments incorporated and final preliminary design material produced.

4.3 DETAILED DESIGN

During detailed design each subsection is designed using a Section Overview Form. A Section Overview Form is used to identify the testable learning objectives for each sub-section. Additionally the Section Overview Form requires identification of the concepts to be learned in the sub-section along with initial suggestions as to material that can be used to illustrate the concept.

   Additionally, an Exercise Overview Form is used to identify the requirement for an exercise, the concept to be reinforced, the placement of the exercise within the sub-section, and whether the exercise is a group or individual activity. The forms permits special notes regarding the solution to be documented.

   A Critical Design Review (CDR) of the detailed design material is held.

4.4 IMPLEMENTATION

Until now, the materials for the course had not been determined. The decision was to have the following for each course, where appropriate:

Student Guide

Presentation Visuals

Exercise Book

Instructor Guide

Additional Handouts

4.4.1 Student Guide

The Student Guide was developed using a learning technology called
Information Mapping[3.4]. Information Mapping brings together current
learning research and instructional technology into a comprehensive
materials development and presentation technology to improve
technical presentations.

The goal of Information Mapping is to make the

    o learning and referencing of material,

    o preparation of learning material, and

    o maintenance of learning material

easier and quicker.

A sample page of the Student Guide for Ada For Experienced
Programmers is shown in Figure 2. In the Student Guide one page
addresses one fact, and that fact is addressed by different named
blocks of information. At the bottom of the page, the reader is
referred to related concepts within the guide. The Student Guide for
Ada for Experienced Programmers is approximately 700 pages long.

4.4.2 Presentation Visuals

The presentation visuals are developed from the Student Guide, thus
ensuring compatibility between the lecture and the reference
material. The student does not receive copies of the visuals. The
student does receive the Student Guide. As a side note, during the
Beta Test (discussed in Section 4.5) for Ada for Experienced
Programmers the students did not open the Student Guide on the first
day of class. On the second day of class one or two students opened
the Guide, and by the middle of the first week the entire class was
following the lecture in the Student Guide.

4.4.3 Exercise Book

The Exercise Book was originally developed by distributing the
Exercise Overview Forms throughout the corporation for implementation
by Ada knowledgeable individuals. There were problems because
although individuals had outlines of the courses, they really were
not in a position to define an exercise that satisfied the
requirements. Currently all exercises are developed by the course

designer.

4.4.4 Instructor Guide

The goal of the Instructor Guide is to aid instructors in the delivery of the course material by tracking material, indicating degree of emphasis (in depth or quick overview), anticipating typical student questions, and so on. The following is taken from Section III of the Instructor's Guide for Ada Impact Issues:

> III. LANGUAGE
>
>> Recall that the DOD wanted to use
>>
>>> o software engineering (last section)
>>>
>>> o a common language (this section)
>>>
>>> o an environment (next section)
>>
>> to combat the software crisis.
>
> These three topics were introduced in foil 8 of Section (1-8). This section addresses bullet 2 of that foil, the common language.

4.5 TESTING PHASE

The testing phase consists of test teaching each course at least twice to ensure the validity of the material and to find and fix bugs. These initial course offerings are called the Beta and Pilot tests respectively and are described below.

4.5.1 Beta Test

A Beta Test is the first teaching of the course designed to iron out major bugs (such as Exercise Book mentioned previously) and minor bugs, like typos. The students in a Beta Test class agree to participate in a constructive manner in this "structured walkthrough" of the course and no tuition is charged.

4.5.2 Pilot Test

The Pilot Test is the second teaching of the course. Hopefully any remaining bugs are identified and corrected. The course is then baselined and is ready for delivery across the corporation.

4.6 MAINTENANCE

IDENTIFIERS

Definition	An <u>identifier</u> is used as a name for an Ada entity. An <u>identifier</u> is a sequence of characters that stands for whatever data may be associated with it when the program is run.

Rules	1. An identifier is composed of
	    o the letters A through Z (upper or lower case)
	    o the digits 0 through 9
	    o underlines
	
	2. An identifier may be as long as a line.
	
	3. Identifiers are <u>not</u> case sensitive.
	
	4. The first letter of an identifier must be a letter.
	
	5. An underline must be embedded between two non underlines.

Examples	Current_Altitude Maximum_Height Front_40 FRONT_40 Stack_Size StackSize Maximum_Altitude_of_Current_Target MAXIMUM_Altitude_of_Current_Target MaximumAltitude_of_Current_Target
Non Valid Examples	Grand_Total_ (underline must be embedded) Hello_ There (underline must be embedded between two non underlines) 4_July (must start with letter) _July_4 (must start with letter) Raise_10% (% not a legal character)
Comment	The identifiers Front_40 and FRONT_40 represent the <u>same</u> data item. The identifiers Stack_Size and StackSize represent <u>distinct</u> identifiers. Choose names that reflect the problem domain. Do not use cryptic identifiers like X, P, CC, etc.
Related Concept	reserved words

Figure 2. Sample Student Guide Page.

4.6.1 Reduced Maintenance

The only revisions made to the Ada Impact Issues course as a result of the Beta Test were to incorporate two sections as subsections of another section and include 2 or 3 visuals that address GD specific information, such as points of contact within the corporation, Ada implementation across the corporation, and course fees.

Ada for Experienced Programmers required only corrections of typographical errors and minor enhancements.

4.6.2 Course Manager

A Course Manager is designated for each course. The course manager attends the Beta Test, is responsible for team teaching the Pilot Test with the course developer, and is the point of contact for the course from that point on.

Use of the principles of software engineering significantly reduces the maintenance effort.

5 SOFTWARE ENGINEERING

The following subsections describe how the principles of software engineering were used to develop the curriculum.

5.1 ABSTRACTION

Abstraction is employed during each step of the process by suppressing non-essential details. First thoughts are to be focused on WHAT the curriculum is to achieve as opposed to HOW it is to achieve it. The curriculum is designed to address

o immediate and long term needs

o software engineering

o the software development life cycle

o Ada

o GD Ada capability

o GD operational divisions

o and so on

Once the initial courses are identified, abstraction is used to focus thoughts on WHAT information is to be provided by each course rather than on HOW the course is to provide information. Use of the Course Overview, Section Overview and Exercise Overview Forms enforced the abstraction.

5.2 INFORMATION HIDING

By confining the details to the subsection level, subsections can be moved around with little impact on the rest of the course. Changes do not ripple throughout the rest of the course.

5.3 Modularity

The curriculum consists of individual modules to permit personnel to select a path appropriate for their needs. Furthermore, should technology change, the identification of those sections requiring modification is greatly simplied.

6 FUTURE PLANS

Demand for all courses is high. As soon as the sources were announced to the user community all available offerings for 1985 were immediately filled.

The high demand created certain resource problems in the areas of classroom space and terminals, compiler access, and the availability of trained instructors.

The current instructor corps was developed by drawing on several sources: Computer Related Training Department Instructors being cross trained to become Ada Instructors; programmer/analysts from the user community who have had experience and/or training in Ada, and, in several cases, representatives from the user community who have been teaching Ada in local colleges and/or universities.

General Dynamics has future plans in the following areas:

o Instructor Corps

o Course Development

o Delivery Enhancements

Each of these areas is discussed below.

6.1 INSTRUCTOR CORPS

Several problems have been identified in this area. The number of instructors will need to be significantly increased to meet the expected demand. Back-up instructors are needed for all courses,

especially for those instructors from the user community who may not
always be able to leave their projects. A "train the trainer"
program is needed to provide non educators with teaching skills and
to offer background knowledge from an Ada expert to the instructors.

Periodic seminars and workshops are required for the instructors to
help them maintain state of the art knowledge regarding the Ada
movement and to discuss teaching techniques and common successes/
problems.

Finally, regular project assignments are necessary for the
instructors to enable those non-user instructors to obtain project
experience.

6.2 COURSE DEVELOPMENT

Courses currently anticipated for 1986 development include: Real-Time
Issues, Quality Assurance, Testing Ada Systems. Development efforts
in 1987 are expected to focus on Analysis and Design methodologies.

6.3 DELIVERY ENHANCEMENTS

All courses developed from 1986 on are expected to move away from
standard presentation visuals and move to a PC-based colour graphics
package for the delivery of the classroom visuals. Additionally,
emulation software for the PC's will permit terminal capability to
in-house hardware hosting Ada implementations.

7 CONCLUSIONS

The success of this Training effort can be attributed to the
following:

    o corporate commitment

    o corporate Ada Training Coordinator

    o involvement of the user community

    o use of software engineering to produce the courseware

    o contractor supplied Ada expertise

    o contractor supplied course development expertise

BIBLIOGRAPHY
[1]   Ross, D.T. Goodenough, J.B. et al. "Software Engineering:
      Process, Principles and Goals". Computer Magazine May 1975.

[2]   PARNAS, D. On the criteria to be used in Decomposing Systems.
      CACM, Vol. 16 pp 1053-1058, December 1972.

[3]   Olympia P.L. "Information Mapped SAS: Teaching SAS for
      Retention" University of District of Columbia.

[4]   "Information Mapped Chemistry". Journal of Chemical
      Education. Vol. 56, page 176, 1979.

A NOVEL APPROACH TO A HANDS-ON ADA COURSE FOR INDUSTRY

J.M. Bishop

Computer Science Department, University of the Witwatersrand, Johannesburg 2001, South Africa.

(on leave at Computer Studies Department, The University, Southampton SO9 5NH, England.)

Abstract. Retraining of programmers is one of the crucial concerns in managing the transition to Ada. Moreover, those making the decision to change also need a thorough understanding of the language and its capabilities. The cost of releasing personnel for courses, and of the courses themselves, can often be prohibitive. Traditional retraining courses often take a week or more and cover the language exhaustively, presenting each feature in turn as if it were new to the audience. An alternative approach is to make the most of the knowledge of experienced programmers and cover *only* those concepts which are not current in the languages they already know. For scientific programmers of the Pascal-Fortran school, these would be: Ada's type system, packages, generics, exceptions and tasking in the full. Such a course has been given in two days to programmers from industry, with half the time being spent on hands-on practical work. The results were startling, with all attendees declaring themselves at least reasonably confident of their understanding of Ada at the end. This paper gives an outline of the course and the practical sessions, a summary of the survey conducted, and suggestions for improvements to the approach and the material.

1. INTRODUCTION

Retraining of programmers is going to become one of the prime concerns of firms wishing to embark on projects using Ada. Rogers [1985] found that those trained in Ada tended to get snapped up by software houses, and that the companies in his survey could only fill 8% of their needs with trained people. The options open to a firm with experienced programmers are:

- send them on a course
- get a course done by in-house personnel
- let the programmers "pick it up" themselves.

There is a decided element of risk in the last option, yet the experience of educators at universities is definitely that students trained in one language properly, can very quickly become proficient in another with no tuition. The way to reduce costs of retraining would be to make use of this phenomenon, coupled with an initial short course of some 2-3 days duration. The essential property of such a course would be that it gives sufficient coverage to the whole language, especially the more advanced topics, so that the programmers will have a feel for what the language can do, and the benefits that will encrue from switching to the "Ada idiom".

Such a course has been given in two days recently to experienced programmers from industry. It was advertised as a "Hands-on Experience" and attracted 30 attendees, mainly from engineering and military establishments. Half the time was spent in lectures and half in practical sessions where Ada programs had to be written and modifed. The course was a success, judging from the assessment of the attendees of their understanding of Ada at the end, and it is believed that the approach could well be adopted on a wider basis.

2.   COURSE CONTENT
2.1 Overall Philosophy

The guiding principle in deciding on the course content was to ignore anything with which the programmers would be familiar, in terms of the languages they already know. There is so much in Ada that is Pascal-based, and so much that is common with any high-level language, that it is a waste of time to cover it in class. The list of common concepts is an impressive one, and accounts for the greater part of four of the fifteen chapters in the Ada manual:

- lexical structure
- comments
- names
- expressions
- assignment
- control statements - loop, if, case, exit, goto
- procedures, functions and parameters
- input-output
- normal scope conventions.

That is not to say that the details of these features are identical across languages - of course they are not - but it is certainly the case that a programmer seeing these kinds of things in an Ada program will have a reasonable idea of what is meant. This "reasonable idea" is all that is necessary during a formal course - an appreciation of the nuances of Ada's semantics will come during the follow-up self-study period, and during practice on the job. It is generally accepted that mastery of the details of a language cannot be transmitted during a lecture: personal experience with using the language is essential. In summary, therefore, in this course we do not waste time on the impossible, but concentrate on what can be done, and on completing the Ada syllabus.

The features that remain to be covered come generally from the latter part of the Ada manual, but it was also decided that a thorough understanding of Ada's type system was vital. The list of topics for the course is:

- history and goals
- types, constraints, literals, aggregates and attributes
- overloading
- packages
- private types
- generic declaration and instantiation
- exceptions
- tasking
- compilation units and structure
- representation and implementation considerations
- standards and compiler availability.

These were all covered in the two-day course, although access types and representation considerations were discussed along with tasking, rather than as topics in their own right.

2.2   The lectures

The material was broken down into four lectures - the first for an hour and a half, the others for an hour as follows:

Introduction to Ada - *history and background, components to be left out, the complete type system, attributes, literals, aggregates, input-output instantiation.*

Ada in the large - *packages, generic instantiation with type, variable, constant and subprogram parameters, default parameters, private types, overloading.*

Real-time programming - *exceptions, task declarations, entry and accept, select, terminate.*

Dynamic Ada Systems - *kinds of tasks, task types, access to tasks, allocating tasks, timed actions, families of tasks, scheduling.*

Each topic was presented in a manner aimed at emphasing how it would be used. Hence, the usual little explanatory examples were avoided in favour of complete programs which illustrated a few points together. This technique also enabled the features not explicitly covered to be evident, and the audience could then pick up the syntax and layout conventions almost unconsciously. As an example, the following program was used to illustrate most of the features of Ada's type system.

```
WITH text_io;  USE text_io;

PROCEDURE array3 is
    SUBTYPE natural is integer range
                        0..integer'last;         -- range constraint
        SUBTYPE real      is float digits 6;     -- digits constraint
        TYPE kinds        is (plain, decimal);   -- enumerated type
        TYPE itables      is array (integer range <>)
                            of natural;          -- unconstrained
        TYPE rtables      is array (integer range <>)   --   array types
                            of real;
    TYPE tablepack
        (length : integer := 100;                -- bound discriminant
         kind   : kinds := plain) is             -- variant discriminant
        RECORD
            CASE kind is                         -- variant choice
                WHEN plain =>
                    itable : itables (1..length);   -- indexed constraint
                WHEN decimal =>
                    rtable : rtables (1..length);   -- indexed constraint
            END CASE;
        END RECORD;

    PACKAGE real_io is new float_io(real);       -- i/o instantiations
    PACKAGE int_io  is new integer_io(integer);  --   for real, integer
    USE real_io, int_io;                         --   and their subtypes

    n, m : integer;

BEGIN
    put_line(" How many elements in a and b?");
    get(n); get(m);  skip_line;
    put(" n has "); put(n); put(" and m has "); put(m); new_line;
    DECLARE
        a : tablepack (n, plain);                -- creating dynamic
        b : tablepack (m, decimal);              --   arrays with variants
    BEGIN
        for i in a.itable'range loop get(a.itable(i)); end loop; skip_line;
        for i in a.itable'range loop put(a.itable(i),6); end loop;new_line;
        for i in b.rtable'range loop get(b.rtable(i)); end loop; skip_line;
        for i in b.rtable'range loop put(b.rtable(i),6); end loop;new_line;
    END;
END array3;
```

This was followed up by an example of defining two procedures to read and write data of an unspecified type into an array of any size and a couple of uses of the routines, such as an array of reals or a table of strings indexed by an enumerated type. The power of generics can then be brought home by encapsulating these routines in a package:

```
WITH text_io;  USE text_io; --to use 'get' and 'put'
GENERIC
    TYPE item   is private;
    TYPE bounds is (<>);
        trailer : item;
    WITH PROCEDURE get(i : out item) is <>;
    WITH PROCEDURE put(i : in item)  is <>;

PACKAGE tabler is
    TYPE      tables is array(bounds) of item;
    PROCEDURE read(table:out tables);
    PROCEDURE write(table:in tables);
END tabler;
```

and suitably instantiating them, as in:

```
--  Instantiation of tabler for an array of reals.
--   Uses a package with single parameter get and put procedures.

SUBTYPE vectorrange is integer range 1..100;
PACKAGE vectormaker is NEW tabler (real,vectorrange,0.0);

--  Instantiation of tabler for an array of strings indexed
--    by an enumerated type. String_io already included in text_io.

TYPE    countries  is (Britain, France, Spain, Italy);
SUBTYPE alfa       is string(1..8);
PACKAGE stringmaker is NEW tabler (alfa,countries,"        ");
```

At this point, overloading is discussed, including the problems that sometimes arise. In general, problem areas were highlighted, rather than glossed over, so that, for example, dynamic and unconstrained arrays were also covered thoroughly.

Tasking was treated in a manner similar to that in Bishop [1986]. Instead of taking the Ada features one by one, the various uses of the rendezvous are explained, and then related to how they would be done in Ada. In other words, we have

general rendezvous feature	Ada feature
synchronisation	order of accepts
multiple rendezvous	nested accepts
different kinds of service	multiple accepts for an entry
alternative services	select
conditional service	conditional select
cancelling a rendezvous	else

The more advanced aspects of tasking - task types, allocating tasks, families of entries - were covered using a generalised client-server adapted from Roubine [1985].

2.3 The practicals

The practicals were the most important part of the course. If the attendees could not write and run real, meaningful Ada programs, then the message would simply not get across. Each lecture was followed by a practical session of from one and a half to two hours, with attendees allocated to individual terminals connected to a large mainframe running the NYU/ED compiler. The version we had was not fast, and required a four megabyte virtual machine per person, but it had the extremely valuable properties of **completeness** and **accuracy**. Anything we threw at it was evaluated precisely according to the manual, and there were no unimplemented features that we could see. Bearing in mind the objectives of the course, completeness and accuracy of the implementation were a *sine qua non,* whereas efficiency would have been nice, but we managed without it.

The four practicals were all related to Fred's garage and his interest in

keeping track of his second-hand cars on the one hand, and developing interesting gadgets
to go in them on the other. Each day started off with a given program that had to be
extended in two ways, one for each session. The given programs were available on file,
and could be run as a first exercise. After each session, a complete solution to the practical
was provided, and attendees could use this for the next session if they had not got the
problem out. In brief, the practicals were:

The Car *(real, integer, enumerated, string and record types; procedures and
parameters; input and output instantiations; for loops)*
Define a record to hold information about a car (make, model, price, year) and two
procedures to read in and write out details of a single car.

The Garage *(packages, private types, functions, generic instantiation with type and
procedure parameters, including defaults)*
Set up an abstract data type for a car including the read and write routines and
comparison functions for each field. Instantiate a given generic package which
creates tables of things, sorts and writes them, and use it to read in, sort and write
out lots of cars.

The Driving Simulator *(exceptions, exception handlers at various levels, task
declaration, select, terminate)*
Given a program which simulates a car driving along, by accepting input from the
keyboard to indicate accelerate, brake, go downhill etc. and thus causing the speed
to alter, add exception handlers for anything that could go wrong. Then change
the speedometer handling package into a task and see that the program runs exactly
as before.

The Cruiser *(synchonising and communicating tasks, use of delay and calendar)*
Add a task to simulate a cruise control mechanism which endeavours to maintain
the car at constant speed despite changes induced by the terrain.

The practicals were carefully designed so as not to require the
development of any complicated algorithms. There was not much need for control
structures, except in the last case, where the algorithm was given. All along the emphasis
was on using Ada, rather than on programming *per se*.

3.   RESULTS

At the end of the course, attendees were asked to fill in a short
questionniare on their background, their performance in the practicals, their understanding
of Ada now, and their perceived need for Ada in the future. The number of returns was
28.

3.1 Profile of attendees

Four questions were asked, with the results as follows:

Type of firm

engineering	military	education	software house	other
43%	25%	18%	7%	7%

Years experience

9 or more	5 to 8	2 to 4	less than 2
46%	32%	21%	0

Languages used

Pascal	Fortran	BASIC	PLM80/86	PL/I	RTL/2	C
64%	57%	32%	25%	18%	14%	14%

Ada knowledge

used it	read about it	none
11%	68%	21%

Thus the profile of a typical attendee would be someone in the engineering or military sphere with nine or more years programming experience mainly using Pascal or Fortran, and who had read about Ada. This was exactly the kind of person we were hoping for, and for whom the course had a good chance of success.

3.2   Performance in the practicals

Attendees were asked how they did in each of the practicals, with the results:

	Done	Nearly	Halfway	Nowhere near
Prac 1 (records and i/o)	54%	39%	7%	0
Prac 2 (generic packages)	14%	46%	32%	14%
Prac 3 (exceptions)	18%	36%	32%	14%
Prac 4 (tasking) (/26)	8%	46%	31%	15%

Adding the figures for the first two columns, we find that 93% could do or nearly do the first practical - not bad in a new language on a new machine (for most) in under two hours. 61% coped with Practical 2, with this figure reducing to 54% for the next two. The quality of the programming was good: attendees readily followed the layout and style conventions that they saw during lectures, although no word was spoken on this aspect.

A possible stumbling block in a course that is not offered in-house is unfamiliarity with the computer system on which the practicals have to be done. In general the attendees coped well with the strange editor and compiling commands. Interfacing to libraries did prove difficult, though, as special filing commands were needed and in some cases inexplicable operating system errors occurred, which definitely contributed to the sharp drop in those completing Practical 2 after Practical 1.

3.3 Understanding of Ada

Attendees were asked to rate their resultant knowledge of Ada now under very broad headings. The intention was to ascertain whether they were confident, reasonably confident or still lost -- overall, and then with the following Ada concepts: scalar types, arrays and records, input-output, packages, private types, generic instantiation, overloading, exception handling, task declarations, entry and accept, select, terminate, loops and procedures. The last two were added to test the hypothesis that concepts could be mastered without formal instruction. They were also asked to state the hardest Ada concept. An analysis of the results revealed that:

Half the attendees were **confident** of their understanding of
- scalar types
- arrays and records
- loops
- procedures

Three quarters were **reasonably happy** with
- everything except generic instantiation

Noone was **still lost** with
- scalar types
- arrays and records
- input/output
- exceptions
- loops
- procedures

The **hardest concepts** were
tasking	44%
generics	30%

Others mentioned were packages, types and dynamic systems.

3.4 Future needs

The perceived need to use Ada on the job was the subject of the final question. The answers showed that 36% felt they would be using Ada soon (including all those from software houses and most of the educators), while 57% responded that they may have to use it. We had thus captured people from both sectors - those needing retraining and those wanting an orientation course.

4. ASSESSMENT and IMPROVEMENTS

The course was an evident success in several respects. The attendees valued the opportunity to get their hands onto an Ada compiler and to really see how it works. Such experience is not easy to arrange otherwise. We would advise anyone contemplating offering or attending an Ada course to ensure that it is **hands-on**. During the breaks, the attendees were able to discuss how others were progressing with the transition to Ada and to swop information and experience. From this point of view, an **open course** offers benefits over an in-house course. It is obviously desireable that the computer system used should be efficient, but it is essential for this kind of course that the Ada compiler be complete and accurate, in other words **validated.**

As far as the material goes, there are two areas where changes are indicated. Firstly, noone had any problems at all with understanding and using **exceptions**. The concept was quite natural, if not familiar, and the Ada semantics not hard to grasp. It is therefore unnecessary to treat them as a separate topic and it would be better to bring them in on the first day, perhaps with packages. Secondly, **generics** were obviously a stumbling block, even though we concentrated on instantiation rather than defining such packages. More time should be spent on generics, and maybe the traditional way of first introducing the idea via a subprogram rather than a package is worth trying. In planning the course, the possibility of starting off with packages was considered. This was rejected because it was felt that the initial practical should relate as far as possible to more familiar ideas i.e. programming in the small. However, it could well be that starting off with a generic instantiation (other than for input-output) could break the barrier that this feature seems to present.

Finally, as stated at the start, such a course should be used as a precursor to further self study and practice on the job and more substantial reference material would be needed than the notes provided. From the **text books** that were on view (nine of them), the consensus among the attendees was that Booch [1983] was the most useful text. They liked his object-oriented approach as well as his emphasis on Ada as a design language, an aspect that there was not really time to cover in the course.

REFERENCES

Bishop J.M., *Data Abstraction in Programming Languages,* Addison Wesley, 1986.

Booch, Grady, *Software Engineering in Ada,* Benjamin Cummings (Addison Wesley) 1983.

Rogers M.W., Companies' acceptance of and attitudes towards Ada, Proceedings of the *Ada in Use Conference,* 1-13, Paris 1985, J.G.P. Barnes and G.A. Fisher Jr eds. Cambridge University Press, 1985.

Roubine O. Programming large and flexible systems in Ada, Proceedings of the *Ada in Use Conference,* 197-209, Paris 1985, J.G.P. Barnes and G.A. Fisher Jr eds. Cambridge University Press, 1985.

EXPLOITING GENERICS IN ADA* TRAINING

J. A. Anderson
The MITRE Corporation
Washington Center
1820 Dolley Madison Boulevard
Mail Stop W429
McLean, Virginia   22102

Abstract. This paper provides the Ada instructor with techniques for teaching generics effectively, and methods to present and reinforce other Software Engineering topics using generics as a focus. Included are design considerations for writing generic templates and a general approach for designing laboratory assignments.

This paper is based on experiences gained by designing and delivering specialized Ada training programs at Texas Instruments and the MITRE Corporation. Although the recommended approach evolved in an industrial training environment, it may be applied in traditional academic environments as well. The approach presented has an impact on the instruction of many Ada topics but focusses on the use of generics and thus does not constitute a complete Ada training program.

INTRODUCTION

Generic constructs incorporate many of the goals of the Ada language effort, and therefore should be used to develop the skills of software engineers in designing and programming higher quality systems. Generics should be introduced early in the Ada curriculum and used throughout to exemplify and reinforce many of the software engineering goals of the Ada language.

Since generic structures are templates for procedures or packages, data and procedural abstraction can be reinforced using the generic as the vehicle. Generic parameters indicate only the assumptions made about the structures to be passed upon instantiation, forcing the implementor to write the template using only the attributes of those structures. These concepts may be exploited to train novice Ada programmers to code without depending on 'hard coded' literals and other poor programming methods. This practice expands the skills of the students in all areas of programming, not just in generic construction.

The Goal: Software Engineering

The primary goal of teaching the effective use of any modern programming language is for the student to look beyond the syntax of the language to its application. Booch (1983) has almost become a standard for introducing Ada to professionals with diverse backgrounds because it applies a software engineering approach to the instruction rather than a purely syntactical view. Because they support so many software engineering goals, generics provide an excellent vehicle for introducing and reinforcing the software engineering aspects of the Ada language.

A PROGRESSIVE APPROACH

Many novice Ada programmers find the concept of generic constructs very appealing. Most texts are successful in presenting the concepts quite well using examples such as a generic value exchange procedure or set package (Barnes 1984, Booch 1983). Unfortunately, when asked to design or write a generic, the student is often in a quandary over where to start. The following is an outline of an approach for instruction and lab assignments that has proven quite effective.

Overview.

Generics should be introduced to the student gradually, emphasizing their use before leading to development and design. Early in the course, students should use Ada generics before learning to write them, reinforcing their concepts and familiarizing them with their facilities. During this early introduction, generics should be used to illustrate various software engineering goals. Exploiting the unique capabilities of generics can be encouraged by using generics to exemplify the goals of the Ada language throughout the course.

After instruction of the more traditional language features, generics are investigated more thoroughly highlighting their abstraction capabilities. Because generics have been used extensively before this, students feel they are no more difficult to design or program than other structures. Finally, the students are provided design guidelines to help expand the applicability of their generics while controlling complexity.

Throughout the course, the students are assigned programs and modules to design, write and test. These assignments are designed so that code from previous exercises is reused in later exercises. The student progresses from implementing simple procedures, to packages of facilities, and finally to writing generic facilities.

A Gradual Introduction

The use of generic facilities is easily incorporated into the instruction of other Ada constructs. Introducing their use slowly while discussing more traditional structures such as procedures and functions avoids the problem of the students later classifying them as something 'different', 'advanced', or 'difficult'.

Introducing the concept. Early in the curriculum, students should use instantiations of existing generic modules such as TEXT_IO.INTEGER_IO, introducing the concept of generics, without exploring too deeply into the details of their structure. While discussion of the syntax and structure of the generic construct itself may be deferred, discussion of the purpose and rationale should not. This is the ideal time to identify the reusability of generics without compromising the strong typing precept of the language. It is essential for the student to develop an appreciation for the checks being done on their code, instead of considering the instantiation for each type as an inconvenience. This topic is often debated by veteran coders who pride themselves on brevity in a language. This is also an opportunity to discuss the possible readability advantages made by the locality of the instantiation, as in the following:

```
type LOAD is INTEGER range 0 .. 100;
package LOAD_IO is new TEXT_IO.INTEGER_IO(LOAD);
```

In the above example, LOAD_IO allows input/output of values of type LOAD without referencing the packages TEXT_IO or INTEGER_IO, and aids in maintainability by citing the type for which it is instantiated.

Only a Template. During this introductory stage of instruction, it is effective to introduce the difference between the generic template and the instantiation. Texel (1984) identified an effective analogy of the generic to the flowcharting symbol template. Just as the cutout on the plastic template is not the actual symbol that will be part of the flowchart, the generic template is not executable code. The flowcharting template is used to draw the specific symbol on the paper, just as the generic template is used to make specific instances of executable code for the Ada program.

Examples for Abstraction. Many novice programmers have difficulty breaking their projects into levels of abstraction, as opposed to simply breaking programs into smaller units of code. Data and procedural abstraction can be introduced and reinforced by using examples that reference existing packages providing support expressed through high level names. In order to build upon this later in the instruction, some of these support modules should be in the form of generics.

Addressing Generics Specifically

After subprograms and packages have been investigated thoroughly, generic constructs should be presented as a separate entity. Because some generics and their instantiations will have been utilized previously, the students are less likely to consider them foreign, or as 'advanced' features that should be avoided until later.

When presenting the material about generics, as with most structures, begin by focussing on the reason for the presence of the structure in the language, rather than only the syntax and semantics. Incorporating the rationale of the generic and each of its components into all phases of the instruction of the generic is essential for the effective retention, acceptance, and eventual application of the structure.

Compare and Contrast. Following the rationale for generics, the structure and syntax should be investigated thoroughly. Comparing and contrasting subprograms and their parameters with generic constructs and their formal parameters is an essential step in learning how the Ada generic facility works. It is important for the students to realize that generic constructs are "a natural extension of subprogram parameterization" (Ichbiah et al., 1979). The specific use of generics to allow subprograms as parameters should be highlighted at this time, stressing the advantages of the checking that will be done at compilation.

Illustrate the Concepts. The graphic symbols used by Booch (1983) are very useful in illustrating the addition of formal parameters to the 'normal' specification and body of subprograms and packages. They also illustrate the fact that generics are only templates and not executable code.

Complete the Picture. By this point in the instruction, the students may be overloaded with new concepts and structures. Since subprogram parameterization may be new to some students, it is important to present 'complete' examples. Booch (1983) provides several instantiations for each of the generics presented, which allows the reader to appreciate the varied applications of the generic. In many cases, however, it has become necessary to present examples of calls to the instantiations along with the generic specification and instantiation. Without all of these, students often confuse the different classes of parameters as well as instantiations with calls. Presenting examples of each on the same page allows discussion of interdependencies, syntax and semantics. Examples having different numbers of generic formal parameters and subprogram parameters also help alleviate some of this confusion.

Self-Documentation. When discussing instantiation and parameter association for generics, there arises an opportunity to reinforce the self-documentation aspects of subprograms. The readability gained by using named association of generic parameters should be highlighted while stressing the similarities to methods of subprogram parameter association. This not only reinforces these concepts presented earlier in the instruction, but illustrates the consistency of notation throughout the Ada language.

Abstraction through Generics. During this detailed investigation of generics, other advantages of using generics may be identified. The curious situation of generic packages with no generic parameters emphasizes both strong typing and abstraction. Habermann & Perry (1983) illustrate this with a package that provides arithmetic operations for number pairs. This package is redeclared as a generic and then can be instantiated for complex numbers, plane vectors, etc.

Efficiency through Generics. Students may be shown how generics can provide opportunities for gaining efficiency. When subprograms include optional processing which depends on the value of input parameters, and the subprogram is called frequently with the same values, efficiency may be gained by transforming the subprogram into a generic. Changing these 'constant' parameters into the generic formal parameters allows the compiler to remove the unneeded code (Ausnit et al., 1985).

Are Generics That Different? Students often ask: "How do I design a general purpose template, if I do not know what structures it will act upon?" It is the instructor's responsibility to impress upon the students that although there may be a few additional considerations that should be taken, the programming task is chiefly the same. The instructor may reinforce this concept by relying on one of the basic principles of software engineering, abstraction. At this point, working with generics builds upon and reinforces the data and procedural abstraction taught previously.

Code Comparison. A useful method of demonstrating that there is usually little difference in coding the body of a generic is to compare a generic module with its similar single-purpose counterpart. Booch (1983) uses this approach effectively with a generic FIFO package after developing a FIFO queue package for Integers earlier in his book. The only changes to the body is a replacement of the word INTEGER with formal type name. This approach can be carried further by using user-defined types, allowing the transformation into a generic module to be performed without any change to the body at all.

Private Types. When discussing generic formal parameters, Barnes, et al. (1984) uses a very effective summary statement, that generic parameters are the assumptions made about the structures to be passed into the template upon instantiation. This is especially useful when discussing private and limited private types. When used in a non-generic sense, the designer still utilizes the hidden capabilities of private types when implementing the body. This can be especially confusing to the people working with packages for the first time.

A different perspective may be gained in using private types as generic formal parameters: The abstraction of the type is held throughout the implementation of the body. Thus generics may be used to focus on the abstraction made by private and limited private types. When writing the generic body, the implementor is much more restricted. The designer must become much more precise in the specification of requirements for the generic formal types. For example, when designing a standard generic sort, many novice programmers first wish to declare the type of the elements as limited private, allowing any type in the list to be sorted. Upon implementation, and a possible iteration through the compiler, they then realize that assignment is required, but not allowed for limited private types. Usually they opt for a private type, which allows the assignment operation.

Opportunity for Individuality. Often programmers are irritated by the rigid restrictions of a language; this often can be alleviated by identifying opportunities for the programmers to reflect their individuality in their code. An opportunity for this arises when discussing the form of the generic part. Bardin & Moon (1985) agree that much can be gained from trying out the generic for several instances. Instantiations and calls of the generic should be written for various applications. By using the generic for more than one application, commonalities in use can be identified. These commonalities can provide the designer with insights into the optimal ordering of the formal parameters and possible default values for them.

DESIGN CONSIDERATIONS FOR GENERICS

Generics are developed to allow the reuse of code within a system and from one system development effort to another. The following design considerations have been collected to assist students in the development of more reusable modules. These considerations may be used as guidelines for implementing laboratory assignments or as a job aid when developing systems. It is hoped that this list will be used to write easier to use, more general purpose generics, and that the list will be expanded as experience grows.

When presenting and discussing these considerations, it is important to stress the a trade-off between usability and versatility in a generic module. We may get guidance from the designers of the Ada language: "writing a generic unit may well require some care; using it, on the other hand, should be extremely simple" (Ichbiah, et al., 1979).

A generic unit is made more versatile by providing more generic formal parameters of various classes. As the number of parameters grows, the more complex the generic unit becomes, perhaps becoming too complicated to understand and utilize effectively. Even when available to designers and programmers, a very useful generic may go unused because its application was not understood. This complexity must be managed; although the general purpose applicability of Ada generics does not come free, reusability will offset this cost if the units are easy enough to use.

Versatility Considerations

Consider usage of the module broader than for which the specific application area calls. A simple example for comparison may be found in (Booch, 1983):

```
generic
  type ELEMENT is (<>);
  type LIST is array (INTEGER range <>) of ELEMENT;
procedure SORT (TABLE : in out LIST);
```

This generic SORT procedure was designed to be general purpose and supports ELEMENTs that are enumeration or integer types and arrays with integer indexes. This may easily be extended for use in other applications by providing a few additional formal parameters:

```
generic
  type ELEMENT is private;
  type INDEX_TYPE is (<>);
  type LIST is array (INDEX_TYPE range <>) of ELEMENT;
  with function "<"(LEFT, RIGHT : ELEMENT} return BOOLEAN is <>;
procedure SORT (TABLE : in out LIST);
```

The expansion of this example may be carried further, if needed. A well documented example of the generic sort expanded to its possibly most general purpose state is provided by Mendal (1985). Of course, the range of applicability to be designed into some generics may be restricted by funding and scheduling constraints.

Provide generic formal subprogram parameters for common user options. Analyze algorithms for places which the user can provide advice to the specific way a situation should be handled. End of processing conditions are prime opportunities for this method, and usually the details are left to a lower level of abstraction. Ausnit, et al. (1985) uses an example of a tape writing process which needs to handle the situation of encountering an end of volume mark:

```
generic
  with procedure END_OF_VOLUME_PROCESSING is
       DEFAULT_END_OF_VOLUME_PROCESSING;
  . . .
package RECORD_IO is
  procedure WRITE (...);
  . . .
end RECORD_IO;
```

The user would provide the routine to handle the situation (possibly mount a new volume and continue), or indicate that processing should be discontinued.

Provide generic (Boolean) constants to allow users to tailor unwanted generality from the reusable component (Ausnit, et al., 1985). When including checks within the generic body for division by zero, checking boundary conditions, etc., these checks may be executed conditionally based on the value of the flag passed as a generic formal constant. This allows the removal of unnecessary checks where the user can show that the case being checked for could never arise.

Usability Considerations

Specify default values wherever possible and logical, especially if a 'normal' case can be identified. This reduces the number of required parameters for instantiation and therefore restores simplicity for the user. Ichbiah, et al. (1979) notes that in many cases it may be possible to have only types as mandatory parameters, providing defaults for operations and constants. Properly named default subprograms also provide additional documentation as to the intended purpose of that parameter and the generic itself.

Write several example instantiations and calls for the generic while designing its specification. As mentioned earlier, using the module in its intended manner in a few examples can highlight commonalities in use. This may identify potential default values as well as simplify the ordering and naming of parameters.

LAB ASSIGNMENTS

Throughout the course, exercises should be assigned which reinforce the topics discussed during the presentations. If carefully planned, the code produced by students in earlier exercises may be reused by them later in their development. This reinforces the readability and modifiability of Ada code, while providing students with an additional reason for completing their exercises when assigned. An added incentive can be gained by assigning the production of components which the student may use after completion of the course, such as the Set package in Booch (1983), or the Safe_IO package (Anderson, 1984) which was developed as an exercise in the Texas Instruments curriculum.

Phase One--Introductory Stage. Subprograms should be written first, as they are the basic executable unit. It has proven very effective to assign small related subprograms, such as a subset of the Set operations, and the test program to exercise these routines. These modules will be stored in a directory and reused again in later assignments as inherited code, Because this is the introductory stage for the use of generic constructs, code for instantiations and calls to generic library units such as TEXT_IO may be provided to the students. Any questions about the use of these generics should be addressed. When examining the specification of a generic package such as TEXT_IO.INTEGER_IO, focus on the subprograms being called. Defer questions regarding the generic part to later when these are investigated specifically, if possible.

When discussing the solutions to these lab assignments, identify the use of attributes as better 'style' over the use of literal values. This point need not be labored however, as later assignments that reuse components from these early exercises will reinforce the concept.

Phase Two--Packaging Related Procedures. Following these introductory exercises, students should collect their related procedures into packages hiding implementation details with private and limited private types. The assignments may also require the students to expand the capabilities of the packages by writing additional functions and procedures, plus their corresponding tests. The main subprograms can therefore perform the same function as in the earlier exercises, but puts the student in the role as the package user, instead of as the designer. This transition highlights the need to provide facilities for what may seem to be primitive operations on the private types and dependencies on implementation details. Additional design problems may be assigned, perhaps simplified by providing support packages and generics in the students' libraries. As the programmers expand their experience in using generics, they import the facilities and create instantiations themselves. This phase should concentrate on data and procedural abstraction. Positive examples of students' solutions as well as 'ideal' solutions provided by the instructor should be disected and discussed. This is an excellent opportunity for expanding the instructors repertoire of examples.

Phase Three--Programming and Designing Generics. After the traditional packages and subprograms are thoroughly investigated, and the students have had extensive experience instantiating and using generics, the design and implementation of generic structures may be assigned. The main purpose of this phase is to allow the students to realize that although a bit more thought must be put into the design of generics, their programming is no more difficult than that of non-generic structures. It is very effective to start with changing a previously developed module into a more general purpose generic template such as an existing stack or queue package into a generic facility.

After completing the transition from package to generic package, an exercise to design and implement a generic for a new application should be assigned. Even with this new assignment, existing library units may be used, whether developed by the students or provided in a library.

The varied backgrounds of participants can be an asset to the discussions resulting from the lab exercises. Students who have few conversions from earlier exercises to the formulation of their generics have incorporated many of the desired characteristics early in the progression. These act as discussion topics for the entire class in interdependencies of code, modifiability and reusability.

SUMMARY

Generics can be a valuable tool for introducing and reinforcing software engineering concepts such as abstraction, strong typing, efficiency, readability, maintainability, and reusability.

The major emphasis in effectively teaching generics is the teaching of their purpose and application, not their syntax and semantics. The introduction should be early and gradual, making use of their facilities before focussing on their design. Generics should not be considered an advanced feature of the language to be treated later or in isolation.

Generics are a natural extension of subprogram parameterization. Students find that generics are not necessarily more difficult to design or implement than other packages and subprograms when the concepts are introduced gradually, providing experience in use before design and development is required.

REFERENCES
Anderson, John A. (1984) generic package Safe_IO. Ada Repository on the
        DDN SIMTEL20. PD:<ADA.COMPONENTS>SAFE_IO.ADA
Ausnit, Christine, et al. (1985) Ada Reusability Guidelines. Technical Report
        ESD-TR-85-142. SoftTech, Inc., Waltham, Mass.
Barnes, J. P. G. (1984) Programming in Ada, 2nd Addition. Reading, Mass.:
        Addison-Wesley Publishers Limited.
Barnes, J. P. G., et al. (1984) Ichbiah, Barnes and Firth on Ada. (Video Tape)
        Waltham, Mass.: Alsys, Inc.
Bardin, Bryce M. & Moon, Marion F. (1985) In Search of "Real" Ada: A Software Saga
        with a Moral or Two. Ada Letters, Special Edition, V, No. 2, 217-228.
Booch, Grady (1983) Software Engineering with Ada. Reading, Mass.
        The Benjamin/Cummings Publishing Company, Inc.
Habermann, A. Nico & Perry, Dewayne E. (1983) Ada for Experienced Programmers.
        Reading, Massachusetts. Addison-Wesley Publishing Company.
Ichbiah, Jean, et al. (1979) Rationale for the Design of the Ada Programming
        Language. SIGPLAN Notices, 14, no. 6, Part B.
Ichbiah, Jean, et al. (1983) Reference Manual for the Ada Programming Language.
        United States Department of Defense.
Mendal, Geoffrey O. (1985) generic package Sort_Utilities. Ada Repository on the
        DDN SIMTEL20. PD:<ADA.COMPONENTS>SORTARRY.ADA
Texel, Putnam (1984) Educating the Educators. Presentation at February, 1984
        AdaJUG - SIGAda Conference, San Diego, California.

Part VI   Formal Methods

ADA AXIOMATIC SEMANTICS: PROBLEMS AND SOLUTIONS

N.H. Cohen
SofTech, Inc., One Sentry Parkway, Suite 6000
Blue Bell, PA 19422, U.S.A.

Abstract. As part of a research project on formal
verification of Ada programs, SofTech has developed an
axiomatic description of the Ada language. Many difficult
problems had to be solved, including the complexity of the
language's compile-time rules; the need for a proof rule
notation accommodating exceptions; the undefined nature of
erroneous execution; exceptions raised independently of the
computation state; different implementations of parameter
passing with different semantics; verification of packages;
concurrency; side-effects in expressions; and optimizations
that affect program behavior. The effort has provided
insight into subtle aspects of the Ada language and issues to
be considered in designing a programming language for
verifiability.

BACKGROUND

SofTech, Inc., is now completing a two-year independent
research and development effort exploring formal verification of Ada
programs (Cohen 1985 a). One of the products of this effort is a formal
axiomatic description of the Ada language. This paper briefly sketches
problems we encountered and solutions we devised in developing the formal
description. See (Cohen 1986) for a more complete account.

When the SofTech project began, there was no formal semantic
definition of the 1983 standard for the Ada language. Existing Ada
formal definitions (Belz et al. 1980, Bjorner & Oest 1980, Drossopoulou
et al. 1982, INRIA 1980) were for earlier versions of the language.
Furthermore, axiomatic semantics is the best approach for specifying the
deductions that may be drawn when constructing a proof about a program,
but none of the existing definitions were axiomatic. Therefore we
undertook our own formal definition. (Dansk Datamatik Center and CRAI
have since begun development of an operational semantics for the Ada
language (Bjorner 1985).)

SCOPE OF THE FORMAL DESCRIPTION

Our formal description of the Ada language is implementation-independent. It based only on rules in the Ada Language Reference Manual that apply to all implementations of Ada. Any program property proven using this formal description is thus a portable property of the program. A verifier based on the semantics of a single compiler is too narrowly applicable to justify its implementation cost. Furthermore, implementation behavior can vary from one release of a compiler to the next, invalidating implementation-dependent proof rules.

Our formal description does not completely define the behavior of an Ada program. Rather, it describes certain aspects of program behavior that can be used as the basis of a proof. Other aspects of program behavior are left unspecified because they are difficult to describe in an implementation-independent way.

We define a verifiable subset of Ada that excludes a few Ada constructs and usages. However, our exclusions are limited to a few rarely used features. Because we envision a scheme by which a large Ada program can be verified unit by unit, the bulk of a program using excluded features can still be verified if the excluded features are confined to a few units. The units using the features must be validated by some means other than formal proof, and the validity of the proof for the remaining units is based on the hypothesis that the unverified units work as specified.

DIFFICULT ISSUES

Source language, assertion language, and metalanguage

A typical verifier uses proof rules specifying an assertion that must hold before a particular language construct is processed, given another assertion that is to hold afterwards. In writing proof rules, we must be concerned with three different languages. The source language is the language in which the program construct is written. The assertion language is a language used to describe conditions that are expected to hold at various points in a computation. Anna (Luckham et al. 1984) is an example of an assertion language. The metalanguage is the language in which the proof rules themselves are written.

The source language. The source language in our proof rules is not the Ada language, but an expanded language in which programs explicitly reflect the static information implicit in an Ada program. This halves the size of our formal description by making it unnecessary to describe Ada's complex static semantics. (Fifty-five per cent of the formal description by Bjorner & Oest (1980) was devoted to static semantics.) It is relatively easy to map the intermediate form typically produced by an Ada compiler to its equivalent in this expanded language.

The assertion language. Our proof rules make minimal assumptions about the assertion language, for example that assertions written in it can be combined using the usual logical operators and that there is a way to substitute a given term for all occurrences of a given logical variable. Given these assumptions, we can write rules for building one formula out of another without considering the structure of the formulas.

The metalanguage. Our proof rules are written in a notation intuitively similar to the weakest liberal precondition (wlp) function of Dijkstra (1976). In Dijkstra's notation, wlp (S, P) is a formula w such that if w is true before statement S is executed and execution of S terminates, then formula P will be true afterward. We add an argument to this notation to account for the possibility of exceptions. Furthermore, it is convenient to define a second-order function, Statement_Precondition, which returns a function mapping a formula to a formula. Applications of Statement_Precondition then can then be composed, avoiding the need for nesting. Using the Ada catenation operator & to denote function composition,

```
Statement_Precondition [begin S1; S2; S3; end, null] (P) =
    Statement_Precondition [S1, null] &
    Statement_Precondition [S2, null] &
    Statement_Precondition [S3, null] (P)
```

This is the formula which, if true before the execution of the block statement **begin** S1; S2; S3; **end,** guarantees that if the block statement terminates, P will be true and no exceptions will be raised. The formula

```
Statement_Precondition [begin S1; S2; S3; end, Constraint_Error] (P)
```

is analogous, but covers the case where Constraint_Error is raised at the conclusion of the block statement if the block statement terminates.

Erroneous execution

Certain Ada language rules need not be enforced either at compile time or at run time, but violation of these rules makes execution of a program erroneous. The effect of erroneous execution is undefined. This allows compiler writers to make simplifying assumptions without establishing the validity of those assumptions.

While the notion of erroneousness simplifies compilation, it complicates verification. No Ada construct has defined semantics once a program is executing erroneously, so no deduction in a proof is valid unless it can also be proven that erroneous execution is impossible. Therefore the precondition given in our proof rules for the processing of any construct includes sufficient conditions to guarantee that processing of the construct will not be erroneous.

Unpredictable exceptions

Some exceptions, for example Constraint_Error, can be avoided by proper programming practices. One can write an assertion whose truth guarantees that such an exception will not be raised. Other exceptions, for example Storage_Error and IO_Exceptions.Device_Error, arise for reasons unrelated to the state of a computation. To the proof rules, the raising of such an exception is a random event.

Consider the following block statement:

```
begin
   A := new Integer'(0);
exception
   when Storage_Error =>
      Standby_Cell.all := 0;
      A := Standby_Cell;
end;
```

If Standby_Cell /= null beforehand, then A.all = 0 afterwards. If the allocation succeeds, this follows from the initial value in the allocator. If the allocation fails, it follows from the two assignments in the handler and the fact that Standby_Cell /= null. However, we have no logical basis for assuming either that the allocation succeeds or that it fails. Therefore, neither line of reasoning can be justified on its own, even though we know that one of them must be valid.

Our solution is to introduce a new <u>uninterpreted</u> <u>logical</u> <u>predicate</u> intuitively indicating whether or not a given "random event" will occur. This predicate becomes part of the precondition for the occurrence of the event and for its nonoccurrence. Nothing may be assumed about the truth or falsity of this predicate. In the example above, suppose the uninterpreted predicate were named Allocation_Succeeds. Then the precondition for successful allocation leaving zero in A.**all** is

Allocation_Succeeds **and** True

The precondition for Storage_Error being raised and the handler leaving zero in A.**all** is

not Allocation_Succeeds **and** Standby_Cell /= **null**

By the proof rule for block statements with exception handlers, the precondition for the block statement leaving zero in A.**all** is the disjunction of these formulas,

(Allocation_Succeeds **and** True) **or**
(**not** Allocation_Succeeds **and** Standby_Cell /= **null**)

Since the formula Standby_Cell /= **null** implies the formula above, it is a sufficient precondition for the block statement leaving zero in A.**all**.

Specification and verification of subprograms

The logical specification of a subprogram consists of a set of precondition/postcondition pairs, one for normal termination and one for each exception that the subprogram may raise. Verifying a subprogram body consists of proving that when invoked with one of the specification's preconditions true, the subprogram terminates with the corresponding postcondition true and with the corresponding exception, if any, raised. In verifying a client, one assumes the validity of the relevant postconditions and proves that the corresponding preconditions hold at the point of call. The proof is based entirely on the logical specifications of the called subprogram, with no reference to its body.

Dependence on parameter-passing mechanisms

Array and record subprogram parameters may be passed either by reference or by copying. A subprogram call is erroneous if its effect

depends on which mechanism is used.   The rules of the Ada language
guarantee that the two mechanisms have equivalent effects except possibly
when the subprogram call generates aliases or when execution of the
subprogram is interrupted by an exception.

Aliases are multiple names for the same variable. They can
arise, for example, when a variable is used as an actual parameter twice
in the same subprogram call. Subprogram calls that generate aliases are
excluded from our verifiable subset whether or not they actually cause
the effect of the program to depend on the parameter-passing mechanism.

In the case of subprograms interrupted by exceptions, actual
parameters of mode **in out** or **out** retain their original values if a
copy-back scheme is employed; but if call by reference is employed, they
assume whatever values were held by the corresponding formal parameters
at the time the exception was raised.   Different mechanisms may be used
for passing different parameters in the same call.   To accommodate all
possibilities, the precondition for a subprogram call is a conjunction,
each conjunct of which specifies the precondition appropriate for a
different combination of calling mechanisms.   The length of the
conjunction grows exponentially with the number of array and record
parameters of mode **in out** or **out**, but the conjunction can be simplified
into a single conjunct when good programming practices are followed.

Verification of packages

The logical specification of a package consists of the
logical specifications of the subprograms provided by the package.   In
the expanded form of an Ada program, each subprogram provided by a
package is augmented with an additional parameter representing the
abstract package state. Formal models may be constructed specifying how
calls on a package's procedures affect the abstract state of the package
and how the abstract state of the package affects the results of the
package's procedures and functions. A package may have many internal
states corresponding to the same abstract state.

Associated with each package body is a package invariant.
This is a formula that is asserted to be true before and after each call
on one of the package's subprograms. The proof rule for elaboration of a
package body generates a precondition sufficient for the package
invariant to be true after execution of the package body's initialization

statements. Within the package body, the package invariant may be assumed true at the start of a call in verifying a subprogram body; but verification of that subprogram body also entails proving that the package invariant is true at the end of a call.

Concurrency

Verification of concurrent programs is still poorly understood. Therefore, our proof rules allow only weak forms of reasoning about concurrent programs. One task "knows" nothing about another task except what can be deduced from calls on that task's entries and the logical specifications of those entries.

Our view of a task is similar to our view of a package. A task has an abstract state that is passed as an implicit parameter to each entry call. An entry has a logical specification like that of a procedure, consisting of a set of precondition/postcondition pairs. A logical specification of a task type consists of the logical specifications of its entries. (See (Cohen 85 b) for a further discussion of analogies between packages and tasks.) Verification of a task body consists of proving that an entry's precondition/postcondition pairs apply at each **accept** statement for that entry.

Our proof rules do not address timing issues or the relative speed of tasks. This is largely necessitated by our requirement for implementation-independent semantics. Among the consequences of this approach are that a delay statement is equivalent (in the absence of an expression with side effects) to a null statement; that selective waits, conditional entry calls, and timed entry calls are all viewed as arbitrary choices among the alternative paths; and that the Priority pragma is ignored in a proof.

Variables shared among tasks are excluded from the verifiable subset. This decision was originally made because of the difficulty in proving that their use in the absence of the Shared pragma would not be erroneous. (See section 9.11 of the Ada Language Reference Manual.) Such a proof would have to reason about the relative timing of the tasks sharing the variables.

Side effects in expressions

Ada expressions may have side effects. This is reflected by proof rules that make evaluation of an expression one of the steps performed in sequence while processing a language construct. Like the execution of a statement, the evaluation of an expression has a precondition and a postcondition.

Many Ada constructs entail the evaluation of two or more expressions "in some order that is not defined by the language." A program contains an incorrect order dependency if the order determines the net effect of evaluating the expressions. In such situations we construct the conjunction of formulas generated for each possible order. The overwhelming majority of Ada expressions are side-effect-free, so their preconditions and postconditions are identical. This allows drastic simplification of the conjunction, usually to the expression's postcondition. Therefore, combinatorial explosion should not be a practical problem except when verifying programs that make profligate use of side effects.

Optimization

Section 11.6 of the Ada Language Reference Manual allows compilers to perform certain optimizations that change the semantics of programs raising predefined exceptions. Operations that may raise predefined exceptions can be moved earlier within a sequence of statements, even though this may change the state of the computation at the time that a handler is entered. This greatly complicates what would otherwise have been a simple and elegant rule for the propagation of an exception from a sequence of statements. Operations that may raise predefined exceptions can be removed entirely, provided that the effect would be the same in the case where no exception is raised. This makes it impossible to write a precondition guaranteeing that a predefined exception will be raised. Fortunately, it remains possible to write a precondition guaranteeing that no predefined exception will be raised.

LESSONS LEARNED

Our work formulating an axiomatic definition of the Ada language has given us a better understanding of subtle aspects of the language. We have often been surprised to learn which aspects of the language create the most difficulties for formal verification, and we have adapted our approach accordingly. We have gained insight into factors that must be considered in the design of a verifiable language.

The raising of predefined exceptions

Our original intent had been to define, for each possible exception, the precondition for a particular construct to raise that exception. This turns out to be impossible, both because the raising of some exceptions is random with respect to the state of the computation and because optimizations are allowed that cause exceptions not to be raised. There are four kinds of states that a program may be in at any point in the program text:

- those might lead to erroneous execution
- those that are guaranteed to allow normal execution
- those that are guaranteed to raise a programmer-defined exception
- those that might result in either normal execution or the raising of a predefined exception

A program relying on the raising of a predefined exception is not portable, because an optimizing compiler may cause it not to be raised. Therefore it can not be verified using our proof rules.

Uncertainty about the raising of predefined exceptions suggests that the following attitude should be adopted: The raising of a predefined exception corresponds to an error, and predefined exceptions should not be raised intentionally. Thus a rational programmer should not be interested in proving that a program component raises a particular predefined exception (which would indicate that the component contains errors), but that it cannot (which would indicate that the component is free of a certain class of errors). This attitude appears to reflect the intent of the language designers.

Disallowing side effects

Our semantics could be considerably simplified if expressions with side effects were eliminated from the verifiable subset. (We do not consider the raising of an exception to be a side effect in this context.) Side effects in expressions arise from function calls and allocators. Side effects in functions can be restricted without ruling out "benign" side effects like those hidden in a package body and irrelevant to the caller. The use of allocators could be restricted to assignment statements of the form

      variable := allocator;

A special proof rule would apply to such a statement (as if it were a special "allocate statement"), rather than the usual proof rules for assignment statements and expressions.

REFERENCES

Belz, F.C. et al. (1980). A multi-processing implementation-oriented formal definition of Ada in SEMANOL. SIGPLAN Notices 15, no. 11, 202-12.

Bjorner, D. (1985). The role and scope of the formal definition of Ada. Document no. Ada FD/DDC/01/v 3.1. Lyngby, Denmark: Dansk Datamatik Center.

Bjorner, D. & Oest, O.N. (1980). Towards a Formal Description of Ada. Lecture Notes in Computer Science 98. Berlin: Springer-Verlag.

Cohen, N.H. (1985 a). The SofTech Ada Verification Project. In AIAA/ ACM/NASA/IEEE Computers in Aerospace V Conference, pp. 399-407. New York: American Institute of Aeronautics and Astronautics.

Cohen, N.H. (1985 b). Tasks as abstraction mechanisms. Ada Letters 5, no. 3, 30-44.

Cohen, N.H. (1986). Ada axiomatic semantics: Problems and solutions. Technical paper TP223. Waltham, Massachusetts: SofTech, Inc.

Dijkstra, E.W. (1976). A Discipline of Programming. Englewood Cliffs, New Jersey: Prentice-Hall.

Drossopoulou, S., et al. (1982). An attribute grammar for Ada. SIGPLAN Notices 17, no. 6, 334-49.

INRIA (1980). Formal Definition of the Ada Programming Language. Preliminary Version for Public Review. Rocquencourt, France: Institut National de Recherche en Informatique et en Automatique.

Luckham, D.C., et al. (1984). Anna, a language for annotating Ada programs: Preliminary reference manual. Tech. Report no. 84-261, Computer Systems Laboratory, Stanford University, Stanford, California.

THE ADA CHALLENGE FOR NEW FORMAL SEMANTIC TECHNIQUES

E.Astesiano
Department of Mathematics, University of Genova, Italy

A.Giovini
CRAI, Rende (CS), Italy

F.Mazzanti
CRAI, Rende (CS), Italy

G.Reggio
Department of Mathematics, University of Genova, Italy

E.Zucca
CRAI, Rende (CS), Italy

Abstract Ada is posing new challenging problems in the field of formal definitions, as it is witnessed by the many attempts at a solution.
We argue that the CEC-MAP project on AdaFD could be considered a new starting point, meeting the challenge to some extent. Indeed, following the SMoLCS methodology, the dynamic semantics is split in two parts, formalizing a model for the underlying concurrent structure and then connecting the abstract syntax to that model by a set of denotational, hence compositional, clauses. The formal model is given as an abstract data type which accomodates an operational semantics of concurrency and a parameterized modular specification of all the needed structures.
We outline how the followed approach can handle some of the basic problems, particularly the interference between sequential and concurrent features, together with permitting a local correspondence with the Language Reference Manual. We also point out some problems still to be settled.

INTRODUCTION AND MOTIVATIONS

The importance of a sound formal foundation for a programming language definition is now widely recognized. Not only because a formal basis is the only reasonable starting point for the development of rigorous software engineering tools and techniques, but also because the formal semantic definition of a language greatly helps in clarifying and making precise the full meaning of the constructs of a language, providing the best support for language implementations, education and good software design. The development of Ada has issued a new challenge in the field of formal definitions, pointing out new problems and presenting old problems from a new viewpoint.

This work has been partly supported by the CEC-MAP project on "The Draft Formal Definition of ANSI-MIL-STD-1815A" (DDC Prime Contractor - CRAI Contractor - IEI Subcontractor - University of Genova (Dept. of Mathematics) and University of Pisa (Dept. of Informatics) Consultants). All the reports quoted in the references are available at the following address: AdaFD - c/o prof. E. Astesiano, Dept. of Mathematics, University of Genova, via L. B. Alberti 4, 16132 Genova, Italy.

The major fundamental difficulties with Ada are related to its concurrent structure, which is not only far more complicated than the concurrent structure of previous languages, but also deeply mixed and interfering with the sequential aspects of the language. The Ada challenge moreover is not limited to the fundamental issue of the interference between sequential and concurrent features, but involves several new aspects rarely taken in consideration in previous languages: correct programs may generate erroneous executions (in the sense of the Language Reference Manual (LRM)), legal Ada programs may contain incorrect constructs (in the sense of LRM)(for both points see Astesiano et al. 1985 a), and the overall effect of a program may be strongly influenced by implementation dependent properties (see Bendix Nielsen et al. 1985). In the end the overall complexity of the language raises the problem of readability and ease of understanding its formal definition, a problem which extends the Ada challenge from the need of new semantic foundations to the need of new modular techniques of "specification" engineering. The experimentation of new formal techniques and methods and the transition from more classical approaches to some new improved specification methodologies thus becomes one of the more significant challenges we have to face if we want not only that Ada is widely accepted, but also well understood, safely used, and taken as a basis for the development of innovative software techniques.

Many early attempts at the formal definition of Ada (see INRIA 1982, Dewar et al. 1983, Bjørner & Oest 1980) witness the importance and the difficulties of this work. A starting point towards a settlement of the above problems could be provided by the CEC-MAP project "The Draft Formal Definition of ANSI-MIL-STD-1815A Ada". The purpose of this project is the production of a draft formal definition of full Ada together with the development of some tools for its use. A preliminary investigation has shown that the main technical difficulties are concentrated in modelling and defining the interference between sequential and concurrent features in the dynamic semantics. Hence it seems interesting to outline the solution which has been proposed and used in the Trial Definition related to a difficult subset of Ada (CRAI & DDC 1986). We will also refer to more detailed presentations of each of the relevant aspects, and point out some still challenging problems.

A PROPOSAL FOR A SOLUTION

The dynamic semantics is currently modelled using the SMoLCS methodology, which is an integrated approach for the specification of concurrent systems (Astesiano 1984, Astesiano et al. 1985 b, Astesiano & Reggio 1985 a) and languages (Astesiano & Reggio 1985 b, Astesiano & Reggio 1986) explicitly devised for tackling the problems of Ada-like languages.

Basically and informally, the approach splits the dynamic semantics definition of Ada in two steps. In one of these steps a model of the underlying concurrent structure is defined as a concurrent system modelling the execution of Ada programs (see Blum 1984 for the importance of the underlying model and Astesiano et al. 1985 c for a preliminary study). The concurrent system is modelled as a labelled transition system, i.e. a triple consisting of a set of states, a set of flags (labels) and a set of transitions, which are triples of the form (s,f,s'), written also $s \xrightarrow{f} s'$ to suggest that the state s is transformed into the state s' by an action represented by the flag f. Here the states of the concurrent system correspond to execution states of Ada programs; each state is composed by some global information and by a set of subcomponent states corresponding to execution states of Ada tasks; also tasks are modelled by means of a labelled transition system. Every state, both of tasks and of the overall concurrent system, is represented by a syntactic term in a suitable language, which we call "intermediate language", adopting explicit combinators for modelling concurrency. The semantics of this language, consisting in the definition of a suitable algebra embodying an observational semantics of the concurrent system, is still given following the SMoLCS approach in a way which will be explained in some more detail later.

Another step connects an abstract syntax for Ada to the underlying model, obeying the following principles:
- each syntactic construct is translated into a term in the above mentioned intermediate language used to represent the underlying model;
- the above translation is compositional in the sense that the term corresponding to a construct is obtained by composing the terms corresponding to its subconstructs;
- the translation is defined inductively on the structure of the abstract syntax;
- the meaning of a syntactic construct is just the interpretation of the corresponding term in the algebra giving the semantics of the intermediate language.

Formally the above principles correspond to what is known as "denotational semantics": the semantics is a homomorphism from the algebra of the abstract syntax into a suitable semantic algebra. In the following two sections we explain the two steps in more detail by some examples; in particular it will be seen how the above homomorphic translation can make explicit what is truly sequential and what is (maybe hiddenly) concurrent in a construct, thus helping to resolve the basic interference problem.

CONNECTING THE SYNTAX TO THE UNDERLYING MODEL

Accordingly to the above schema, to each state of an Ada program execution is associated a state of a concurrent system, which consists of a set of *behaviours* (states of the labelled transition system associated to tasks) and a *global information* (a structure containing, among others, the storage, the environment and in general the information which has to be shared by the tasks). In the following we give some idea of how this association is defined; but note that our examples are an illustration somewhat simplified , for sake of clarity and lack of room, w.r.t. what is found in the Trial Definition (CRAI & DDC 1986).

The starting point of this association is provided by the following clause, where p is the abstract syntactic representation of a program:

$$exec\text{-}Program \ (p) = (\{exec\text{-}System\text{-}Task \ (p)\}, \text{Initial\_Global\_Inf}).$$

The function *exec-Program* has functionality PROGRAM → STATE; the function *exec-System-Task* associates to a program the initial state of the execution of the system task corresponding to that program (see LRM 10.1(8)); since a task will be represented by an object in the domain of behaviours, the function *exec-System-Task* has functionality PROGRAM → BEHAVIOUR. Hence the result of *exec-Program* on p consists simply in adding to the behaviour *exec-System-Task* (p) an initial global information.

The behaviour associated to p by *exec-System-Task* , and more generally the behaviour associated to the syntactic representation t of a task, is defined inductively on the structure of t by composing the meanings of its subconstructs (e.g. declarations, statements and expressions). The term of the intermediate language which is associated to a declaration, statement or expression is also a behaviour, as the elaboration of a declaration, the execution of a statement, the evaluation of an expression are necessarily fragments of the activity of a single task. In order to define the meaning of those subconstructs an auxiliary structure is needed (which we call the *local information*) which keeps track of the information local to the task which executes the subconstructs (e.g. the name of the task). The behaviours corresponding to those subactivities are composed to give the behaviour of the whole activity by means of combinators, as will be illustrated in the next examples.

Consider for example how the function *exec-Body* , with functionality BODY → (LOCAL-INF→ BEHAVIOUR) is defined inductively using the functions *elab-Declarative-Part* and *exec-Sequence-of-Statements* , corresponding to the elaboration of the declarative part and to the execution of the sequence of statements of a body (where for simplicity we do not treat task declarations and exception handlers):

> *exec-Body* (**declare** dec-part **begin** seq-of-stat **end**) local-inf =
> **def** local-inf' =*elab-Declarative-Part* (dec-part) local-inf
> **in** *exec-Sequence-of-Statements* (seq-of-stat)local-inf'

The construct "**def..in..**" is an example of a combinator on behaviours: given a behaviour bh1 and a behaviour bh2(v), where v is a variable, the resulting behaviour **def** v = bh1 **in** bh2(v) is a behaviour modelling the following activity: the activity of bh1 goes on until a resulting value v_0, if any, is obtained and then the activity of the behaviour bh2(v_0) starts. If the first activity terminates abnormally (e.g. because of an exception) without the production of a value, then the second behaviour is not executed, and the control is transferred to some enclosing behaviour. We do not detail here how the abnormal transfer of the execution is treated.

As another, more complex, example of a clause, showing again the inductive pattern and the combinators, consider the semantics of an assignment statement:

```
0   exec-Stmt ( name := expr ) local-inf =
1       def (left-val,type-den) = eval-Name (name) local-inf
2       and val = eval-Expr (expr) local-inf
3       in  def val' = make-Subtype-Conversion (val,type-den) local-inf
4           in
5           choose UPDATE-STORAGE(left-val,val',...) Δ
6               skip
7           or ERR-UPDATE(left-val,...) Δ start-erroneous-execution
8           or MAKE-UNDEFINED(left-val,...) Δ
9               complete-abnormally (local-inf)
```

The constructs "**choose..or..**", "**..Δ..**" and "**def...and...in...**" are other examples of combinators on behaviours. The first, given two behaviours bh1 and bh2, produces the behaviour **choose** bh1 **or** bh2, which models a nondeterministic choice between the activities modelled by the two behaviours (this operator is canonically extended to an arbitrary number of behaviours); the second, given an action ACT and a behaviour bh produces the behaviour ACT Δ bh, which models the execution of the action ACT followed by the activity of the behaviour bh. Indeed an action models an indivisible activity, i.e. an activity whose intermediate states are of no interest. A possible execution of an activity is indeed modelled by a sequence of actions. The third combinator builds a behaviour which models a nondeterministic choice of the order in which the first two behaviours are executed. Finally **skip** is a term representing a behaviour which models the termination of an activity and the consequent transfer of the control to some subsequent activity.

The above clause can be accompanied by a line-by-line natural language explanation (based on LRM quotations) as follows:

```
0   The execution of an assignment consists in:
1   evaluating the variable name
2   and the expression, in some order which is not defined by the language;
3   then the needed checks and subtype conversions are performed;
5   finally, either the variable is updated with the value of the expression
6   and the execution continues,
7   or, if an assumption on shared variables is violated, then an erroneous
    execution starts
8,9 or, if the task which executes the assignment is abnormal, then the value of the
    variable can become undefined as effect of the abnormal completion of the task.
```

The clause on the assignment shows how the interference mentioned in the introduction between sequential and parallel aspects of the language is treated: sequential aspects are fully modelled (for example the fact that executing an assignment consists in first evaluating the name and the expression, then converting the value and so on) and concurrent aspects are made apparent by suitable combinators on the behaviours that will be defined formally as part of the underlying model.

We end this section recalling, for the reader acquainted with denotational semantics techniques, that functions like *exec-Program, exec-System-Task, elab-Declarative-Part* and so on are the so called "semantic functions" components of the (many-sorted) homomorphism mapping the algebra of abstract syntax into the semantic algebra. The domains like LOCAL-INF $\rightarrow$ BEHAVIOUR, STATE are semantic domains, carriers of the semantic algebra. Some of these domains, like STATE and BEHAVIOUR, are carriers of the algebra (the Concurrent Algebra mentioned later) which represents the semantics of the intermediate language, formalizing the underlying model.

FORMALIZING THE UNDERLYING MODEL

The concurrent aspects made explicit by the denotational clauses illustrated above are modelled in the concurrent system which formalizes the underlying concurrent structure of Ada and provides a semantics for the intermediate language. Following an operational intuition, a concurrent system is seen as a labelled transition system (as e.g. in CCS, see Milner 1980). Moreover our model for Ada is *flat* in the sense that we do not consider any inner hierarchical structure for the tasks, based e.g. on visibility or dependences. The motivations for this flat structure are discussed in Astesiano et al. 1985 c. Note that a rather similar choice underlies the early definitions by NYU (Dewar et el. 1983) and DDC (Bjørner & Oest 1980).

As a consequence we have in our model of Ada two labelled transitions systems:
- the Task Transition System (TTS), in which every state represents an execution state of a single task;
- the Program Concurrent System (PCS), in which every state represents an execution state of a program.

Following the SMoLCS approach, PCS and TTS are specified as abstract data types obtained by instantiating a parameterized schema embodying an operational intuition of concurrency. Later we will briefly discuss the use of this algebraic approach; for now we illustrate the operational schema.

Task Transition System.The states of TTS are behaviours, elements of the intermediate language encountered when describing the denotational clauses. As it was already seen the behaviours are obtained inductively as terms built from some combinators. For example if ACT is an action, x a variable, v a value and bh, bh_1, bh(x) are behaviours then ACT Δ bh, **choose** bh **or** bh_1, **def** x = bh_1 **in** bh(x) and **return** v are behaviours (the last modelling intuitively the termination of an activity with the production of the final value v). The transitions of TTS are given by means of axioms; here are some examples.

$$\text{ACT } \Delta \text{ bh} \xrightarrow{\text{ACT}} \text{bh}$$

is an axiom defining a transition for ACT Δ bh (see CCS, Milner 1980); moreover transitions are given also by means of inference rules, like e.g.

$$\frac{bh_1 \xrightarrow{ACT} bh_1'}{\textbf{choose } bh_1 \textbf{ or } bh \xrightarrow{ACT} bh_1'} \qquad \frac{bh_1 \xrightarrow{ACT} bh_1'}{\textbf{def } x = bh_1 \textbf{ in } bh(x) \xrightarrow{ACT} \textbf{def } x = bh_1' \textbf{ in } bh(x)} ;$$

finally equalities on combinators are defined, like e.g.

$$\textbf{choose } bh_1 \textbf{ or } bh = \textbf{choose } bh \textbf{ or } bh_1$$
$$\textbf{def } x = \textbf{return } v \textbf{ in } bh(x) = bh(v)$$

These rules and equalities, which are just axioms of an algebraic specification, formalize the intuitive explanation of these combinators given when discussing the denotational clauses.

Program Concurrent System. The states of PCS are couples; each couple consists of a set of behaviours (states of TTS) and a term representing some global information. The states of PCS are themselves terms of the intermediate language, target of the denotational clauses; we have seen how the initial state of a program is obtained by the function *exec-Program* and consists of just one behaviour corresponding to the system task and an initial global information. Then the rules corresponding to creation and termination of tasks generate states with a varying number of behaviours. The transitions of a state s of PCS, say $s=(\{bh_1,...,bh_n\},i)$, are obtained by composing the transitions associated by TTS to $bh_1,...,bh_n$, in three steps. First are produced the (synchronous) transitions which correspond to synchronizations of TTS transitions (e.g. rendezvous between tasks); then are produced the transitions which correspond to allowed parallel executions of synchronous transitions (thus resolving problems like e.g. mutual exclusion); finally general monitoring conditions are imposed (e.g. priorities between tasks) in order to select those parallel transitions which become transitions of PCS.

We clarify now this schema by means of a small example. Consider the two transitions of the labelled transition system for tasks:

$$bh_1 \xrightarrow{\text{QUEUED-CALL(entry-id,called-task,pr,....)}} bh_1' \text{ and}$$
$$bh_2 \xrightarrow{\text{ACCEPT(entry-id,called-task,pr,....)}} bh_2'$$

which model respectively the possibility that the task modelled by the behaviour bh_1 (which has priority pr), whose call to the entry entry-id of called-task has been queued, starts the rendezvous, and the possibility that the task modelled by the behaviour bh_2 (identified by the name called-task) executes an accept statement for the same entry.

Starting from these two basic transitions, in the first step the following synchronous transition is produced under the condition (here not formalized) on the global information i that the calling task is not abnormal:

$$(\{bh_1,bh_2\}, i) \xrightarrow{\text{RENDEZVOUS(called-task,pr)}} (\{bh'_1,bh_2'\}, i').$$

That transition models the fact that the two tasks modelled by bh_1 and bh_2 have the possibility of synchronizing starting a rendezvous. The global information i is changed into i' to record the needed changes but we do not detail it further.

In the second step we consider the two tasks as part of the whole system. In this case, as the start of a rendezvous can be executed in parallel with any other action, then all the transitions

$$(\{bh_1, bh_2, bh_3, ..., bh_n\}, i) \xrightarrow{\text{RENDEZVOUS(called-task,pr) // PAR-FL}}$$

$$(\{bh_1', bh_2', bh_3', ..., bh_n'\}, i'')$$

are defined, where PAR-FL is any other (parallel) flag (possibly none), the symbol "//" denotes the parallel composition of actions and i" is obtained by composing the transformations associated to RENDEZVOUS(called-task,pr) and PAR-FL. That transition models the fact that the whole system has the possibility of performing an action which consists in starting the rendezvous between bh_1 and bh_2 together with some other activity of $bh_3, ..., bh_n$, modelled by PAR-FL.

Finally, in the third step we define in which cases a parallel action (here RENDEZVOUS(called-task,pr) // PAR-FL) becomes an action of the overall system PCS; in the example considered we require that there is no other possible rendezvous for the called task with a higher priority (formally, there does not exist any other possible action of the system with a flag having as a component RENDEZVOUS(called-task,pr') with pr' > pr). That completes the three steps schema.

As already mentioned, the whole concurrent system described until now is presented by an algebraic specification, which defines static and dynamic structures as abstract data types (as examples, the terms of the intermediate language are just terms on the signature of PCS; the global information is given as another abstract data type). In general the algebraic techniques allow a complete modularization and parameterization of the description: for example some of the implementation dependent features are modelled as a set of parameters (e.g. the bounds of the predefined type INTEGER, or the checks on the correctness of the values read by an I/O operation), which are algebraic specifications on which the definition has to be instantiated.

For what concerns the semantics of the concurrent system, it can be given operationally and observationally.

The operational semantics consists in associating, starting from the transitions, a (possibly infinite) labelled tree to each state of the system and hence also to the programs via the corresponding initial states. This gives a meaning to an Ada program in the sense that the tree (modulo some permutations and identifications of subtrees) represents already an abstraction (for the acquainted reader, corresponding to Milner's strong equivalence (Milner

1980)). We say that two states (programs) are operationally equivalent iff their trees coincide.

However it happens that two programs modelled by different trees have to be considered equivalent depending on the kind of observations which can be made. Thus the whole specification includes also an *observation part* , which contains a set of observation functions which check whether a state satisfies an observation.Then two states (programs) are observationally equivalent iff they statisfy the same observations (formally if the observation functions coincide on the two given states). Once we have fixed the observations, it can be proved that under some conditions (see Astesiano & Reggio 1986, Astesiano et al. 1985 d) there exists an algebra, the Concurrent Algebra, in which two states are equal iff they are observationally equivalent; this algebra gives thus a semantics to the states of PCS and to each of the subcomponents of those states, like behaviours (i.e. tasks), terms corresponding to subprograms and so on (formally: the observational equivalence is a congruence).

Since the right hand sides of the denotational clauses,which are terms of the intermediate language, are subcomponents of the states of PCS, they can be interpreted in the Concurrent Algebra. In this way the denotational clauses define a homomorphism from the algebra of the abstract syntax into a semantic algebra, some carriers of which are the carriers of the corresponding sort in the Concurrent Algebra.

CONCLUDING REMARKS

The approach we have presented permits a splitting of the semantics definition of Ada which has some pragmatic advantages. It is sufficient a general semiformal comprehension of the combinators on behaviours and of the synchronization, parallelism and monitoring steps for understanding the denotational clauses. Moreover the combination of compositionality and of the operational modelling of the tasks allows a full local correspondence with LRM; each clause can be accompanied by a natural language explanation which is almost as rigorous as the formal clause itself.

There are some other advantages which, for lack of room, are not fully explained in our presentation; most importantly the algebraic parameterized specification approach used in the definition of the concurrent system, which permits a complete modularization of the definition of the structures (which are just abstract data types) and an easy solution for most problems related to the issue of implementation dependent features (see Bendix Nielsen et al. 1985).

However there are still some important problems to be settled; we mention just two. First, it is not at all clear which should be in general the observational semantics of an Ada program, except for the simple cases in which one is interested in input/output (final and finite) semantics. Once that is defined, we should look for an explicit characterization of the semantic equivalences among programs, tasks and other subcomponents, at a more abstract level than the present labelled trees, to get what is called an explicit fully abstract semantics.

Then by a further step we should look for proof systems, starting with the one characterizing the semantic equivalences, and this could be a difficult task.

Hence what we have accomplished is far from a complete solution. Nevertheless we believe that the result of our work can be a starting point since it provides a complete formal setting for full Ada. Indeed it seems worthwhile to end this paper with a warning: it has become quite common and fashionable to present some work on semantics and proof methods for Ada, Ada tasking and so on, while considering extremely simplified subsets of Ada (typically tasks without shared variables, or even tasking reduced more or less to CSP). From our experience we see this as a bad and dangerous attitude: full Ada is incomparably more complex and poses completely different problems, so that many of these partial attempts are of no use at all when coming to real Ada. The Ada challenge cannot be answered just by forgetting the real problems.

REFERENCES

LNCS n. xxx stands for: Lecture Notes in Computer Science, n. xxx, Springer Verlag, Berlin and AdaTFD xxx stands for: The Trial Definition of Ada, Deliverable xxx of the CEC MAP project: The Draft Formal Definition of ANSI/MIL-STD 1815A Ada.

Astesiano, E. (1984). Combining an operational with an algebraic approach to the specification of concurrency. To appear in Proc. Workshop on Combining Methods. Nyborg, Denmark. also Cnet report n.127, ETS Pisa.

Astesiano, E. & Giovini, A. & Mazzanti, F. & Reggio, G. (1985 a). Modelling Erroneous Executions and Incorrect Order Dependences. In AdaTFD 7.

Astesiano, E. & Mascari, G.F. & Reggio, G. & Wirsing, M.(1985 b) On the parameterized algebraic specification of concurrent systems. In Proc. CAAP '85. - TAPSOFT Conference, LNCS n.185.

Astesiano, E. & Mazzanti, F. & Reggio, G. (1985 c). Towards a SMoLCS based abstract operational model for Ada. In AdaTFD 5a.

Astesiano, E. & Reggio, G. (1985 a). The SMoLCS approach to the specification of concurrent systems.In CNET - Distribute Systems on Local Network, vol 2, pp. 237-254, ETS Pisa.

Astesiano, E. & Reggio, G. (1985 b). A syntax-directed approach to the semantics of concurrent languages.Submitted for publication.

Astesiano, E. & Reggio, G. (1986). The SMoLCS methodology - An Introduction to the Methodology for the dynamic semantics. In AdaTFD 7.

Astesiano, E. & Reggio, G. & Wirsing, M. (1985 d). Relational specifications and observational semantics. Submitted for publication.

Bendix Nielsen, C. & Botta, N. & Fantechi, A. & Mazzanti, F. (1985). Modelling implementation dependent aspects. In AdaTFD 7.

Bjørner, D. & Oest, O. (1980). Towards a formal description of Ada. LNCS n.98.

Blum, E.K. (1984) An Abstract System Model of Ada Semantics. TRW Redondo Beach CA.

CRAI & DDC (1986) (Astesiano, E. & Bendix Nielsen, C. & Botta, N. & Fantechi, A. & Giovini, A.& Inverardi, P. & Karlsen, E. & Mazzanti, F. & Reggio, G. & Zucca, E.). AdaTFD 7.

Dewar, R. & Froelich, R.M. & Fisher, G.A. & Kruchten, P. (1983). An executable semantic model for Ada, Ada/Ed interpreter Ada Project, Courant Institute, NYU.

INRIA (1982). Formal Definition of the Ada Programming Language,Honeywell Inc,CII Honeywell Bull.

Milner, R. (1980). A calculus of communicating systems. LNCS n.92.

PROGRAM DEVELOPMENT BY
SPECIFICATION AND
TRANSFORMATION IN ADA/ANNA

B. Krieg-Brückner, Universität Bremen
H. Ganzinger, Universität Dortmund
M. Broy, Universität Passau
R. Wilhelm, U. Möncke, B. Weisgerber, Universität des Saarlandes
A. D. McGettrick, University of Strathclyde
I. G. Campbell, SYSECA Logiciel
G. Winterstein, SYSTEAM KG

1 Summary

The PROSPECTRA project aims to provide a rigorous methodology for developing *correct* software and a comprehensive support system. It is sponsored by the Commission of the European Communities under the ESPRIT Programme, ref. #390.

The *methodology* integrates program construction and verification during the development process. User and implementor start with a formal specification, the interface or "contract". This initial specification is then gradually transformed into an optimized machine-oriented executable program. The final version is obtained by stepwise application of transformation rules. These are carried out by the system, with interactive guidance by the implementor, or automatically by compact transformation tools.

The final version is correct by construction: only the applicability of transformation rules needs to be verified at each step, assisted by the system. Transformation rules are proved correct, analogously to theorems. They form the nucleus of an extendible knowledge base, the method bank, together with pre-fabricated program components, previous program versions, and entire development histories that can be replayed.

The strict methodology of Program Development by Transformation (based on the CIP approach, see e.g. [Bauer, Wössner 82, Bauer et al. 85]) is completely supported by the system, enabling the construction of "a priori" correct programs from formal specifications. However, the system also allows other program development styles where the user assumes responsibility for unguarded development transitions. Moreover, it will be possible to integrate existing program components based on their specification, and to develop them further.

The *system* comprises basic components for the application of individual transformation rules and of compact development methods described as transformation scripts; these provide its real power. Any kind of system activity is conceptually and technically regarded as a transformation of a "program" at one of the system layers. This provides for a uniform user interface, reduces system complexity, and allows the construction of system components in a highly generative way.

2 Objectives

Engineering Discipline for Correct SW: Current software developments are characterized by ad-hoc techniques, chronic failure to meet deadlines because of inability to manage complexity, and unreliability of software products. The major objective of the PROSPECTRA project is to provide a technological basis for developing *correct* programs. This is achieved by a methodology that starts from a formal specification and integrates verification into the development process. Complexity is managed by abstraction, modularization and stepwise transformation. Programs need no further debugging; they are correct by construction with respect to the initial specification. Testing is performed as early as possible by validation of the formal specification against the informal requirements (e.g. using a prototyping tool). Adaptative maintenance is greatly facilitated by replay of developments.

The methodology does not aim at helping in the analysis of requirements at the "requirements engineering" stage, nor does it help in the development of the initial formal requirement specification that is its starting point. It is sufficiently rigorous, on a solid formal basis, to allow verification of correctness during the complete development process thereafter. Thus it is deemed to be more realistic than the conventional style of a posteriori verification: the construction process and the verification process are broken down into manageable steps; both are coordinated and integrated into an implementation process by stepwise transformation that guarantees a priori correctness with respect to the original specification.

Efficiency considerations and machine-oriented implementation detail come in by conscious design decisions from the implementor when applying pre-conceived transformation rules. A long-term research aim is the incorporation of goal orientation into the development process. In particular, the crucial selection in large libraries of rules has to reflect the reasoning process in the development.

The PROSPECTRA project aims at making software development an engineering discipline. In the development process, ad hoc techniques are replaced by the proposed uniform and coherent methodology, covering the complete development cycle. Programming knowledge and expertise are formalized as transformation rules and methods with the same rigour as engineering calculus and construction methods, on a solid theoretical basis. Individual transformation rules, compact automated transformation scripts and advanced transformation methods are developed for Ada/Anna to form the kernel of an extendible method bank analogously to a handbook of physics. Rules in the method bank are proved to be correct and thus allow a high degree of confidence. Since the methodology completely controls the system, reliability is significantly improved and higher quality can be expected.

Specification: Formal specification is the foundation of the development to enable the use of formal methods. Existing specification techniques are consolidated and made amenable to mechanical verification. High-level development of specifications and abstract implementations (a variation of "logic programming") is seen as the central "programming" activity in the future. The abstract formal (e.g. algebraic) specification of requirements, interfaces and abstract designs (including concurrency) relieves the programmer from unnecessary detail at an early stage. Detail comes in by gradual optimizing transformation, but only where necessary for efficiency reasons. Validation by formal verification is integrated into the construction process. Specifications are the basis for adaptations in evolving systems, with possible replay of the implementation.

Programming Language Spectrum: Ada/Anna: Development by transformation receives increased attention world-wide. However, it has mostly been applied to research languages. Instantiating the general methodology and the support system to Ada and Anna (its complement for formal specification, see [Luckham et al. 84, von Henke et al. 85]) make it realistic for systems development including concurrency aspects. Ada/Anna taken together cover the complete spectrum of language levels from formal specifications and applicative implementations to imperative and machine-dependent representations. Uniformity of the language enables uniformity of the transformation methodology and its formal basis.

Stepwise transformations synthesize Ada programs such that many detailed language rules necessary to achieve reliability in direct Ada programming are obeyed by construction and need not concern the program developer. In this respect, the PROSPECTRA methodology may make an important contribution to managing the complexity of Ada.

Research Consolidation and Technology Transfer: Research in language design and methodology has traditionally come from Europe; strong expertise in formal methods is concentrated here and has had considerable international influence. Ada will become central for a common European technology base. The PROSPECTRA project aims at contributing to the technology transfer from academia to industry by consolidating converging research in formal methods, specification and non-imperative "logic" programming, stepwise verification, formalized implementation techniques, transformation systems, and human interfaces. A consortium of a Spanish an a French company are expected to start an ESPRIT demonstrator project for the methodology in an industrial context soon.

Industry of Software Components: The portability of Ada allows pre-fabrication of software components. This is explicitly supported by the methodology. A component is catalogued on the basis of its interface. Formal specification in Anna gives the semantics as required by the user; the implementation is hidden and may remain a company secret of the producer. Ada/Anna and the methodology emphasize the pre-fabrication of generic, universally usable components that can be instantiated according to need. This will invariably cut down production costs by avoiding duplicate efforts. The production of perhaps small but universally marketable components on a common technology base will not only foster a European market but also assist smaller companies in Europe.

Tool Environment: Emphasis on the development of a comprehensive support system is mandatory to make the methodology realistic. The system can be seen as an integrated set of tools based on a minimal Ada Program Support Environment, e.g. the planned ESPRIT Portable Common Tool Environment. Because of the generative nature of system components, adaptation to future languages is comparatively easy. Existing environments only support the conventional activities of edit, compile, execute, debug. Existing transformation systems are mostly experimental and hardly have production quality in user interface, efficient transformation or library support. Conventional verification systems are monolithic and only support a posteriori verification.
     The support of correct and efficient transformations is seen as a major advance in programming environment technology. The central concept of system activity is the application of transformations to trees. Generator components are employed to construct transformers for individual transformation rules and to incorporate the hierarchical multi-language approach of Ada/Anna, TRAFOLA (the language of transformation descriptions), and CONTROLA (the command language). Generators increase flexibility and avoid duplication of efforts; thus the overall systems complexity is significantly reduced.
     Choosing Ada/Anna as a standard language, and standard tool interfaces (e.g. the ESPRIT Portable Common Tool Environment, PCTE), will ensure portability of the system as well as of the newly developed Ada software.

3   The PROSPECTRA Methodology

The Development Model: Consider a simple model of the major development activities in the life of a program:

(1)   *pre-development phase:*

ANALYSIS of requirements and informal problem definition

(2)   *development phases:*

SPECIFICATION of the problem (formal requirement specification)
       - interface between user and implementor, the "contract"
       - prototype modelling allows validation of informal requirements
       - formalization allows rigorous verification of implementations
       - restriction to necessary requirements leaves design choices open

IMPLEMENTATION
       by decomposition ("top-down" hierarchy)
              * design: design specification of components
              * verification: of design specification against interface
              * construction: by implementation of components
              * installation: of components by integration
       by instantiation ("bottom-up")
              * design: selection of pre-fabricated components from stock
              * construction: by specialization / parameterization
              * verification: of instantiated component specification against interface
              * installation: of instantiated component

(3) *post-development phase:*

EVOLUTION in response to changes in requirements
- evaluation, inducing changes in requirements
- leads to re-development, starting with changes in the specification
- requires re-implementation, possibly by replay and adaptation of previous
  implementations or of previously discarded variants.

Dimensions of Development: In adaptation of the conventional view of a life-"cycle", one can distinguish several dimensions along which program development activities take place (see fig. 1):

(1) *revision*　　　change of a specification/implementation to adapt to new requirements
(2) *variation*　　　alternate implementation for the same interface specification
　(2a) *decomposition* (hierarchy of recursive developments):
　　　specification and implementation of components
　(2b) *abstraction / instantiation* (pre-fabrication and use):
　　　generalization/parameterization of components to/from stock
(3) *transliteration*　　transformation, possibly to different language style

Transliteration does not invalidate previous design decisions as a variation would. It may make the design more detailed, and translate into a more machine-oriented language style or a different implementation language. A conventional compilation is a transformation in this sense. Similarly, a specification can be transformed into a different language style.

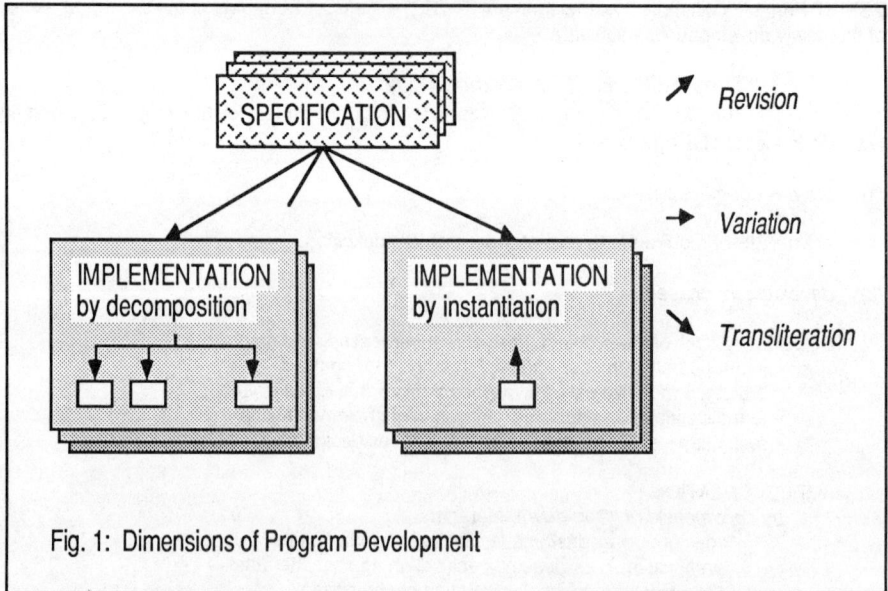

Fig. 1: Dimensions of Program Development

Development by Transformation: Each transition from one program version to another can be regarded as a transformation in an abstract sense. It has a more technical meaning here: a transformation is a development step producing a new program version by applic ation of an individual transformation rule, a compact transformation tool, or, more generally, a transformation method invoking these. Before we come to the latter two, the basic approach will be described in terms of the transformation rule concept. A transformation rule is a schema for an atomic development step that has been pre-conceived and is universally trusted, analogously to a theorem in mathematics. It embodies a grain of expertise that can be transferred to a new development. Its application realizes this transfer and formalizes the development process.

Not only is the program construction process formalized and structured into individual mechanizable steps, but the verification process is structured as well and becomes more manageable. If transformation rules are correctness-preserving, then only the applicability of each individual rule needs to be verified step by step. Thus a major part of the verification, the verification of the correctness of each rule, need not be repeated. Verification reduces to verification of the applicability of a rule, and program versions are correct by construction (with respect to the correctness of the original version). The design activity consists in the selection of an appropriate rule, oriented by development goals, for example machine-oriented optimization criteria.

Transformation Rules and Transformation Scripts: Although program development by stepwise transformation has attracted considerable interest and substantial work has been carried out by various groups; no production-level system to support this method has yet appeared (see [Partsch, Steinbrüggen 83]).

Experiments with prototype systems showed clearly that the problem of systematically using a large collection of transformation rules has to be solved. The problem is to structure the transformation bank in such a way as to reflect the systematic, goal-oriented reasoning necessary to select a transformation. It should then be possible to automatically support each development step in an effective way without abolishing the guiding intuition of the programmer. The long term research goal is to develop transformation methods that relieve the programmer from considerations about individual rules to concentrate on the goal oriented design activity. Some of these methods may be quite application oriented, for example to develop programs with strong concern for properties of concurrency.

Some catalogues of transformations have been assembled for various high-level languages. Of particular interest is the structured approach of the CIP group. The program development language CIPL is formally defined by transformational semantics (see [Pepper 79; Bauer et al. 85]), mapping all constructs in the wide spectrum of the language to an applicative language kernel that is defined denotationally. These basic transformation rules have an axiomatic nature: compact rules for program development can be derived from them in a formal way.

A stock of basic Ada/Anna transformation rules and methods is the basis for program development in the system. Whereas basic transformation rules have to be correct in terms of the underlying formal semantic model of specification and computation, the correctness of derived transformation rules can be inferred from the correctness of the basic ones. These derived rules / scripts are then used in program development by transformation.

4   The PROSPECTRA System

4.1   User Interaction with the System

The system provides for various kinds of user activity. The principal goal is to develop and implement a uniform concept of user interaction. As the methodology for program development in the system will be that of transforming programs and specifications by applying transformation rules, it seems natural to view user interaction on each system level as invocation of manipulations on (attributed) trees. It seems that the concept of transformation (as tree manipulation) can be generalized to all processes in the system initiated by user interaction, at various nested levels. This view subsumes command "sequences" in the conventional sense.

Levels of Interaction: The development of powerful personal workstation computers with high-resolution graphic display and pointing devices together with highly interactive user interfaces and program environments has set new standards of user interaction. Common features are windows for pursuing distinct activities in parallel, and uniform commands to edit data, invoke system activities, select parameters of commands, manipulate windows, etc. Some systems support language-dependent generation of user interfaces (MENTOR [Donzeau-Gouge et al. 80], Cornell

Program Synthesizer [Teitelbaum, Reps 81], ALOE [Medina-Mora, Feiler 81; Habermann et al. 82]).

Important aspects are not covered by today's systems. Firstly, a program system, if it is designed according to the principles of modularity and information hiding, is hierarchically structured. This means that user commands have arguments that may result from computations performed on lower levels of the system. The principles of abstraction and information hiding should be reflected in the system's ways of guiding user interaction through the levels in the hierarchy. Secondly, in an interactive system, the user manipulates the internal state of the system by inputing new data or invoking commands. The presentation of the resulting system state (input parameters of commands, results of calls, internal module state) is, however, the responsibility of each single module. Uniformity of externally presenting internal data in a way that suits their intuitive meaning is therefore not guaranteed. (In the following we will call the process of external representation of internal data *paraphrasing*.) An interactive framework for a program system should therefore provide for mechanisms that generate paraphrasers for internal representations of data from high-level descriptions.

4.2   System Development Components

Generator Components: Having achieved the reduction of the system's complexity to a few principles mentioned above, it is now possible to achieve corresponding reduction of the complexity of implementation. For that purpose, the development of a few basic generator components is conceived. The development of parameterized or generative system components is an undispensable concept of the PROSPECTRA project, both from a methodological and a technical point of view.

Reducing a systems complexity to a few principles, developing models as formal abstractions of these principles, and implementing highly parameterized software modules as their concrete representations is a generally accepted principle in software engineering. This is especially important in the PROSPECTRA project, since here a system is to be developed whose complexity is orders of magnitude beyond what can realistically be managed by naive ad-hoc implementation techniques.

The PROSPECTRA system is a multi-language program development environment: besides Ada and Anna, TRAFOLA, the language for describing transformation rules, and CONTROLA, the command language. Editors, paraphrasers and transformers should, nevertheless, provide uniform operating principles. This requires that these modules are based on a uniform mechanism, which then, however, has to be parameterized by language descriptions. On the other hand, such parameterization increases the flexibility in systems design considerably. Changes in TRAFOLA or CONTROLA, for example, need then not lead to a redesign of all system modules. A parameterized module is called a *generator*, if upon instantiation with an actual parameter a nontrivial analysis of this parameter is performed to increase the module's performance. We will distinguish below between generators and parameterized system components.

It is expected that during the lifetime of the PROSPECTRA system new expertise in program development will be gained so that the system must be conceived from the beginning to allow its incorporation. Technically speaking, the user may input, at the transformer development level, transformation scripts or methods representing new development strategies. If these are not formally derived from existing ones, the user assumes full responsibility and may have to be specially authorised.

Parameterized Structure-Oriented Editor: If a user is faced with the development of a program for a new or for a modified problem, s/he has to input new specifications, program fragments, or transformation rules to the system. All these data are conceptually regarded as tree-structured. New trees with possibly *new meanings* are obtained by editing already existing ones. Editing is done by invoking a syntax-oriented editor (see [Bertling, Ganzinger 85]). The operations of a tree editor can be reduced to the three basic operations "cut", "copy" and "paste".

As far as syntactic issues are concerned, the generation of syntax oriented editors from context-free grammars is well-understood. Editing of semantic information represented in terms of attributes in abstract syntax trees is not supported by conventional systems, in particular, if attributes may themselves contain program fragments of other languages represented as trees.

There is no semantic relationship between the trees before and after editing. In particular, correctness of static semantics cannot be guaranteed. Therefore, editors have to call upon incremental attribute evaluation for re-evaluating semantic attributes. Editor commands are invoked by appropriately interpreting user activation of input devices (keyboard, mouse). Since the user is allowed to act in terms of the intuitive external 2D representation of a tree, and since this representation is specified in the paraphrasing description, this decoding is the task of the paraphraser.

Paraphraser Generator: At any time, the user of the system sees external ("paraphrased") representations of the internal attributed tree. As described above, this tree contains too much information that is relevant at other levels of user interaction only, at any stage. In order not to irritate the user with irrelevant information, a level-dependent external tree representation is strictly required. Since particularly important interaction levels correspond to classes of transformation rules, and since the system has to allow for adaptation to new transformation strategies, the tree representation process must be adaptable. A paraphraser generator is, therefore, an indispensable component of the final system to assist the dynamic evolution of the envisaged program development system.

Editing of trees is always closely connected to paraphrasing (formatting), as the user is allowed to act (select nodes and operations) in terms of an intuitive external representation of the tree - its paraphrased version. Yet it is a separate logical process. The way in which editing commands are recognized as user activation of input devices, or in which edited trees are paraphrased on the screen by invoking operations of a virtual I/O-driver is completely independent of the editing process itself. This conceptual distinction is not clearly made in existing editor/formatter generators (MENTOR, Cornell Program Synthesizer).

Transformer Generator: Transformers are generated for (classes of) rules and scripts. In analogy to LALR parser generators, the tree transformer generator analyses the properties of a rule in the context of other rules to compute application strategies etc. at transformer generation time. This allows a significant increase in efficiency at transformer execution time, in particular for scripts, i.e. sets of rules to be applied together. In existing systems, applicability conditions for rules are either expressed purely syntactically or as verification conditions about the context to be proved on the side. Applicability conditions are described in terms of semantic attributes. This is appealing from a conceptual point of view since it relates to the well-understood notion of attribute grammars. On the implementation side, a considerable increase in efficiency of transformation application can be expected, as context information is available locally and can be incrementally updated.

The proposed program development methodology and the subject languages, Ada, Anna etc, need basic transformation rules with the following properties:
- input and output templates of transformation rules may have a regular structure, i.e. containing list-of-nodes. Access to list components must be made possible explicitly, i.e. using indices, implicitly by specifying a property accessed components must have, or through iteration.
- iteration operators may have to be specified, thereby differentiating between depth- and breadth-iteration.
- the domains of template parameters may be restricted by syntactic typing, i.e. specification by a grammar.
- output templates may contain "free" parameters. Their value in the case of rule application must be supplied from either the user or a program fragment library.

The OPTRAN system is the basis for the work done in the PROSPECTRA project [Möncke et al. 85, 86]. It has been designed to provide generative support for transformations on programs represented as attributed trees. It contains generators for efficient tree pattern matching and attribute reevaluation. The tree pattern matcher generator works incrementally and thus allows for addition of rules at any time. It also provides for transformation scripts ("T-units"), i.e. collections of transformation rules with an application strategy.

The transition from collections of individual rules to scripts is a major step forward in the mechanisation of transformation descriptions. Rules are described uniformly, whether used individually or incorporated into a script. Optional application strategies are furnished separately. Scripts can be seen as a structured breakdown of monolithic optimizers; they can be applied individually under the methodology, guided interactively by the user.

Attribute Evaluation Generator: Transformation strategies are expressed in transformation scripts. These include attribute grammar specifications for the computation of semantic information needed during transformation. Different transformation strategies require different kinds of semantic information. For example, attributes for transformations on the specification / applicative level will be defined. This corresponds to context information in a conventional compiler front-end. Similarly, attributes for data flow analysis may be needed on the imperative level. At the transformer development level, the user must therefore be able to input new attribute evaluation rules as part of new transformation strategies. Corresponding attribute evaluators are then generated.

4.3   Transformation Development Components
TRAFOLA Editor: TRAFOLA is the language for the definition of transformation scripts, including strategies of rule application. Interactive input and modification of transformation rules is done via a structure-oriented editor. The user is responsible for delivering correctness proofs for edited transformation rules.

Method Bank: Transformation methods are collected in a method bank. Initially, it contains an extendable library of transformation rules and tools that embody the expertise about the program development process gathered so far. One can compare it to an encyclopedia of mathematical methods for engineers. It can not be expected that a universal closed method will be found, just as there is no single closed formula for the solution of differential equations.
Apart from this general portion of the Method Bank there are individual portions for archiving program versions and histories of previous developments. Replay of developments may make an adaptation of previous versions possible during a revision, depending on the nature of the changes. Analysis of development histories may also allow a suitable abstraction and generalization of a development to a method for future use.

4.4   Ada/Anna Development Components
Ada/Anna Subset Front End: A front end for a subset of Ada/Anna including the specification, applicative level and package interfaces is developed that can be used as part of the Ada/Anna Editor. It will be derived from an existing attribute grammar for Ada, extended by those parts that are necessary for Anna. Expertise gained from the existing SYSTEAM Ada front end (see [Uhl et al. 82; Winterstein, Mulder 84]) is used in the development of this new component. As far as possible, this front end is interactive allowing incremental re-evaluation of attributes.

Ada/Anna Subset Editor: The input of new specifications and/or programs at the applicative level of Ada/Anna is assisted by a specifically instantiated structure-oriented editor. As mentioned before, there is no guarantee that editing preserves correctness. Therefore, static semantic re-analysis of edited Ada/Anna programs is required using the Ada/Anna Front End. At this point it is not yet clear to what extend this analysis can be performed incrementally during editing. Some semantic attributes will have to be computed incrementally, in particular those which occur in applicability conditions of transformation rules.

Transformers: A hierarchy of transformation rule classes will be defined. The classes constitute levels of Ada/Anna transformation components corresponding to program development phases such as specification, applicative level, mapping to the imperative level. For these classes, transformers are generated. Different classes of transformation rules require different sets of semantic attributes in their applicability conditions.

Verifier: Automatic verification systems do exist but the most successful of these are not distributed due to severely restricted circulation because of the commercial or national security considerations resulting from the obvious benefits in terms of reliability.
Existing systems tend to be designed along the following lines. Starting from a given specification and a given program, a verification condition generator will produce a set of logical expressions whose truth would guarantee the correctness of the program. The processing

of these logical expressions is then accomplished by a theorem prover (perhaps using an algebraic simplifier) in an attempt to establish the truth of the logical expressions.

There is general agreement that these early systems had considerable deficiencies, partly due to the difficult theoretical problems which dictate that the verification process cannot be completely automated. Further shortcomings stem from the fact that the user interfaces were traditionally very poor: should the theorem prover fail to prove that a verification condition is true, a user would typically be confronted with an awesome expression which bares little relation to the original program; small changes to a program would require to start the complete verification process again.

The advances of a verifier integrated into the process of program development by transformation are several. Firstly, since verification conditions are produced by means of a sequence of transformations and since the system possesses a mechanism for remembering, it becomes a simple matter to relate back to the original versions in a user-friendly manner. Secondly, changes to a verification condition need only be made incrementally with respect to the previous version. Thirdly, theorem provers that interact to enlist the help of the user offer substantial advantages both in terms of their efficiency and their capability over alternative approaches.

4.5 Control Components

Virtual I/O Driver: The Virtual I/O Driver is a PROSPECTRA high-level system interface that maps to the window manager and input device drivers provided by PCTE or a particular workstation manufacturer.

CONTROLA Editor and Controller: CONTROLA, a language for formulating control commands, forms the top level of the system hierarchy. Atomic elements of CONTROLA interface to the various system components. Command trees are input via the corresponding structure-oriented editor. Interpretation of a command leads to interaction with corresponding system components. CONTROLA trees, together with their tree-structured atomic leaves that represent lower-level system actions, form a complete history for development activities. Complete re-interpretation of a tree means automatic replay of development processes.

Library Manager: A library manager has to provide for storing and accessing trees and their tree-structured atomic elements of all system levels. The system hierarchy is mirrored in the library hierarchy. Additional structure comes from version management and from the application problem structure.

The library manager interfaces to a lower level of an object oriented database provided by PCTE or such like. This needs to provide DB-objects and relationships with attributes (preferably in a typed manner) to implement relationships of the system hierarchy, versions, and, as far as possible, information that enables the goal-oriented selection process of the method bank.

5 Conclusion

In the first year, the PROSPECTRA Project has made considerable progress, according to schedule, in the areas of the definition of the editable Anna/Ada subset for formal specifications and applicative implementations, now called $PA^{nn}dA$-S, and its formal semantics [Krieg-Brückner 85a, b; Broy, Nickl 86], structure editing [Bertling, Ganzinger 85], the implementation of a protoype Basic System, and work towards the final transformation system [Badt et al. 85; Heckmann 85; Möncke et al 86, 87].

References

[Badt et al. 85] Badt, P., Möncke, U., Raber, P.: Attribuation Schemata for List-Structured Nodes. PROSPECTRA Study Note S.1.3-R-1.0, Universität des Saarlandes, 1985.

[Bauer, Wössner 82] Bauer, F.L., Wössner, H.: *Algorithmic Language and Program Development.* Springer 1982.

[Bauer et al. 85] Bauer, F.L., Berghammer, R., Broy, M., Dosch, W., Gnatz, R., Geiselbrechtinger, F., Hangel, E., Hesse, W., Krieg.-Brückner, B., Laut, A., Matzner, T.A., Möller, B., Nickl, F., Partsch, H., Pepper, P., Samelson, K., Wirsing, M., Wössner, H.: *The Munich Project CIP, Vol. 1: The Wide Spectrum Language CIP-L. LNCS 183,* Springer 1985.

[Bertling, Ganzinger 85] Bertling, H., Ganzinger, H.: A Structure Editor Based on Term Rewriting. in: Proc. 2nd ESPRIT Technical Week, Brussels (1985).

[Broy, Nickl 86] Broy, M., Nickl, F.: PA^{nn}dA-S Semantics. PROSPECTRA Study Note M.2.1.A1-SN-2.1, Universität Passau, 1986.

[Donzeau-Gouge et al. 80] Donzeau-Gouge, V., Huet, G., Kahn, G., Lang, B.: Programming Environments Based on Structure Oriented Editors: The MENTOR Experience. Rapport de Recherche 26, INRIA 1980.

[Habermann et al. 82] Habermann, A.N., et al.: The Second Compendium of Gandalf Documentation. Dept. Comp. Sci., Carnegie-Mellon Univ. (1982).

[Heckmann 85] Heckkmann, R.: Manual for the ELL(1) Parser Generator and Tree Generator Generator. PROSPECTRA Study Note S.1.1-R-2.0, Universität des Saarlandes, 1985.

[Krieg-Brückner 85 a] Krieg-Brückner, B.: Transformation of Interface Specifications. in: Kreowski, H.-J. (ed.): *Recent Trends in Data Type Specification.* Informatik Fachberichte 116, Springer 1985, 156-170.

[Krieg-Brückner 85 b] Krieg-Brückner, B.: PA^{nn}dA-S, its Canonical Syntax and Alternative Paraphrasings. PROSPECTRA Study Note M.1.1.S1-SN-7.1, Universität Bremen, 1985.

[Krieg-Brückner 85 c] Krieg-Brückner, B.: Informal Specification of the PROSPECTRA System. PROSPECTRA Study Note M.1.1.S1-SN-9.0, Universität Bremen, 1985.

[Luckham et al. 84] Luckham, D.C., von Henke, F.W., Krieg-Brückner, B., Owe, O.: Anna, a Language for Annotating Ada Programs, Preliminary Reference Manual. Technical Report No. 84-248, Computer Systems Laboratory, Stanford University, June 1984.

[Medina-Mora, Feiler 81] Medina-Mora, R., Feiler, P.: An Incremental Programming Environment. *IEEE Transaction on Software Engineering 7:* 5 (1981) 472-482.

[Möncke et al. 85] Möncke, U., Weisgerber, B., Wilhelm, R.: Generative Support for Transformational Programming. in: Proc. 2nd ESPRIT Technical Week, Brussels (1985).

[Möncke et al. 86] Möncke, U., Pistorius, S., Weisgerber, B.: OPTRAN under UNIX. PROSPECTRA Study Note S.1.6-R-3.0, Universität des Saarlandes, 1986.

[Partsch, Steinbrüggen 83] Partsch, H., Steinbrüggen, R.: Program Transformation Systems. *ACM Computing Surveys 15* (1983) 199-236.

[Pepper 79] Pepper, P.: A Study of Transformational Semantics. in: Bauer, F.L., Broy, M (eds.): Program Construction. *LNCS 69* (1979) 322-405.

[Teitelbaum, Reps 81] Teitelbaum, T., Reps, T.: The Cornell Program Synthesizer: A Syntax-Directed Programming Environment. *CACM 24:* 9 (1981) 563-573.

[Uhl et al. 82] Uhl, J., Drossopoulou, S., Persch, G., Goos, G., Dausmann, M., Winterstein, G., Kirchgässner, W.: An Attribute Grammar for the Semantic Analysis of Ada. *LNCS 139,* Springer 1982.

[von Henke et al. 85] von Henke, F.W., Luckham, D.C., Krieg-Brückner, B., Owe, O.: Semantic Specification of Ada Packages. in: Barnes, J.G.P., Fisher, G.A. jr (eds.): *Ada in Use,* Proc Ada Int'l Conf. 85 (Paris), Ada Companion Series, Cambridge University Press 1985, 185-198.

[Winterstein, Mulder 84] ANSI Ada Compiler; Global Design; Front End. SYSTEAM KG, Karlsruhe 1984.

Part VII Design Methods

A STRUCTURED TECHNIQUE FOR CONCURRENT SYSTEMS DESIGN IN ADA

P.H. Welch

Computing Laboratory, University of Kent at Canterbury, CT2 7NF, ENGLAND.

Abstract. Ada tasks define both network components and the connections between those components. This means that we cannot naturally define components with raw Ada tasks that are independent of the network in which they are to be embedded. Further, hierarchical structures of networks are difficult to implement. This causes severe problems for the design, implementation, testing, integration, maintenance and reusability of multi-tasking algorithms. This paper presents a model of tasking with increased powers of abstraction that overcome many such difficulties. Transformation rules down to legal Ada are given. The extra information provided by this model not only improves the life-cycle project management of large multi-processor embedded systems, but it also enables the compiler to produce code with lower overheads for inter-task communication.

INTRODUCTION

One of the more bewildering problems encountered by software designers when considering their first "large" Ada-based projects is which Ada concepts to use and where to use them. In particular, information hiding may be achieved through packages and tasks in ways that are not entirely complimentary. For real-time multi-processor embedded applications, the approach which seems to offer the best returns both from the viewpoint of performance (through concurrency) and understandability (through discrete components) is that of tasking. It is therefore somewhat alarming to confront the reusability and life-cycle management problems that arise through the naive use of Ada tasks whenever *high* levels of parallelism are involved (e.g. in the "real world"). This is particularly worrying in view of the special benefits that Ada is supposed to confer on just these areas.

Consequently, various "higher level" methods to support concurrent designs are being adapted and/or invented for Ada — for instance, MASCOT (Basdell et al., 1984) and DIADEM (Nissen et al., 1986) Our approach reflects that of Occam (Inmos Ltd., 1984), which has very simple yet powerful capabilities for expressing concurrent systems. Occam is related to Ada through the concept of the "rendezvous" for inter-task control that was first defined by CSP (Hoare, 1978). The views and methods reported in this paper are derived from experiences gained by the author when working with colleagues at GEC Avionics (Rochester) on an experimental Ada design for a "real" real-time control system — see Acknowledgements.

We consider two principles of software engineering: *abstraction* and *structure*. For any object, we need to be able to abstract sufficient information into its *specification* so as to allow its most general area of *application* without commitment to any particular *implementation*. So long as object application and implementation are independent of one another, reusable components can be built and life-cycle problems managed.

The second principle allows objects to be structured hierarchically. For instance, we must be free to implement an object specification, *A* say, by using (i.e. applying the specifications of) other objects. Of course, such an implementation must abide by the first principle and not force any changes to the specification of *A*, nor to any application of *A*.

Let us see how Ada tasks stand up to these principles.

RAW ADA TASKING

We assume the reader is familiar with the concept of Ada tasking as defined in section 9 of the Language Reference Manual (AJPO, 1983). Communication between tasks transfers information and achieves synchronisation. Communication is based on the "server/actor" model and is asymmetric. The server task provides an *entry* on which any other task may call — the server task does not know who his callers may be. The actor task makes a call on a specific entry of a specific task — the actor task does know the name of the server upon whom he is calling.

We present a (greatly) simplified example of a real-time control system. We shall concentrate on tasking and will not concern ourselves with orthogonal issues (like sensible datatypes). We represent communicating processes diagrammatically as follows :—

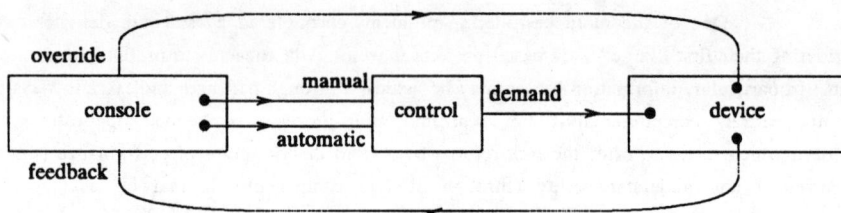

override

console   manual   control   demand   device

automatic

feedback

There are three communicating tasks: *console*, *control* and *device*. Task *control* is a "pure server" in that it only provides the entries *manual*, *automatic* and *demand*, upon which other tasks may call. Task *control* calls no task itself. Task *device* is a "pure actor" and provides no entries for other tasks. Task *device* makes specific calls on *control.demand*, *console.override* and *console.feedback*. The fact that *device* needs to know the name and entry of the tasks it is calling is indicated in the diagram by the communication lines starting from inside the body of *device*. Task *control* does not know the tasks that call its entries and so the communication lines do not reach inside *control*. Task *console* is a "transducer" of information — behaving sometimes as an "actor" (by calling *control.manual* and *control.automatic*) and sometimes as a "server" (by providing the entries *override* and *feedback*). The direction of data-flow is independent of the server/actor relationship and may be bi-directional. In the diagram, this direction is indicated by the arrowheads.

Of course, the relationship between these tasks is a little contrived but it was designed to illustrate the problems that arise for these varieties of task.

In Ada, the raw task specifications only declare entries, informing us that we have the following components :—

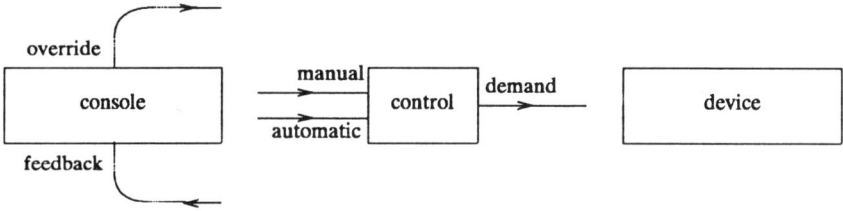

override

console

feedback

manual

automatic

control

demand

device

The components are *applied* (i.e connected into the required network) only through *implementing* their bodies. This breaks the principle of abstraction that implies the independence of application and implementation. The only component which is independent of its environment, and thus reusable and testable in some general purpose test environment, is *control*. Only "pure servers" satisfy this principle and the trouble is that you cannot build a network out of server tasks alone :—

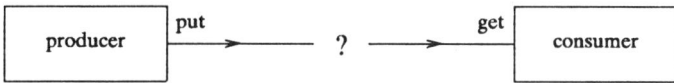

producer

put

?

get

consumer

They must either be connected with purpose-built plugs :—

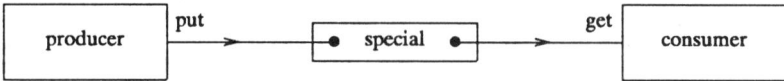

producer

put

special

get

consumer

(which introduces extra buffering that may affect network characteristics and is inefficient) or one of the servers must be patched to turn an accept into a call :—

producer

get

consumer

(which is not always possible, violates abstraction and loses many of the benefits of reusability).

With this natural method of using Ada tasks, overall system design is expressed by individual task implementations. This has serious implications for systems testing, integration and maintenance. For example, we might have to change the implementation of a well-tested component simply because we have re-designed some other part of the network with which it communicates.

We interpret the principle of structure for tasking as meaning that we can construct them by means of a sub-network of parallel task components. This is a very natural method of design that reflects the way hardware engineers have always worked. Contrary to the case for abstraction, it is only "pure actors" that satisfy this principle. For instance, suppose we decided to implement the task *device* by a network of sub-tasks :−

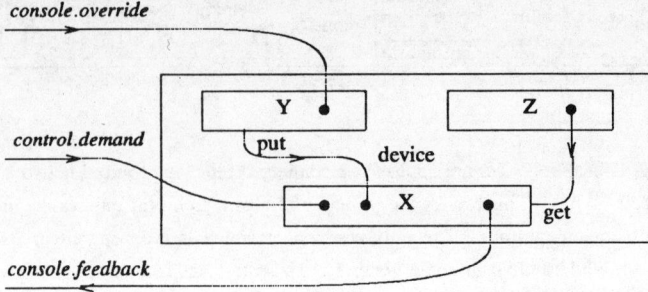

The body of *device* would consist just of the specifications of the three tasks *X*, *Y* and *Z* followed by their implementations (which define the connections within the sub-network and between the sub-network and the main network). The specification of *device* (which never contained a great deal of information anyway!) would remain unaltered along with the rest of the main network.

However, when we try to do the same with the other components, problems arise. Suppose we wished to implement the *console* by means of the sub-network :−

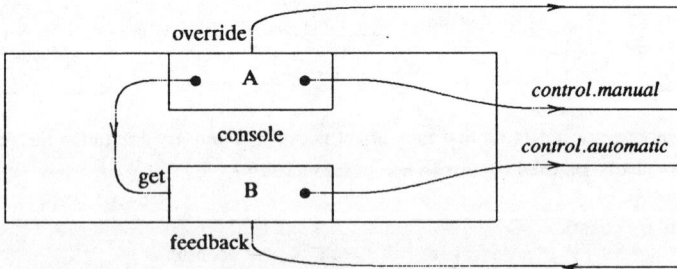

If tasks *A* and *B* are declared within the body of *console*, they not allowed to accept the entry calls *override* and *feedback* on behalf of their parent. In an earlier paper (Welch, 1985), many attempts are described to try to overcome this problem. The conclusion reached was that, *with this simple method of using Ada tasks*, all that could be done was to replace the *console* task with the tasks *A* and *B* and abandon the principle of structure so far as Ada source code was concerned. Unfortunately, we then run into the abstraction problem in that we have to change the implementation of *device* so that it calls *A.override* (not *console.override*) and *B.feedback* (not *console.feedback*).

The difficulties are even worse for the "pure server" task *control*. If we try to make a parallel implementation, changes are forced on the implementations of both *console* and *device*. The final network of tasks with all these parallel implementations is "flat" with all structuring information lost.

ABSTRACT STRUCTURED PROCESSES

We present, by example, a formal design language for designing structured networks of parallel components. All connections for communication lines are abstracted into the component specifications. Consider the following :—

```
process console_task
  (port feedback (x : in float);
   port override (x : out float))
  ->
  (port manual (x : in float);
   port automatic (x : in float));

process control_task
  (port manual (x : in float);
   port automatic (x : in float);
   port demand (x : out float));

process device_task
  ->
  (port override (x : out float);
   port demand (x : out float);
   port feedback (x : in float));
```

The ports *before* the arrow (—>) will correspond to task entry *declarations*. The ports *after* the arrow abstract out the entry *calls* made by the process. These specifications capture :—

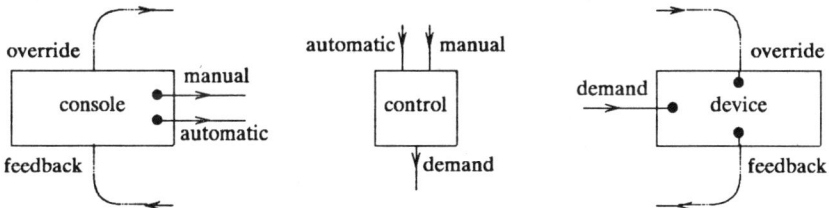

The components are connected (i.e. *applied*) independently of their *implementations* :—

```
process overall_system_task;

process body overall_system_task is

  channel manual (x : in float);
  channel automatic (x : in float);
  channel demand (x : out float);
  channel feedback (x : in float);
  channel override (x : out float);

  console : console_task (feedback, override) -> (manual, automatic);
  control : control_task (manual, automatic, demand);
  device : device_task -> (override, demand, feedback);

end overall_system_task;
```

The **channel** names need not match the corresponding **port** names but the parameter structures must be the same. In such an implementation, each **channel** name must be used exactly once somewhere on the left-hand side of the arrow ($->$) of a **process** instantiation *and* at least once on the right-hand side. Of course, the channels may be declared in any order and the processes instantiated in any order.

The processes are implemented quite independently. For example :−

```
process body console_task is
    ...
    ...   -- accepts of feedback & override
    ...   -- calls to manual & automatic
    ...
end console_task;
```

The abstraction principle has been satisfied.

Hierarchical structures of (even "non-pure actor") processes present no difficulties now. Consider the parallel structure of the *console* drawn in the previous section. The sub-components *A* and *B* are specified :−

```
process A_task
    (port override (x : out float))
    ->
    (port put (x : in float);
     port manual (x : in float));

process B_task
    (port feedback (x : in float);
     port get (x : in float))
    ->
    (port automatic (x : in float));
```

The *console* may now be implemented :−

```
process body console_task is    -- parallel

    channel c (x : in float);

    A : A_task (override) -> (c, manual);
    B : B_task (feedback, c) -> (automatic);

end console_task;
```

The **port** names *manual, automatic, feedback* and *override* refer to the **port** declarations in the specification of *console_task*. Their parameter structures must match those of the corresponding **ports** of the sub-processes being instantiated.

ABSTRACT STRUCTURED ADA TASKING

A **process** specification is represented in Ada by a **generic package**. The accept-ports (which are those *before* the arrow) are declared as **procedures** in the visible package specification and the **pragma** *inline* invoked. The **call-ports** (those *after* the arrow) are declared as **generic procedure** parameters. For example :—

```
generic

    with procedure manual (x : in float);
    with procedure automatic (x : in float);

package console_task is

    procedure feedback (x : in float);
    procedure override (x : out float);

    pragma inline (feedback, override);

end console_task;
```

```
generic package control_task is

    procedure manual (x : in float);
    procedure automatic (x : in float);
    procedure demand (x : out float);

    pragma inline (manual, automatic, demand);

end control_task;
```

```
generic

    with procedure override (x : out float);
    with procedure demand (x : out float);
    with procedure feedback (x : in float);

package device_task is
end device_task;
```

Processes are applied as follows. The **channels** which are used to connect **process** instantiations are first declared as **procedures** and the **pragma** *inline* invoked. The process instantiations are **generic package** instantiations. In Ada, only the **call-ports** may be supplied here. Finally, the **accept-ports** are installed by implementing the **channel procedures** as single calls to the appropriate **accept-port procedures** exported by the **generic package** instantiations. For example :—

```
generic package overall_system_task is
end overall_system_task;
```

```
package body overall_system_task is     -- parallel

  -- channels

  procedure manual (x : in float);
  procedure automatic (x : in float);
  procedure demand (x : out float);
  procedure feedback (x : in float);
  procedure override (x : out float);

  pragma inline (manual, automatic, demand, feedback, override)

  -- processes and calls

  package console is new console_task (manual, automatic);
  package control is new control_task;
  package device is new device_task (override, demand, feedback);

  -- entries

  procedure manual (x : in float) is
  begin
    control.manual (x);
  end manual;

  ... -- similarly, the other channels are implemented
  ... -- by making the appropriate entry call.

end overall_system_task;
```

We distinguish two types of **process** implementation: *sequential* and *parallel*. For a sequential implementation, a **task** is declared in the **package body**, with a set of **entries** that match the pseudo-**entry** **procedures** declared in the **generic package** specification. These **procedures** are implemented by single calls to the corresponding **task entries**. Finally, the sequential implementation of the **process** is coded within the **task body**. Calls to external processes become calls to the appropriate **generic procedure** parameters. This is the only occasion whenever a raw Ada **task** is used.

For instance, a sequential implementation of the *console* process is :−

```
package body console_task is     -- sequential

  task console is
    entry feedback (x : in float);
    entry override (x : out float);
  end console;

  procedure feedback (x : in float) is
  begin
    console.feedback (x);
  end feedback;

  procedure override (x : out float) is
  begin
    console.override (x);
  end override;
```

```
task body console is
    ...
    ...     -- accepts of feedback and override
    ...     -- calls to manual and automatic
    ...
end console;

end console_task;
```

A parallel implementation is just the instantiation and interconnection of sub-processes (as for *overall_system_task* above) together with connections to any external circuitry. Actual **generic** parameters of the sub-process instantiations are either local **channel procedures** (as before) or the formal generic parameters of the **process** being implemented. The pseudo-entry **procedures** declared in the **generic package** specification are implemented by single calls to the appropriate **accept-port** procedures exported by the local **generic package** instantiations.

For example, the parallel implementation of the *console* **process** is as follows. Translate the **process** specifications of *A_task* and *B_task* into **generic package** specifications using the rules given earlier :—

```
generic
    with procedure put (x : in float);
    with procedure manual (x : in float);

package A_task is

    procedure override (x : out float);

    pragma inline (override);

end A_task;
```

```
generic
    with procedure automatic (x : in float);

package B_task is

    procedure feedback (x : in float);
    procedure get (x : in float);

    pragma inline (feedback, get);

end B_task;
```

Then :—

```
package body console_task is        -- parallel

  -- channels

  procedure c (x : in float);

  pragma inline (c);

  -- processes and calls

  package A is new A_task (c, manual);
  package B is new B_task (automatic);

  -- external entries

  procedure feedback (x : in float) is
  begin
    B.feedback (x);
  end feedback;

  procedure override (x : out float) is
  begin
    A.override (x);
  end override;

  -- local entries

  procedure c (x : in float) is
  begin
    B.get (x);
  end c;

end console_task;
```

EXTENSIONS (SELECTIVE CALLS, ABORTIONS AND ENTRY FAMILIES)

Having abstracted tasks as generic packages and entries as procedures, we appear to have lost some of the "higher level" Ada capabilities for inter-task control. Only an innermost body of a process can see a raw task and its entries. Thus, a calling process may not make a selective call. Similarly, aborts are not possible! While we would not wish to claim that such a "loss" is really a "gain", there is certainly merit in not having these capabilities by default (see the Conclusions section below).

For those occasions when our system design demands such techniques, we can get them — but we have to make a positive request. In the Ada manifestation of such a design, extra machinery needs to be created to operate on the raw tasks remotely. Run-time overheads are eliminated through *inlining*. For instance, if we wish the *console_task* process to be abortable, we must so declare it :—

```
abortable process console_task
   ...
```

In Ada, this is handled by exporting an extra parameterless procedure (*exterminate* say) from the corresponding **generic package**. In a sequential implementation, *exterminate* simply aborts the task declared in the **package body**. In a parallel implementation, it makes calls on the corresponding *exterminate* procedures it can see in the sub-process generic package instantiations — of course, sub-processes of abortable processes must themselves be abortable.

Entry families, together with timed and conditional entry calls, may be catered for with similar techniques. The details will be reported in a later paper.

RESTRICTIONS

The major problem left with this technique is that we would very much like to treat our processes in just the same way as we can treat most other objects in Ada — we would like to use them as building blocks for other objects. For instance, we might want to declare :–

system_bank : **array** (0..99) **of** overall_system_task;

In Ada, we cannot declare an array of generic package instantiations. Nor could we have one as a field in a record. Nor can we manage them dynamically with access types.

Although we can do all these things with task types, their lack of abstractive and structuring powers make them very difficult objects with which to work. In particular, the body of a task type has to be able to make all the connections on behalf of all of its instances and, of course, it has to be told, through some initial rendezvous, what particular instance it is!

It seems likely that hierarchically structured generic packages will play a leading role in the development and application of fields other than those concerned with high levels of concurrency — for instance, abstract data-types and object-oriented design. This lack of rights for objects declared through generic package instantiations may prove very difficult for many methodologies for working with Ada.

CONCLUSIONS

The structured technique for tasking developed above provides an effective solution to the problems caused by the weak abstraction mechanism of raw Ada tasks. Sadly, it does seem to fight the language as is evidenced by the somewhat lengthy, repetitive and trivial sections of code that need to be constructed. This could be overcome by appropriate software tools to generate and manipulate the text. With good *inlining*, nothing in the way of executable object code is produced from all this text, so that there is no run-time overhead in applying the method.

The technique provides several other benefits. The information captured by the design language documents many more properties of the objects being specified than are provided by raw task specifications. The fact that **ports** have to be *declared* as being called through **conditional** or **timed** selects will enable better management control of project development. Similarly, **processes** have to be *declared* as being **abortable**.

Secondly, when the design of a communicating system does not require selective calls, the default position is that these facilities are not granted. Since the compiler can now know that such rendezvous cannot be "backed off" by the caller, it can arrange for the run-time kernel to implement them with a simple and fast "hand-shake". For many applications, a greatly reduced overhead for task communication may be very important and well-worth some loss of flexibility.

Finally, there is a gain in safety through processes not being abortable by default. We can be sure that no "time-bombs" can explode.

For implementation on multiple processors, the model provided by the design language fits well with how hardware components are put together. The code for an instantiated **process** running on its own processor will just be a collection of Ada tasks. The tasks call one another internally by direct entry calls (with the intervening **procedures** generated by the **process-to-task** mapping removed through *inlining*). External calls are clearly identifiable by the compiler and would be routed by the run-time system through whatever physical inter-processor media existed. The top-level **process**, with the insertion of suitable configuration *pragmas*, would cause the compiler to generate the load modules for the distributed processors.

ACKNOWLEDGEMENTS

I am very grateful to the Science and Engineering Research Council and the Royal Society who jointly sponsored me for a one year Industrial Fellowship (to May, 1985) at GEC Avionics, Rochester. I am also grateful to my GEC colleagues for their openness and collaboration in this work. Further, I am thankful to Grady Booch and Larry Druffel of Rational Inc. for providing a broader understanding and insight into the strange game being played by Ada tasks, packages and generics. Particular thanks are also due to Bob Gautier and others on the working party on Software Reuse of Ada-Europe for their encouragement and feedback on these issues. Finally, a major debt is owed to the designers of Occam for showing how elegantly and efficiently concurrent systems can be put together.

REFERENCES

Ada Joint Program Office (1983). Ada Language Reference Manual.

Basdell, B.W., Leigh, P.M. & Lovell, A.C. (1984). MASCOT in the Ada/APSE Era. Contract A28B/348 for the Procurement Executive, Ministry of Defence : Royal Signals and Radar Establishment, Great Malvern, Worcs..

Hoare, C.A.R. (1978). Communicating Sequential Processes. *In* Communications of the ACM, Vol. 21, No. 8, August 1978, pp. 666-676.

Inmos Ltd. (1984). Occam Programming Manual : Prentice-Hall International.

Nissen, J.C. et al. (1986). A Compiler-Independent Approach to Distributing a Single Ada Program. First report of DIADEM (MAP Project 770) : Commission of the European Communities (to appear).

Welch, P.H. (1985). Structured Tasking in Ada? *In* Ada Letters, Vol. 5, No. 1, July/August 1985.

Expressing Module Interconnections in Ada

Vinod Grover
SofTech Incorporated, Waltham, MA 02254, U.S.A

Ernesto Guerrieri
SofTech Incorporated, Waltham, MA 02254, U.S.A

Abstract In this paper we show that a subset of general module
interconnection language constructs exists in Ada. We
describe a variety of techniques for expressing module
interconnections in Ada. A module is taken to mean either a
specification or an implementation of some abstraction. In
our technique, modules are represented by generic packages.
The formal parameters of the generics are viewed as import
lists and the visible parts of the package represent the
export list of the module, respectively. Module
interconnections are expressed by instantiating generic
packages with actual parameters selected from the export lists
of other packages. Using this technique we show that module
specifications can be connected to module implementations and
cyclic interconnections can be expressed by multi-level
generic instantiation.

INTRODUCTION

It has long been recognized that programming-in-the-large,
especially with a large team of programmers, is a challenging,
time-consuming, and an error prone task. In particular, the problems and
issues concerning precise interface control, reuseability, and
configuration management arise most frequently in this context. The most
widely accepted approach for addressing these problems require the use of
programming or software engineering environments (Wolf et. al. 1984).
Recent progress in the development of Module Interconnection Languages
(MILs), coupled with modern software development methods such as
abstractions, offer a more systematic and uniform solution to these
problems (Burstall & Lampson 1984, Mitchell & Plotkin 1985). Using this
approach the problem of pogramming-in-the-large is effectively reduced to
that of programming-in-the-small with modules.

One of the key elements used in the management of complexity
is the notion of abstraction. However, abstraction by itself can lead to
its own problems: proliferation of seemingly unrelated abstractions. In
general it becomes essential to describe how various abstractions are
related and can be combined to form a whole. This is accomplished by
using some form of module interconnection description technique. A module
interconnection language is concerned with describing the large-scale
structural and combinational properties of abstractions which are
represented as modules.

In this paper, we show that Ada can be used to describe a set

of module interconnections. In our approach abstractions are represented
by using modules, and modules are represented by generic packages which
can be interconnected in a flexible but secure manner to form larger
systems. A large class of module interconnections can be specified in Ada
alone, and lead to easily enforceable configuration management practices.
This approach has at least two distinct advantages over the previous
approaches. First, the reliance on software engineering environments can
be reduced for the task of achieving precise interface controls and some
degree of configuration management. Second, since Ada itself is used as
the module interconnection language, no special implementation of the
module language is required; an Ada implementation would suffice. We will
describe the power of these techniques by using simple typical examples.

OVERVIEW OF MODULE INETRCONNECTION LANGUAGES

In our approach, a module is meant to denote abstractions, and
Ada packages denote modules. Below we give an informal overview of some
of the essential properties of abstractions and modules.

An abstraction, for our purposes, effectively hides certain
parts of a domain of discourse. The hidden part of an abstraction is
normally termed as the body or an implementation of the abstraction. The
body or the implementation of an abstraction is considered to be
irrelevant to the external user of the abstraction. What is considered
important, from the user's viewpoint, are the list of entities not hidden
in the abstraction. These are termed as the specifications of the
abstraction.

The body of an abstraction consists of some combination of
primitive or constructed abstractions that are already provided. The
specification of an abstraction consists of a list of entities. This list
can be divided into two parts: things exported to a user of the
abstraction and things imported from some user(s) of the abstraction.

Within the body of the abstraction the imported items can be
freely referenced and combined with the rest of the body or with each
other. Within an abstraction it is irrelevant who provides these items.
However, outside an abstraction only the exported items can be combined to
form "higher" abstractions. Thus an abstraction can be viewed as a fence
used for separating concerns on either side.

Modules are treated as syntactic devices used for representing
abstractions in a concrete way. A module is introduced by an explicit
declaration of a module specification, module implementation, or a module
construction from existing modules. A module has input parameters, called
an import list, and a number of output parameters, known as an export
list. Ideally these parameters may be any form of modules (i.e.
specifications, implementations, or constructions).

Module interconnections are specified by module construction
rules. Module constructions are simply applications of module
specifications or implementations to actual parameters. This simplicity
coupled with the range of parameters allowable can lead to considerable

power. For example, a wide range of module specifications can be
constructed from an existing set of module specifications. Also, a module
implementation can be passed as a parameter to a module specification,
under certain conditions, to yield different implementations of common
interfaces. Thus it is easy to see how programming with modules can
provide valuable support for the development of reuseable software.

REPRESENTING MODULES IN ADA

          In this section, we will systematically illustrate through
various examples how the concepts of module interconnection languages can
be represented using Ada. The concepts that we elaborate here are import
and export lists, module specifications, module implementations and module
constructions.

          Import Lists are represented by using input formal parameter
lists of entities that will represent module specifications and module
implementations. The main reason for this choice is that in this manner
import lists are not related in any a prior manner to existing modules.
This is in keeping with the spirit of abstractions.

          Export Lists in the same manner are to be treated as output
formal parameters. The reasons for this choice are similar to those for
import lists.

          Module Interconnections are naturally represented as
applications of modules specifications or implementations to actual
parameters. That is to say exported parameters or identifiers serve as
actual paremeters.

          Module Specifications and Implementations are to be
represented as a generic packages. The formal parameters of the generic
represent the import parameters and the declarations in the visible part
of the package specifications represent the export parameters of the
module. If a module is to have no import parameters, then an ordinary
package or a parameterless generic is adequate. Module interconnections
are represented by instantiating generic packages with parameters selected
from the export list of other modules.

          We now describe the manner in which specifications and
implementations of modules are distinguished. First of all we realize
that module implementations can be connected together to one or more
module implementations to provide concrete modules representing useable
abstractions. However, since we cannot pass generic packages as
parameters which is how interconnections are specified, we must find some
other mechanism for doing so. Passing a package as parameter really means
passing every thing exported by the package that is to be passed as a
parameter. Thus, the import parameters of module specifications are
divided into two parts: the part that will be imported from a specific
module implementation. This is called the implementation import list.
The signature of the implementation import list is isomorphic to the
signature of the export list. The other part of the import list

represents the real import list (see example 3). The package body of the
generic simply "connects" or maps the implementation import list to the
exported items via such features such as renaming, type conversions, and
type derivations.

        Module implementations are generic packages that may have a
null implementation import list. This means that such generic packages
must provide a specific implementation for its exported operations. Note
that all those modules that are required to have a fixed implementations
can be 'optimized' to be replaced by a single generic package whose body
provides the implementation of the operations directly.

        We are now ready to give several examples of module
interconnections in Ada. In our examples, we shall depict modules (or
generics) as rectangular boxes. The imported parameters would appear as
labeled arrows pointing inwards to tha box. The exported parameters would
appear as labeled arrows pointing outwards from the box.

        Example 1.   -- A Stack Module

        The first module we show describes a Stack module . This
module imports two parameters: A stack size and the type of stack
elements. It exports the standard operations Push and Pop.

```
generic
    StackSize : Positive;
    type Element is private;
package StackPackage is
    procedure Push(Item : in  Element);
    procedure Pop (Item : out Element);
end StackPackage;
```

is represented as:

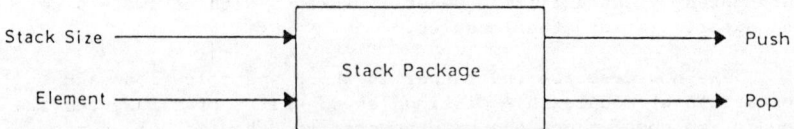

Next we describe how this module imports a maxSize from package
ConstantDefs, and the type BucketType from the package BucketOps to yield
a module representing Stack operations on elements of BucketType.

```
with ConstantDefs, BucketOps, StackPackage;
pragma Elaborate (StackPackage);
package BucketStack is new
    StackPackage (ConstantDefs.maxSize,
                  BucketOps.BucketType);
```

Pictorially this looks like this:

Bucket Stack

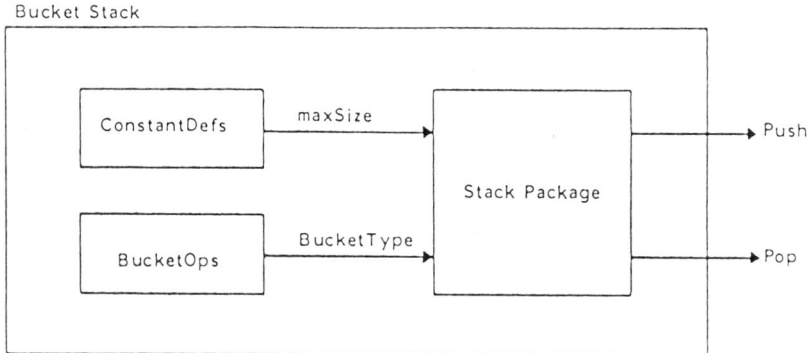

Note that pragma Elaborate is needed to avoid getting PROGRAM_ERROR if the body of StackPackage has not been elaborated. The pragma is not needed for BucketOps or ConstantDefs, since no operations are imported. Precise interface control is achieved through the generic formal matching rules of Ada.

However, the module interconnections that are possible from this obvious approach seem to be limited to describing only acyclic directed interconnections. In some cases a need for cyclic interconnections arises, and we have found that we can do so by multi-level generic instantiations or exporting modules. We describe this technique in the next example.

Example 2 -- Expressing Cyclic Interconnections

The example we describe here is a simplified version of a distributed mail program in Ada. There are two nodes in the distributed system (each modeled by a library package). Each of the nodes provides three procedures: ReadMessage, SendMessage, and ReceiveMessage. Each node encapsulates a mailbox for storing messages. ReadMessage is invoked to provide a listing of the current message in the mailbox of the node. ReceiveMessage is invoked to update the mailbox of the node. SendMessage invokes the ReceiveMessage of the other node to transfer a message to that node. In this system each of the node imports an operation (i.e. ReceiveMessage) from the other. Each node exports all three operations. This situation clearly requires the capability to describe cyclic connections. Furthermore, since each of the nodes is identical in functionality and its implementation it would be advantageous to implement this as a single generic package that can be instantiated for either node.

However, this means that each instantiation requires an actual parameter from the other instance.

This problem can be solved by using nested generics packages and multi-level instantiation. The following program fragment describes the solution.

```
generic
package Node is
    procedure ReadMessage;
    procedure ReceiveMessage;
    generic
        with procedure UpdateMailBox;
    package SubNode is
        procedure SendMessage;
    end SubNode;
end Node;

with Node;
package Node1 is new Node;

with Node;
package Node2 is new Node;

with Node1, Node2;
package SubNode1 is new Node1.SubNode(Node2.ReceiveMessage);

with Node1, Node2;
package SubNode2 is new Node2.SubNode(Node1.ReceiveMessage);
```

This effectively describes the following module interconnection diagram:

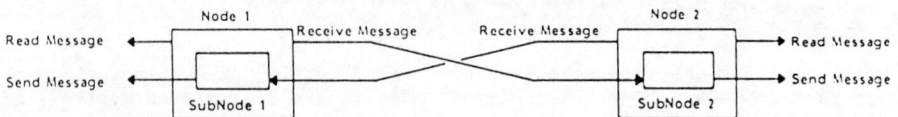

Note that the module Node, effectively exports another module that can import items from other modules including other instances of the exporting module. This technique can be used to export parameterized implementations.

Example 3 -- Module Specification

In this example we describe how a module specification might
be implemented. We describe a simple list module specification. This
module specification describes a List data type with an operation for
inserting items in the list. It has two additional parameters for
importing specific implementations of list type and the single operation
Insert. This forms the implementation import list. The generic package
performs a simple identity mapping of these parameters to the exported
items. Through these parameter declarations concrete implementations can
be passed as parameters.


```
generic
   type ElementType is private;
   type ListTypeImplementation is private;
   with procedure InsertImplementation
           (E : in ElementType; L : in out ListTypeImplementation);
package ListPackage is
   type ListType is private;
   procedure Insert
           (E : in ElementType; L : in out ExportListType);
private
   type ListType is new ListTypeImplementation;
           -- re-exporting the ListType
end ListPackage;

package body ListPackage is
   procedure Insert
       (E : in ElementType; L : in out ListType) is
       TempL : ListTypeImplementation := ListType(L);
   begin
       InsertInsert(E, TempL);
       L := ListType(TempL);
   end;
end;
```


DISCUSSION

This approach has some of the appealing characteristics that
are found in other module interconnection languages such as Pebble
(Burstall & Lampson 1985). It is possible, to some extent, by using
generics to represent modules to describe configurations of modules.
Also, since Ada is strongly typed, precise interface controls are reduced
to type checking operations performed by the implementations. It is not
possible to pass certain kinds of parameters directly using Ada, but for a
few exceptions it is possible to achieve the desired effect.

CONCLUSIONS

We have used this technique for building moderately sized applications where modules are designed using generic packages. From our experiences we have found, even though limited by the range of parameters that can be imported, this method to be useful in describing design configurations, and providing precise interface controls. We have also experimented with this technique for formulating and communicating designs. It forced us to observe and understand module connections for maximum reuseability. This form of module interconnections are based on syntactic (or structural) compatibility among modules. That is two or more modules can legally be connected with each other if they have an appropriate set of matching export and import lists. In the future, we would like to see an amalgamation of this methodolgy with a more semantic approach to specifying Ada modules such as ANNA (Luckham & Von Hencke 1984) along similar lines as described in (Sannella & Tarlecki 1985).

REFERENCES

Burstall, R. & Goguen, J. (1977). Putting Theories Together to form
        Specifications. In Proceedings of the 5th IJCAI,
        Cambridge.
Burstall, R. & Lampson, B. (1984). A Kernel Language for Modules and
        Abstract Data Types, Digital Systems Research Center, Palo
        Alto, Technical Report 1.
Grover, V. (1985). On Expressing Module Interconnections in Ada,
        ACM Ada Letters, Vol. VI (4), pp. 90-93
Luckham, D. & Von Hencke, F. (1984). Overview of ANNA, a Specification
        Language for Ada. In Proceedings of the IEEE Conference on
        Ada Applications and Environments, St. Paul.
Mitchell, J.C. & Plotkin, G.D. (1985). Abstract Types have Existential
        Type. In Proceedings of 12th ACM Symposium on Principles
        of Programming Languages. New Orleans.
Sannela, D. & A. Tarlecki, A. (1985). Program Specification and
        Development in Standard ML. In Proceedings of 12th ACM
        Symposium on Principles of Programming Languages. New Orleans.
Wolf, A.L., Clarke, L.A. & Wiledon, J.C. (1984). An Ada Environment for
        Programming-In-The-Large. In Proceedings of the IEEE
        Computer Society 1984 Conference on Ada Applications and
        Environments, pp 52-62, St. Paul.